Road to Damascus

Elaine Rippey Imady

For information, contact
MSI Press
1760-F Airline Highway, #203
Hollister, CA 95023

Library of Congress Control Number 2008928671

ISBN 978-1-933455-13-6

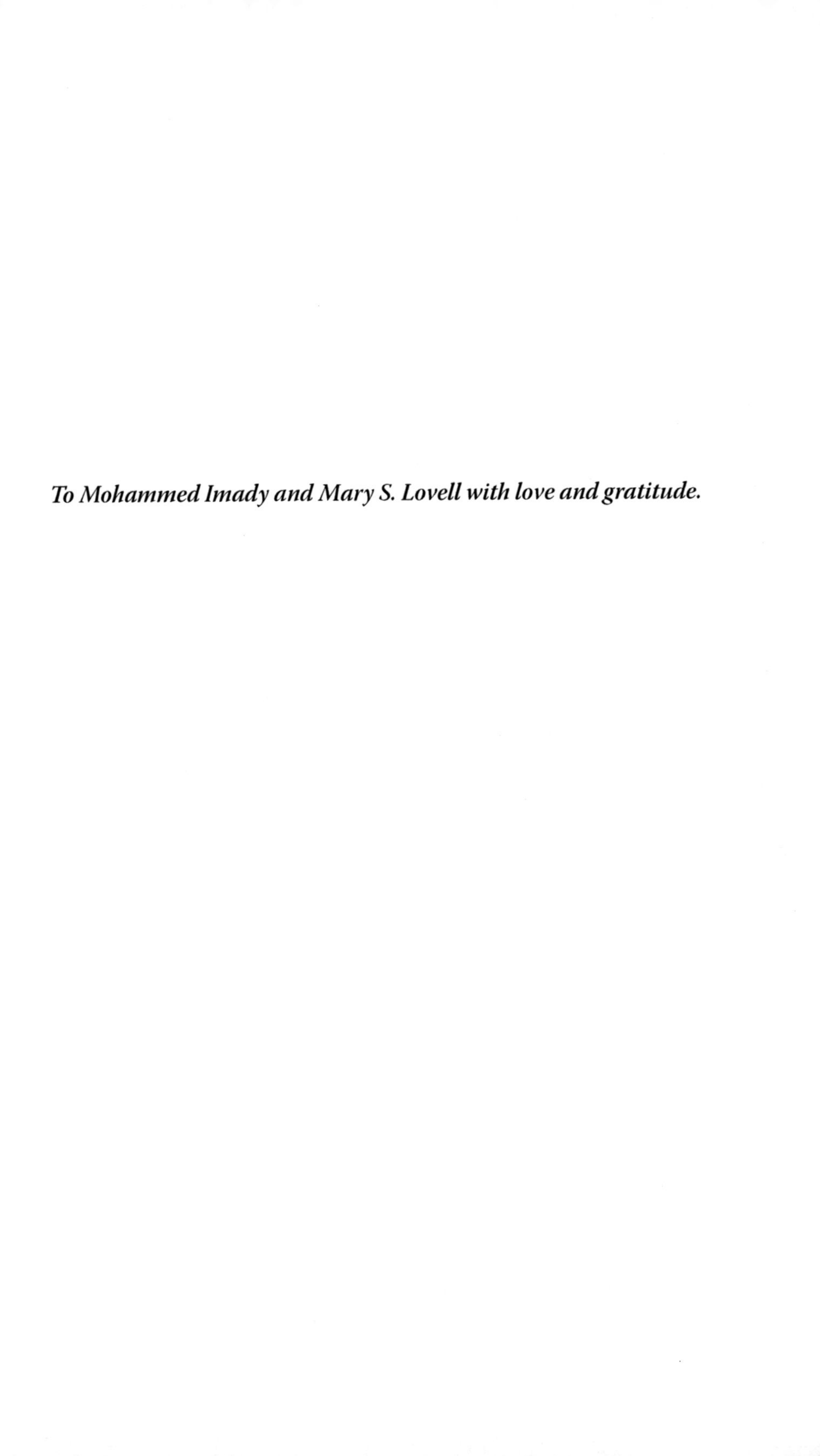

To Mohammed Imady and Mary S. Lovell with love and gratitude.

Table of Contents

Prologue

Many years ago, I fell in love with Mohammed Imady, an Arab student at New York University and, as the old saw goes, thereby hangs a tale. I married him and soon afterwards left New York to live in his city, Damascus. I believed we would only be in Syria for several adventurous years, perhaps the eight years he owed the government for sponsoring his scholarship. We took our two-year-old daughter with us and several years later, another daughter and a son were born to us in Damascus.

At this time Syria was barely on the world screen. Few Americans had heard of it and fewer still had visited it. As we sailed away that cold February morning, my mother feared she would never see us again. I, on the other hand, was serene and optimistic. I felt this journey to Syria with my husband and child was *maktoub* – that is, ordained, destined - and that all would be well.

When I arrived in 1960, Damascus was a small, but proud, city of 400,000. It boasted of being the "oldest continuously inhabited city in the world" and at its heart, lending veracity to this claim, was the Old City, a magical place of winding alley ways and lanes that led to domed mosques, beautiful old houses hidden behind shabby facades, ancient stone khans, crowded souks or markets, an Ottoman palace, Roman ruins and the Biblical "Street Called Straight". Far from being an empty, preserved historical site, or an area tricked out to be a tourist attraction, the Old City was a living, dynamic part of Damascus, a place where people lived in the old homes centered around a courtyard, where merchants sold every conceivable item under the sun and where the Umayyad Mosque was regularly filled with Damascenes making their daily prayers. Although inroads have been made on the Old City since 1960, most of this is still true today.

The area on the slopes of Jebel Qassioun (Mt. Qassioun) where we lived was called Mohajareen and many of the families in this area, like my husband's family, had moved there from the Old City a generation or so earlier. It was a respectable, rather conservative, middle class neighborhood where quite a few people still lived in the traditional one- or two-story family homes. Mohammed's father, in fact, was the first on the block to tear down his old-style home and build a four-story apartment building. One apartment in this building would be our home for seventeen years.

There were few privately owned cars at this time and donkeys, mule carts and, in the autumn, even camels laden with wood for sale were a common sight. Garbage was collected by men pushing small wheeled bins – and the streets were cleaner than they are today. The weather was mostly wonderful. For months there would be clear skies; hot, dry days, but cool nights.

The families of most people in the city had lived there for generations and everyone seemed to know everyone else. I would tell my sister-in-law, Kawsar, about someone I had met and she would look thoughtful and then tell me in great detail how he or she was related by blood or marriage to the Imadys or to neighbors or friends of the Imadys.

Telephones and privately owned cars were rare, but there were taxis, buses and the tram which made it easy to get around the city. Drinking water piped to our home came from a spring called *Fijeh* in the hills outside the city and was cold, pure and delicious. Electricity was chiefly used for lighting and for the radio. Not many people had refrigerators, vacuum cleaners or other electrical appliances. Television arrived in the city in the summer of 1960.

Despite my original understanding that we would spend a few brief years here, Mohammed and I are still living in Damascus and so are our three married children, our eleven grandchildren and our two great granddaughters. Now that almost half a century has elapsed since I arrived, the city I write of so fondly in these pages has, in many respects, disappeared. Gone are the pristine, unpolluted skies, the clean air and the unhurried pace of life. The streets have become congested with thousands of cars and parking has become a major problem. The population has grown as people from all over the country flocked to the city and has probably reached more than four million today. The sounds of donkeys braying, peasants calling out their produce for sale and roosters crowing have been replaced by the din of automobiles, microbuses and trucks and by people talking loudly into their cell phones as they walk the streets and by television sets blasting from open doors and windows. Almost every block has someone renovating his home to the accompaniment of loud poundings as cement walls are knocked down with sledge hammers and tile floors are polished with loud electric machines. However, five times a day, the call to prayer still rises serenely above the noise of the city and, in our garden, the *bulbul* (nightingale) sings its sweet song as the sun goes down.

Perhaps it is social customs which have eroded the most. Weddings which used to be simple affairs held in the grooms's home, are now elaborate events which take place in impersonal, ornate wedding halls or hotels. Most of the young women are employed and have no time for *isti'bals,* the once-a-month "at home" day their grandmothers kept. Some of the traditions connected with death and condolence visits are no longer strictly observed.

On my first visit back to the States, people often looked at my "normal" clothes and then asked, "But what do you wear in Syria?" My answer was always, "The same as I wear here." Actually, I dressed a bit more conservatively. Those first years in Damascus I never wore sleeveless dresses or trousers outside the house. For weddings and evening parties or receptions I often wore long evening gowns. To this day, you won't see shorts in the streets of Damascus, but women in pants - jogging suits, jeans and pant suits are a common sight – often with a scarf on their heads.

Nowadays when "Islamic dress" is such a controversial issue, you may wonder why there is little or no mention of it in this book. In fact, Syria was far more secular in the sixties than it is today. I never heard the word *hijab* in my first thirteen years in Damascus, the time frame covered by this book. Mohammed's oldest sister, Kawsar, was the only one of his sisters who covered her head. She wore what was called an *esharb,* coming from *echarpe,* the French word for scarf, and it was exactly like the triangular scarf we American girls wore in rainy weather in the forties and fifties. Although all the Imadys kept the Ramadan fast, none of them prayed faithfully five times a day, except Mohammed. When I arrived in Syria, secularization and Westernization seemed to be the wave of the future.

Two factors reversed this tide beginning in the late sixties: one was the blanket support of the West for Israel, particularly after the 1967 War, which has tarnished the appeal of Western ideas and culture and the second was the appearance of several *sheikhas* or female Islamic scholars. Young girls were attracted to these charismatic teachers and adopted the *hijab* from religious conviction. These *sheikhas* encouraged their students to get the best education possible and many of these girls became medical doctors, pharmacists, engineers, members of Parliament, bank directors and teachers. They actually achieved more than many of their feminist mothers had. All this would come to pass after 1973, the year when my book ends.

This book tells of my first years in Damascus and also has four chapters with stories about the Imady family and their city as told to me by members of my new family. I hope I have done justice to the city that I have come to love so well, this city which I have now embraced as my home. I also hope I have given a fair and loving account of all the dear family members who made me welcome here so many years ago and of all the close friends who shared so many good and bad times with me.

Elaine Imady,
Damascus, Syria
December, 2007

Author's Note

This book has been five years in the making and without the encouragement of my husband and children it would still be a work in progress. My daughter, Sawsan, helped give it direction and many family members helped me with the family stories: my husband; my son Omar; my daughter, Muna; my sisters-in-law, Lamat and Riad; and my brother-in-law Abdo. It was my friend, Mary S. Lovell, the internationally known author, who first suggested I should write my story and her guidance and advice have been invaluable and are greatly appreciated. I am also very grateful to my patient editor, Geri Henderson, who helped in so many ways to give the final shape to the book. Finally, I am extremely grateful to Dr. Betty Lou Leaver, my publisher who took my book under her wing.

The transliteration of Arabic words into English is a dilemma for any writer, particularly one who is not an Arabic scholar or native speaker. My solution has been to write the Damascene dialect as it sounds to me and to avoid odd looking diacritical marks. An English translation usually follows directly after most Arabic words and phrases I use and the standard Arabic word of most dialect words is given (transliterated) in the glossary. Although there are no capital letters in Arabic, in my transliterations I start sentences with a capital letter and capitalize some proper nouns such as *Allah*, names of holidays and months. Many Arabic family names are preceded by the prefix "al". I use this prefix the first time a name is mentioned and subsequently usually omit it (e.g. al-Imady, Imady). I have pluralized most Arabic words by adding an "s".

In Arabic, there is a specific name for numerous relatives connected by blood and marriage and these are in common use. I learned to call relatives by the same names my sisters-in-law used. For example, they called their Uncle Ghaleb, "Khalo" (maternal uncle) – and so did I – and so I do in the book. This is true not only for Khalo, but for all the Imady relatives. However, when I write about the past I often use their given names.

Finally, I am solely responsible for any inconsistencies or errors in Arabic as well as for any factual inaccuracies in the book.

AL-IMADY FAMILY TREE

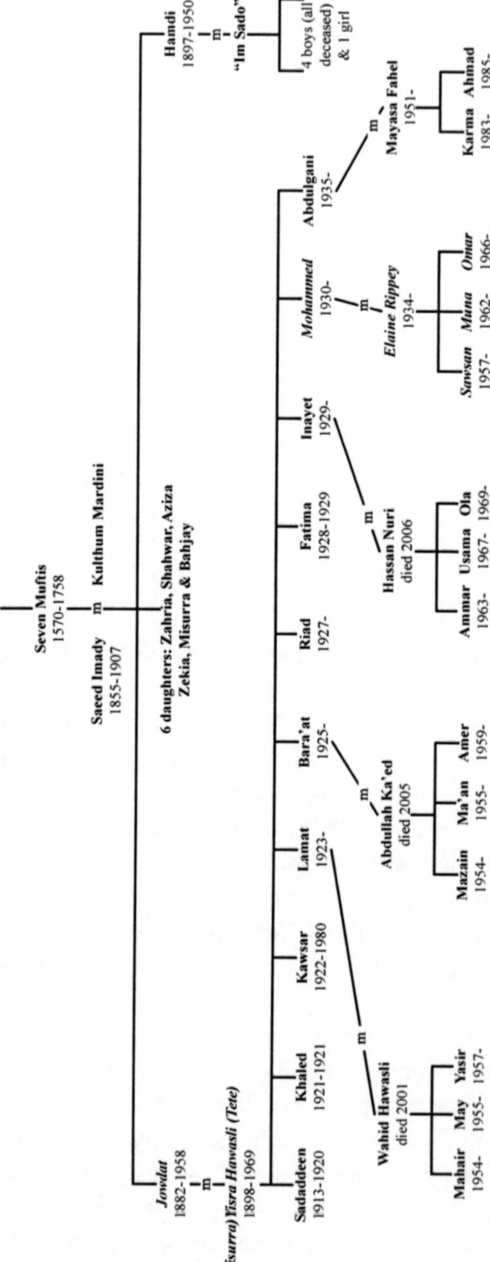

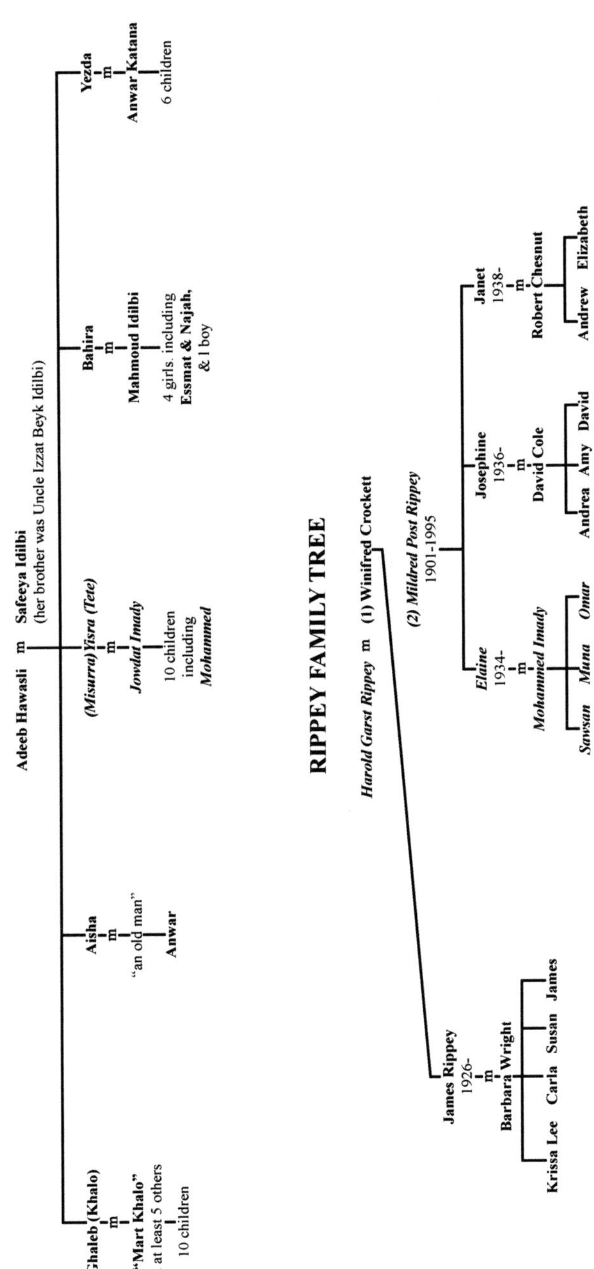
AL-HAWASLI FAMILY TREE
Adeeb Hawasli m Safeeya Idilbi
(her brother was Uncle Izzat Beyk Idilbi)
Ghaleb (Khalo)
m
"Mart Khalo"
& at least 5 others
10 children
Aisha
m
"an old man"
Anwar
(Misurra) Yisra (Tete)
m
Jowdat Imady
10 children
including
Mohammed
Bahira
m
Mahmoud Idilbi
4 girls, including
Essmat & Najah,
& 1 boy
Yezda
m
Anwar Katana
6 children
RIPPEY FAMILY TREE
Harold Garst Rippey m (1) Winifred Crockett
(2) Mildred Post Rippey
1901-1995
James Rippey
1926-
m
Barbara Wright
Krissa Lee
Carla
Susan
James
Elaine
1934-
m
Mohammed Imady
Sawsan
Muna
Omar
Josephine
1936-
m
David Cole
Andrea
Amy
David
Janet
1938-
m
Robert Chesnut
Andrew
Elizabeth

Glossary

abi; Baba: my father; Daddy.

afwan: you are welcome; answer to **shukran**,"thank you".

agha: a Turkish honorific; originally a para-military chieftain, later on, a title for a high-ranking notable. In the Ottoman Empire, Turkish honorifics designated a specific rank or office. In Damascus today they are used simply to show respect.

ahlan wa sahlan: welcome.

akhi: my brother.

ala rasi: literally, "on my head"; usually means, "your wish is my command".

al a'yan: "the notables" the class of scholarly, wealthy, landowning and governing families of Damascus.

al hamdu lillah: thanks be to God.

al hamdila asalamay: thank God for your safe return.

Allahu akbar: God is most great.

Allah yer hama (f)/hamu (m): may God have mercy on her/his soul.

amti: my paternal aunt.

amo: paternal uncle or father-in-law.

argheelay: Damascene dialect for **narghile**, water pipe.

asreeyeh: Damascene women's condolence reception, from **asr**, afternoon, the time when the visits are held.

Baath Party: the ruling party of Syria which came to power in 1963.

Baathist: a member of the **Baath** party.

Belad Esh-Sham: the lands of Syria – "Greater Syria".

beyk: Damascus dialect for **bey**, a Turkish honorific for a high ranking notable; see **agha**.

bukra: tomorrow.

burghol: cracked wheat, a staple of rural Syria; used in making **kibbeh**.

Dimashq: standard Arabic for Damascus.

dra': an arm's length, an old fashioned unit of measurement.

effendi: a Turkish honorific for a high ranking notable; see **agha**.

eid: feast, festival.

Eid al-Kabeer: The Big Feast - the four-day feast that ends the time of pilgrimage. Also called **Eid al-Adha** - the Feast of Sacrifice.

Eid al-Melad: Christmas - literally, "the Feast of the Birthday".

Eid al-Sagheer: The Small Feast - the three-day feast that ends the month of Ramadan.

fatiha: the first seven verses in the Qur'an which are repeated in each of the required daily five prayers, as well as on many other occasions.

fatwa: a legal decision by a scholar of Islamic law, usually a **mufti.**

fellah: peasant.

Ghouta: the green belt of farms and orchards to the east of Damascus

habeebi (m), habeebti (f): my darling, my love.

hijab: literally, "a cover." Often called women's "Islamic dress" which in Damascus usually consists of a scarf which completely covers the hair, a coat to mid-calf and opaque stockings.

Hijira: the Prophet's migration from Mecca to Medina. The Islamic lunar calendar is dated from this event.

hajj: pilgrimage to Mecca.

hajjay: Damascene dialect for **hajji,** female pilgrim.

Hijri calendar: Islamic calendar as above.

hammam: public bath.

ibni: my son.

imbarakay: a party to celebrate a wedding or the birth of a baby; literally, "the blessing".

iftar: the sunset meal that breaks the Ramadan fast.

im; immi: mother; my mother. Damascene dialect for **um**; **ummi**.

imam: leader of the congregational prayer.

in sha' Allah: God willing; used often as "I hope", "I wish".

irs: party to celebrate the wedding night.

isti'bal: Damascene dialect for **istiqbal** - a once a month "at home" or reception day for Damascus women. The visits begin in the late afternoon.

jahennam: hell.

jebel: mountain.

Jebel Qassioun: Mt. Qassioun, the mountain of Damascus.

Jebel Sheikh: Mt. Hermon.

jiddo: grandpa.

jinn: supernatural beings.

Kawsar: Damascene dialect for **Kawthar**, the name of Mohammed's oldest sister.

khalo: maternal uncle.

khalti; khali: my maternal aunt; maternal aunt

khanum: a Turkish honorific. Originally, the wife or daughter of an important notable; now used to show respect.

khatabeen: a delegation of women looking for a bride.

kibbeh: a Damascene speciality. A paste is made of **burghol** and meat which then is shaped into hollow ovals and stuffed with nuts and meat. Can be fried or boiled in yogurt **(kibbeh b'labaniyeh).**

kitab: wedding - this is when the marriage contract is drawn up and signed, making the two parties legally man and wife; literally, "the record".

mabruk: congratulations.

madrasa: school or Qur'anic school.

maktoub: destiny; literally, "it is written".

malemti (f); maalmi (m): my teacher.

maleysh: never mind or it's okay.

marhaba: hello.

mart amo/ami: paternal uncle's wife or mother-in-law.

mart khalo: maternal uncle's wife

ma salamay: good-bye; literally, "(go) with safety".

ma sha' Allah: may you (it) be protected; used to ward off the evil eye; literally, "what God wills".

maylaweeyeh: Damascene dialect for **mawlawi,** a Sufi order whose members perform a dance as part of their striving for spiritual enlightenment; called "whirling dervishes" in English.

mazote: fuel oil.

(ya) meet ahlan wa sahlan; (ya) meet marhaba: one hundred welcomes; one hundred hellos.

meloukhia: a dark green leafy vegetable often cooked with chicken. Cooked meloukhia has a glutinous texture.

mufti: muftis were the highest legal authorities in the Ottoman Empire. They interpreted religious law and issued binding legal decisions called **fatwas.** The **fatwas** of today's **muftis** have only moral authority.

mukhabarat: secret police.

musaher: the man who walks the streets at night in Ramadan beating a drum and calling out to wake people for **suhoor.**

Nakba : The Catastrophe. The 1948 declaration of the State of Israel.

ou lee!: good grief!

pasha: the highest ranking Turkish honorific. Pronounced "basha" by Damascenes; see **agha.**

Safar Barlik: World War I; literally, "The Long March"; a Turkish expression

s'eefay: storage loft.

(Esh) Sham: Damascene dialect for **Dimashq,** Damascus.

Shia; Sunni: the two main sects of Islam.

shukran: thank you.

Shwam: Damascus dialect for **Dimashqiyoun,** Damascenes.

(ya) sidi: sir; literally, "my master".

sitt bait: housewife

sitt salon: "lady of the salon" or cultured woman

soba: heater using **mazote.**

souk: market, often covered.

suhoor: the meal eaten before sunrise in Ramadan.

tafuddali (f) tafuddul (m): come in or sit down.

tanjara, tanajer (pl): round cooking pot without handles.

tarboosh: fez.

tayara: a room on the roof of a house with windows on four sides.

tete: Damascene dialect for grandma; pronounced "TAY tay", like "MAY day".

ti'ibreeni (f); ti'burni (m): Damascene terms of endearment; literally, "may you bury me". In other words, "may you outlive me".

timsayeh: men's condolence reception.

ulama': religious scholars of Islam.

waqf: a philanthropic or family endowment.

ya: a vocative expression; sometimes translated as, "Oh".

yalla: hurry or let's go.

zaatar: a mixture of thyme, sesame seeds, sumac and salt.

zalageet: Damascene dialect for **zagareed**, the eerie, high-pitched trilling sound made by Arab women to express joy; typically heard at weddings.

1.

Maktoub

Arabs say that from the day of your birth the name of your beloved is invisibly engraved on your forehead. Perhaps this is true and explains the mysterious flicker of recognition I felt the day we met.

December 15, 1955 was a cold, overcast Thursday, and snowflakes were swirling down from dark skies, blown by gusts of biting, cold wind. I took the earliest bus into the city, and, as I hurried up the steps of the Main Building of New York University, I glanced at my watch. Eight o'clock. Good, I thought, three hours to review for my Russian exam at eleven. I had to do well because the possibility of a full scholarship hung on my grades this semester.

Looking back, I know it was actually fate that propelled me out of bed before dawn that day. Fate, destiny–the Arabs have a better word for it. They would say our meeting was *maktoub* or "written". Omar Khayyam put it nicely: "The Moving Finger writes; and, having writ,/ Moves on: nor all thy Piety nor Wit/ Shall lure it back to cancel half a Line...."

I pushed open the heavy door of Reading Room 202, easing myself and my heavy load of books into the vast and quiet study hall. Pausing to shake the snow off the hood of my duffle coat, I headed for my usual table near the windows facing Washington Square Park. Suddenly, a student at this table got to his feet and said, "Mademoiselle, may I hang your coat?"

I handed him my coat wordlessly, stunned by his good looks, his French accent and his Old World courtesy. European, I thought, French, maybe Polish or Scandinavian. He hung my coat on the clothes tree, pulled out a chair and sat me down next to him. I dutifully opened my Russian book but knew he was staring at me. I raised my head, and our eyes met. His gray-green eyes were shining.

He smiled and asked me with ingenuous directness, "Have you seen film *Bandora*?" I didn't answer immediately, not sure what he had said, so he leaned forward and repeated the immortal words that have become legend in our family: "Have you seen film *Bandora*?"

"No," I said.

"You look just like Ava Gardner in it."

"Ava Gardner?" I laughed at this absurd idea.

Years later, I learned that this movie was actually called *Pandora and the Flying Dutchman*, but, to this day, I have never seen it nor can I find the slightest resemblance between Ava Gardner and me. However, I have to admit this was a novel way to begin a conversation, and he had succeeded in getting my complete attention. I closed my Russian book and looked him over.

This strangely familiar young man was strikingly handsome. His fair, pink-cheeked face was topped by dark-blond, wavy hair and punctuated by a deep chin dimple. Not only his accent, but also his clothes marked him as a foreigner. He wore a gray turtleneck sweater under his suit jacket, somehow making me picture him on skis. The sweater looked either very expensive or hand-knit, and the shoulder pads of his jacket were too wide. And who wore a suit with a turtleneck sweater in the fifties?

As we smiled at each other, there was a *frisson*, a feeling that somehow we knew each other. Time seemed to slow down while somewhere, where these things are decided, signals flashed, gears were engaged and our lives changed direction forever. Unknowingly, I had taken the first step on the road to Damascus.

Our names were a mutual surprise. He balked at the name Mildred. "Meel-drrred," he repeated doubtfully after me, strongly rolling the r's. Then he frowned and asked if I didn't have any other name. Happily I told him my middle name was Elaine, and I have been Elaine from that day on. In turn, his name, Mohammed, was certainly unexpected, and I was now at a complete loss as to what his nationality might be. Syrian, he said, but that didn't help. The only thing that came to mind was Byron's *The Assyrians came down like the wolf on the fold.* Assyrians, Syrians—were they the same?

Damascus was yet another surprise. To me, it was a Biblical city. Did it still exist? The Middle East had not yet landed on the world stage in 1955, and, like many American college students then, I had only a dim mental picture of the area. I am ashamed to admit that I didn't even know that Syrians were Arabs. Arabs, I thought, lived in Arabia. Oddly enough, I had heard of Palmyra and Queen Zenobia and, of course, Damascus and St. Paul but had no idea all these were part of the history of Syria.

We spent the entire morning talking, and I learned he was a graduate student who had arrived in New York only a month earlier and was currently taking an intensive English course. We talked about our studies–his, economics, and mine, English literature–our families–his large and mine small, and discovered we both loved cats. In passing, he mentioned that, being a Muslim, he did not drink, welcome news to me, the child of an alcoholic father.

Suddenly it was noon, and we had lunch together in the university cafeteria. Before parting we arranged to meet in the same study hall the next day. That afternoon I checked out a book from the library on Syria, but I did not take my Russian exam and I did not get the scholarship. However, that evening I told my mother that I'd met the man I was going to marry (she laughed), and seven months later I did just that.

When we had been married thirty years or more, Mohammed told me the startling fact that he had noticed me in the halls of NYU before we met and determined to get to know me. In the fifties, NYU was the largest private university in America, and we students called it "The Factory", so it is hard to imagine I had been noticed, let alone singled out even before the day fate brought us together. This only reinforces my belief it was no accident we met.

By the next day I was sure I had become an expert on Syria and showed Mohammed the library book. He wasn't impressed and looked dismissively at the pictures of tattooed Bedouin women, camel herds, tents and ruins. It was the kind of book that refers to Islam as "Mohammedanism" and had far more chapters on the Bedouin than on the peasants or city dwellers although the latter two groups, Mohammed told me, constitute an overwhelming 99% of the Syrian population.

"These are not Syrians, and this is not Syria today at all," he protested as he thumbed through the pages, and, true enough, the book dated from the early 1930's. Also, if Mohammed said the book misrepresented his country, you had to believe him. He had a quiet and very convincing air of authority about him even then. But at least, I told myself, I now knew where Syria was and that Syrians were Arabs.

Actually, I knew more about Syria than I realized. At home we had an outsized book by Richard Halliburton about famous ancient ruins. One chapter was devoted to Queen Zenobia with several large photographs of the ruins of her city, Palmyra. I remembered the story of Zenobia very well but had forgotten Palmyra was in the Syrian desert. Further, I had forgotten that Jane Digby, a woman whose story intrigued me, also ended up in Syria. In the summer of 1955, my librarian mother, handed me a new book she thought I might enjoy. It was *The Wilder Shores of Love* by Lesley Blanche and told of several nineteenth century women who found love and adventure in the Middle East. The best of these true stories was about the beautiful and talented Jane Digby. She was born into an aristocratic family in England and, as a teenager, was married to Lord Ellenborough, who later became Viceroy of India.

He was merely the first in a series of husbands and lovers she acquired in her tempestuous life, but her last husband and true love was, improbably, a Bedouin sheikh in–where else?–Syria. I had not forgotten Jane and Zenobia, but Syria had made no lasting impression on me. That failing was soon to be corrected.

Mohammed wanted to take me to a movie our first Saturday, but I said he had to meet my mother and sisters first. So it was that he agreed to come to Palisades on Saturday for dinner. Poor fellow, I'm sure he had no idea of the trip he'd let himself in for. Altogether, it would take at least one and a half hours to get from his hotel on 17th Street in Manhattan to Palisades by subway and bus. And that is if you know your way and don't get lost–which he did.

I gave him directions: "Take the subway–the A train Express up to the Red and Tan bus terminal at 168th Street. Once there, take the 12:20 bus, the 9A bus, to Rockland County. You'll get to Palisades at 1:00. I'll be waiting for you at the bus stop," I promised.

It was another cold day, and there were snow flurries when I went up to the bus stop on 9W. No Mohammed got off the bus. Back home my sisters ribbed me about my foreign boyfriend.

"Guess he stood you up," they said.

Somehow, I was still sure he would come.

Then the phone rang, and it was Mohammed. "Where are you? You promised to meet me at the bus stop."

"Where are *you?*" I countered.

"Palisades Park", he said.

"Oh, no! You're in New Jersey. You're twenty miles south of Palisades, New York. You took the wrong bus."

"Tell me what to do."

Amazing, I thought. He still wants to come. "Okay", I said, "take any bus back to the 168th bus terminal and then take the 9A bus, the *9A bus* that comes every hour at twenty minutes after the hour. Sit up front and ask the driver to tell you when you get to Palisades. And call me before you get on so I know what bus to meet."

More than two hours later he arrived, smiling triumphantly and with a big box of chocolates under his arm. He handed me the beribboned box, and when I thanked him, he said it was nothing; he'd found it on the subway. Although I'd never heard of anyone finding anything so nice on a subway, I was naïve enough to believe him. Only years later did I realize that he had bought the chocolates for me. Gift giving, I discovered, is done in a very unobtrusive manner in Syria, and gifts are seldom opened in front of the giver. Often Syrians will leave a present in your house to be found after they depart. To attract attention to a gift if you are the giver or to make a fuss over it if the gift is for you is simply not done. Not for Syrians any of our effusive

American giving and receiving–"I tried to find something special, something you would really like!"–"Lovely! Just what I wanted!"

But if he played a gentle joke on me, I did the same to him. My sisters and I had made a large batch of decorated Christmas cookies, something we did every year. There were stars, crescents, camels, Christmas trees and bells - the usual. Before Mohammed left, I gave him a large tin of the cookies and told him the camels and crescents were made especially for him, and he believed me.

He ate dinner with us, helped with the dishes and then asked where he could pray. Mother acted as if this were an everyday request and led him to the parlor where, she said, he could be alone.

We walked up to the bus stop in the dark, holding hands and although every inch of that familiar walk was imprinted on my brain, I felt I'd stepped into a new dimension. The same old stars swirled in the velvet heavens above, and, as I looked up, I saw Orion and wondered what my departed grandmother, who taught me what I know of the constellations, would think of my new friend. It was bitterly cold, but we two walked in an envelope of warmth past the stark tall trees iced with snow. His curls fell over his forehead and his eyes shone as we kissed goodbye. He murmured I was his "silver moon".

"How ridiculous!" I thought. "How wonderful!" Then the bus came, and he climbed aboard.

"See you Monday," I said, and he waved goodbye from the bus. I felt abandoned as the bus drove out of sight.

That was the first of hundreds of trips the two of us made on "Bus Number Nine". The bus drivers got to know us and smiled when we got on together, and when it was just one of us, they would ask about the other. They had a warm spot for young lovers.

Mohammed won over my mother and my sisters as effortlessly as he had me. He was charming and at ease with females of any age, maybe because he had grown up with five sisters. He was only insecure about his halting English. He said that he was "a cripple" in the language, and sometimes even I had to guess what he was trying to say. He would be starting his graduate classes in January, and this worried him.

I also wondered how he would manage in his first two classes, but there was no need for my concern. His determination was phenomenal, and his books from that semester testify to his persistence. On every page are the decorative squiggles that make up Arabic writing. He had patiently looked up the Arabic equivalent of many unfamiliar words and had written explanatory notes in the margins. He ended up getting an "A" in both subjects, and I stopped worrying about his studies.

That winter was a magical time. We were young, we were in love and the town of Manhattan was ours to enjoy. I recall–was it in January or February?–there was an unusual blizzard in the city. The snow fell all one day and the next night and the city came to a standstill. Mohammed had never seen anything like it, and even for me, it was extraordinary. We walked from Washington Square Park up Fifth Avenue through virgin snow. The city was transformed. There was no traffic at all, and the snow was past our knees. All sound was muffled by snow, and few people were out in the blocked streets. We walked hand in hand, marveling at the enchanting world the snow had created. The ordinary had been transformed into a whimsical beauty. Parked cars wore thick capes of white, and lowly garbage pails were topped with a cupcake twist of white icing. Was it really that beautiful, or was it the eyes of young love that made it seem so? I know both of us will remember that day forever.

The next few months passed in a dizzying blur as we went everywhere together. In those days you could have a wonderful time in New York on a shoestring. We saw the panoramic views from the top of the Empire State Building and the Statute of Liberty and rode rented bicycles through Central Park. On a clear, calm night, the nickel ferry ride to Staten Island was very romantic. We would stand on the deck with our arms around each other, staring across the harbor at the brilliant lights of Manhattan. We checked out the Damascene room in the Museum of Modern Art and the dinosaurs in the Museum of Natural History. In Coney Island, we rode the roller coaster, ate Nathan's kosher hot dogs and, on warm summer days, we joined the thousands cooling off there on the beach. There wasn't a Chinese restaurant or a Jewish deli in Greenwich Village that we didn't try, but our favorite place for good coffee and sandwiches was the student diner just across from NYU. For a special treat, we took in a Broadway play or a movie at Radio City where we were dazzled by the elaborate shows and the Rockettes. That spring, I remember the two of us walking through Washington Square Park with our arms twined around each other, and a girl I knew who saw us commented later that I looked blooming, like a fertility goddess. I took it as a compliment.

After I took Mohammed around *my* New York, he surprised me by opening up a new world to me in the city I thought I knew so well. With him leading the way, I discovered new neighborhoods, new food and new music. He took me to Atlantic Avenue in Brooklyn where whole blocks of stores, movie theaters and restaurants were owned by Arab immigrants. Every establishment had its name printed in the curlicues of Arabic calligraphy, the streets were filled with the sound of Oriental music and the grocery stores were full of unfamiliar items with enticing odors. We would eat in one of the Lebanese Mom and Pop places where menus were in Arabic and the food was divine. I seldom knew what I was eating, but I loved it all.

Then there was the office of the Organization of Arab Students (OAS) which was located near Columbia University, up on Broadway and 116th Street. This was the favorite hangout of all the homesick Arabs studying in New York, and soon I was as familiar with the place as any Arab. The voice of Ismahan singing insistently, *Emta, habibi, emta?* ("When, my love, when?") will forever conjure up this place for me. Arabic in all its myriad dialects swirled around with the clouds of cigarette smoke as earnest young students endlessly debated the merits of Nasser, unity and socialism and the threats of Zionism, colonialism and imperialism.

In February, 1958, Syria's president, Shukri Kuwatly, and President Nasser of Egypt, signed the document that created the United Arab Republic with Nasser as president of this newly minted country. Most Arab students, including Mohammed, were ecstatic with joy, and Nasser was their hero.

Unity was the grand ideal in the fifties, the banner around which all Arab students rallied, and they would argue for hours about what was the best unifying principle in the Middle East. Not Islam, for then the Christian Arabs would be excluded. Not Arabism, for then the Kurds, the Druze and the Armenians would be left out. In the end, it was the Arabic language and a shared history and culture that won out. It was agreed that those who spoke Arabic and were part of the history of the Middle East were brothers and sisters.

None of us suspected then how unity would prove to be a chimera which these young hopeful students would never achieve. Who would have imagined in 1960 that in 2007 the Europeans, with all their different languages and their history of centuries of conflict, would be living in a practically borderless European Union with a unified currency while the Arab countries would be more divided than ever.

It is strange, but true, that Mohammed never asked me to marry him. He didn't have to. Within a week of meeting, we were talking about names for our children, and he was introducing me to his friends as his fiancée. Every week we went to the movies, and, after all these years, remembering how his eyes shone when he looked at me in the dim light of the theater, can still constrict my heart. Maybe we saw too many films because we sometimes worried that love like ours could only end tragically. We were drawn to each other by an attraction so strong it frightened us both. We had no confidence then that we would be the lucky ones.

Our story began that December day when we fell in love at first sight, but what follows in these pages is not a love story. Or, perhaps I should say it is *more* than a love story. Without our love, there would be no story; love explains not only why I went to Syria, but also why I stayed. Before long, I also fell in love with Mohammed's family and his city so this is also a valentine to the Imady family and to Damascus.

My mother always thought our story resonated with the ancient tale of Naomi and Ruth. Of course, the difference is that I followed my husband to his foreign country while Ruth, a widow, followed her mother-in-law, Naomi, to Naomi's foreign country. But Ruth's words to Naomi could be mine to Mohammed:

"Entreat me not to leave you, or to return from following after you; for where you go, I will go; and where you lodge, I will lodge; your people shall be my people, and your God, my God. Where you die, I will die, and there will I be buried: the Lord do so to me, and more also, if even death part you from me." [Ruth:16,17]

Looking back after all these years, it is hard to remember that we started out as total strangers with different nationalities, different mother tongues, different religions and different cultures. How did we bridge all these profound differences so easily? To this day, I don't know for sure. I can only say we simply never felt like strangers.

We found it easy to talk to each other, and we talked non-stop about everything, telling each other our life stories. My life was as exotic to him as his was to me. We talked while walking or eating together. We talked on the phone and ran up terrible bills. We never ran out of things to talk about (we still haven't): his sisters and brother, my sisters, his childhood, my childhood, his dreams and ambitions and mine. He was charming and gentle with an old-world courtesy. He made me feel cherished. How different he was from the aggressive, crude, groping boys I had gone to school with, boys who, where girls were concerned, had only one thing on their minds. Mohammed had an innate kindness. It was foreign to his nature to knowingly hurt any one or any creature. He told no dirty jokes nor used any four-letter words but was romantic, chivalrous and loving.

Certainly, there was a powerful physical attraction between us. But there was more, much more to it than that. We both had the certainty that in finding each other, we had stumbled onto a path we were destined to take together. We knew our love was meant to be, was *maktoub*.

We got our first marriage license when we had known each other only three months, but I tore it up on our way to the justice of the peace because Mohammed looked like he was going to a hanging. The problem was that he hadn't told his family, and he agonized over how to tell them since he was the favorite son on whom they had pinned all their hopes. He was afraid they would feel he had abandoned his studies and the bright future they hoped for him and might never return to Syria. To make it worse, he was on a government scholarship, and the family home was the collateral to insure his return. We sat in a coffee shop with the torn license on the table between us. Mohammed tried to tape it together, but I didn't let him. The time wasn't right, and the proper time would come.

We talked a great deal about Islam and, as a disillusioned Christian, I listened with interest. To tell the truth, at this time in my life, my understanding of Islam was quite superficial. I merely felt that if this religion was Mohammed's religion, it must be good. I asked my mother (poor Mom!) to have my letter of confirmation in the Palisades Presbyterian Church removed and made the *shahada*, the profession of faith in Islam, in front of two witnesses. That is all there was to it. I was now a Muslim.

Some time after this, I saw a film about the Middle East at the OAS. In one scene, there was a man in flowing robes praying in the desert while the voice-over–first in Arabic and then in English–recited one of the famous verses from the Qur'an: *Qul hua Allahu ahad* ... Say, God is One... The voice seemed to speak directly to me, and I was electrified. This was the moment of truth that sealed and affirmed my acceptance of Islam.

April came and, with it, my first Ramadan. I told Mohammed that I intended to fast, but the first day of the Fast he found me in the university cafeteria drinking coffee.

"I thought you were going to fast," he said.

"I am fasting, I haven't eaten a thing."

"But you're drinking coffee!"

"You mean you aren't supposed to eat *or* drink? You didn't tell me that."

The next day I was caught smoking a cigarette, and the third day I was chewing gum, two more things that broke the fast. Finally, I got it sorted out. I remember one afternoon mowing the lawn in Palisades while watching the slow, the very slow progress of the sun across the sky. It wasn't easy, but I fasted all that Ramadan without any more mistakes and was thrilled to have shared this special month with Mohammed.

Sometimes Mohammed took me with him to the Islamic Student Organization of New York, and we would join the small number of Muslims who gathered for Friday prayers. Half a century ago there was not a single mosque in New York City, and we Muslims had to make do with a chapel on the campus of Columbia University which we shared with Christians and Jews. On Fridays, we would unroll the beautiful Persian carpet donated by the government of Saudi Arabia and conduct our prayers. Students took turns being the *imam*, the one who leads the prayers and gives the sermon. Things were much more relaxed in those days. We girls prayed in skimpy scarves that did not really conceal our hair; only nylon stockings covered our legs and some of us even had bare arms sticking out of short sleeves. None of this would be acceptable today.

I had always been a rebel. In my very Republican high school, I was the student who shocked my fellow students when I stood up in our current events class and criticized my government for its part in overthrowing the popular Iranian Prime Minister, Mohammed Mossadegh. In my first year of college, I got in with a crowd of leftists, which explains my interest in Russian - not the usual choice of language for a student of English literature. At the height of the McCarthy investigations, I joined a student organization called, "Students for Academic Freedom," which was protesting the firing of three NYU professors for taking the Fifth Amendment. I am still proud to have opposed McCarthyism but now realize it is quite possible that this organization was a Communist front. My left-wing activities gave my mother a lot of grief, but they came to an abrupt end when I met Mohammed.

My life now revolved around Mohammed. Although I would have been insulted if someone had said it to me back then, rebel or not, I was very much a child of my time. For most of us women of the Silent Generation, love and marriage outclassed personal ambition. True, I was quite an outspoken member of this generation and my choice of husband was far from typical, but like many women who came of age in the fifties, I instantly abandoned my plans for a university degree and a career when the right man came along. I walked away from NYU with hardly a backward glance and helped Mohammed with his term papers and later his two theses even though economics was not my cup of tea. This was an era when a man earned a PhD and his wife contented herself with a "PHT ("put hubby through").

Around this time, a young man I had dated who was away at another university wrote and very unexpectedly asked me to marry him. "Get rid of that Arab you are seeing," he wrote. "You can't really be serious about him."

I turned him down without a second thought.

* * *

My father was always the outsider in our family, the one with the funny Missourian accent, who said "Miz", "naught", "bucket" and "skillet" instead of "Mrs.", "zero", "pail" and "frying pan," who spoke slowly and who moved deliberately. We–Mother and we three sisters–were the fast-moving, fast-talking, mercurial Easterners who got impatient with Dad's phlegmatic, Midwestern ways.

Dad only had his mother, our Grandma Rippey, but Mother, who had been a Post, had aunts, uncles, first and second cousins galore. In Palisades, everywhere you turned, there were Posts, relatives all. Actually, Dad's relatives probably outnumbered Mom's, but they were far away in Missouri and we only saw them once when they came east. So, as I said, Dad was an outsider.

He was also a drinker. At the end of our days with him, drink was more important to him than anything else in the world. He swallowed it down, and it swallowed him up. I'm not too sure he was very aware of our presence except when we got too rambunctious. Then he would take off his belt and strap us.

But before things got this bad, there were some good times and a few glorious days that shine out undimmed by all the years that have gone by. The first was when Dad took me to the World's Fair in 1939 when I was five years old. I remember the thrill of being singled out for this trip, and though much of what I saw has blurred in my mind, impressions are left of huge buildings with bright lights where strange, shiny objects were on display–odd looking things like nothing I'd ever seen before. I remember the boxes that showed moving pictures, just like tiny movie screens. Dad said this was "television". Even at that young age, I caught some of the grown-ups' enthusiasm for the future and the coming marvelous inventions that were soon to change our world. We ate hotdogs and drank soda pop (at least I did), and I was enthralled by everything I saw but most of all by just having Dad to myself for a whole day.

We got home near midnight, and Mother was worried. I was exhausted, but my flushed, happy face made her hold her criticism. This day might not be so vivid after so many years if it had been only one of many such days, but of course it remained unique. I never again spent a whole day alone with my father.

My father worked for the Bobbs Merrill publishing company at this time, and all our presents from him as young children were books. Some I still remember, and some I still have. Best of all were the Richard Halliburton books about the wonders of the ancient world and faraway places, including Palmyra. I remember being impatient to learn to read and, in fact, Dad taught me to read at four before I started school. Since then, I have hardly passed a day without a book in my hand. Dad taught me to read, and my mother, who also loved books, encouraged my sisters and me to read.

My half-brother, who last saw my father as an infant, says the only thing he owes our father is "good genes". I was thirteen when my father sent my mother back to her father–and us with her. I used to think he'd given me nothing. My bitterness at his drinking and abandoning us blinded me for a long time to the earlier, happier years.

Mohammed met my father twice. The first time was in Pennsylvania Station where we were seeing my sisters, Jo and Jan, off to college in Ohio. It was one of those infrequent occasions when my parents met after their separation in 1948.

Dad said to Mohammed something like, "Take good care of her. She'll do fine in Syria; she comes of good pioneer stock."

Sure, I thought bitterly to myself, "Take her, she's yours." It sounded to me like he was relieved. Now I'd officially be off his hands.

The second time we met in Hoboken, New Jersey, where Dad lived, and Mohammed took us out to dinner. It was a disaster. Dad was in a provocative mood–I'd forgotten how mean he could be. He spent the entire evening talking about the Middle East, praising the Israelis and disparaging the Arabs. Mohammed, ever the diplomat, was unfailingly polite and would not allow himself to be goaded into an argument, but I was hurt and saw to it that they did not meet again.

Our first summer came, and Mohammed decided to move out of the apartment he had been sharing with four other Syrian students up near Columbia University and move to a place nearer NYU. This triggered our decision to marry regardless of his family, his scholarship–regardless of anything and anybody. Mohammed reasoned that if we kept it a secret from his fellow Arab students, the family back in Damascus would not find out until he was ready to break the news to them gradually. I wasn't too happy or convinced about the need for all this secrecy, but I went along with it.

First, we applied for a marriage license in New Jersey. I had not brought any proof of age with me, and to my surprise we were flatly turned down. The official refused to believe I was of age and warned me that Muslims could marry four wives. I insisted truthfully that I was twenty-two, but he was adamant and told me he could not authorize such a terrible mistake. We were insulted and decided to be better prepared next time.

The following day, I brought along my driving license, and we applied in New York City. Everything went smoothly, and we planned to marry without any fuss at city hall. But this was before my mother got into the act. She was incredibly understanding and supportive of our marriage even though she knew from the first–as did I–that Mohammed would be going back to Syria and that I would be going with him. Her only objection was to an impersonal city hall wedding. She told me she hoped I would not be the third generation in the family to marry without any friends or relatives present. My mother and both grandmothers had eloped, and all three couples had found some minister or other to marry them. In each case, the minister's wife was the sole witness.

"Why not get married at home?" said my mother.

Mohammed and I loved the idea and felt that this would be a much more auspicious beginning to our life together. We set the date for August 24th and, in contradiction to all Western wedding traditions, we went shopping together to buy my wedding dress. Instead of a traditional wedding gown, we chose a simple sleeveless red and white silk dress from Lord and Taylor. Mohammed would be looking elegant, as always, in his best suit.

Mother prepared a festive wedding dinner, but Mohammed and I couldn't eat a bite. I remember someone asked him to make a toast (with juice!), and he said some romantic and poetic words in Arabic and then translated them to the delight and merriment of my two younger sisters. My grandmother was present, as well as Margaret and Jim Anderson, good friends of ours. Margaret made the wedding cake, and she and her husband were our witnesses. We were married in the parlor, and Mohammed put his unique touch to the service. Every time Judge McCormack asked Mohammed a question, he looked at me lovingly and said "Surely" instead of "I do". At the end of the service the judge asked him if he would say "I do" just once, and he said yet again "Surely!"

The moment the judge pronounced us man and wife, my youngest sister, Jan, said, "I don't believe it! Do it again!"

Then my grandmother cornered Mohammed and told him how lucky he was to get the best catch among her three granddaughters, as if his only choice of a bride could be from the Rippey sisters! I'm afraid my sisters overheard, but they were used to Grandma Rippey and her tactless tongue.

Finally, it was time to go. My sisters showered us with confetti, and sister Jo offered to drive us down to the George Washington Bridge. We got a lot of friendly stares and smiles that night on the subway since our faces were radiantly happy and our clothes were sprinkled with confetti.

So, I had no elaborate wedding, no wedding gown and no honeymoon. What I did have is the most important thing for any bride–the right man. For eight days, I was the happiest woman in the world.

But nine days after our wedding, Mohammed set off with four of his friends on a car journey to Oklahoma! I can laugh about it now, but at the time it was no joke. I bitterly called it his "bachelor honeymoon." The five young Arabs drove off to attend the annual meeting of all the OAS chapters in the United States, which was held in Stillwater, Oklahoma that year. I'd known for months that Mohammed planned to make this trip, but when the departure date turned out to be just a few days after our wedding, I thought he would change his mind and not go. But he went. He said if he didn't go it would look very suspicious to his friends: they would guess we'd been married, and then the news might filter back to his family. The trip was supposed to last ten days but turned out to be fifteen days, some of the longest days of my life.

At the time I was very upset, but, in retrospect, I can see how important this convention was to Mohammed. It was a great opportunity for meeting and sharing ideas with other students from various Arab countries. These Arabs studying in America were the elite young people of the Arab world and would, in the future, form an "old boy" (and "girl") connection. Many of them would become prominent leaders in their countries: cabinet ministers, bankers, doctors, engineers and businessmen, and the friendships formed when they were students would endure.

The meeting only lasted three days, but the trip there and back by car took twelve. Mohammed's friends were determined to see everything they possibly could along the way. They told me later, after they found out that Mohammed had just been married when the trip began, that they finally understood his strange behavior on the way back. They say he sat in the car with a map on his knees and a ruler and a pencil in his hands, plotting the shortest route to New York City from wherever they happened to be. They claim he hardly looked at the scenery and couldn't understand his odd behavior. "What's your hurry," they would ask him. "Do you miss your studies so much? Enjoy the trip!"

Every day he sent me a postcard with quaint romantic and flowery messages addressed to "Lulu", his pet name for me to this day: "Lulu, my darling, I am remembering you in every step and wishing you were with me. – Lulu, my beloved, I am coming in a few days with my half heart to find the other half. – When I saw this waterfall I remembered your love which is flowing like this water from your golden heart.

– Don't think that I forgot you for one single minute. – Ask the silver moon about me, the man who loves you forever and ever. – I swear that I love you, and believe me that I wish I didn't go on this trip. Please forgive me, I was really wrong. – Lulu, my spirit, heart and mind, I am trying to make my friends drive quickly so I can see my love soon. Last night I couldn't sleep, not one second. I missed you and your blue eyes. – My beloved Lulu, I hope I will be in New York with you as soon as possible. All have become angry at me because I have tried to make them drive back fast."

Today the messages sound very loving, but they didn't mollify me at the time. Four days before he got back, he telephoned, and I cried. I also said some angry things, but my anger evaporated when he walked in the door.

2.

From New York to Beirut

We moved into a cold-water flat on East 6th Street near NYU, and I decided to make another try at getting my degree. I transferred to Hunter College, which was free, and signed up for five night courses. I also got a secretarial job with North American Philips in a skyscraper just around the corner from the New York Public Library. I had only been working a short time at Philips when some of my new colleagues came running over to my desk, saying excitedly that "they are bombing your husband's country!" Actually, this was the Suez crisis, and it was Egypt, before the union with Syria, which was being attacked. However, it gave me a scare to think Mohammed's family might be in danger.

The next day Mohammed and I joined a large group of young people from the OAS in front of the United Nations to protest against the attack. As we left our apartment, Mohammed reminded me to take off my wedding ring so none of our Arab friends would discover we were married, and you can be sure I wasn't very happy about that. It was a cold windy day, and I remember I held my placard in one hand while I kept putting my other hand in my coat pocket to reassure myself that my ring was still there.

I was an old hand at picket lines from my activist days, but this would be the last time I ever joined a protest demonstration. Once again, as with my opposition to McCarthyism, I have no apologies about participating in this protest and feel I was on the "side of the angels". Even my country opposed this attack by France, England and Israel, and it was widely seen as the last gasp of old fashioned heavy-handed colonialism in the Middle East.

By the time we had been married two months, I was expecting a baby. With what seemed like remarkably bad timing, my first appointment at the local Family Planning Center was scheduled for the same day I got the results of my positive pregnancy test. My pregnancy was an ordeal. I was afflicted with "morning sickness" twenty-four hours of the day and had to quit my job at Philips and drop three of my courses at Hunter College. I lost weight alarmingly and spent days in bed back with Mother in Palisades. Finally, by the fourth month I began to feel human once again.

Although our little Susan, called "Susu" to this day, was not a planned baby, no child could have been more welcome. She was my mother's first and much loved grandchild, but Mother had to wait for my sisters' children to come along before she was called "Grandma". Mother was always "Mommy" to Susu and all my children.

Although I was Rh negative and Mohammed was positive, our baby girl was not affected at all. At birth, Susu had blond fuzz for hair, wise blue eyes and incredibly long legs. The nurses in the hospital correctly predicted she would be tall. She was also an extraordinarily colicky baby which made our induction into the role of parents a baptism of fire. For three months, Susu shrieked for two hours and slept for two hours a day. Nothing we did helped. We used to spell each other to save our sanity. Mohammed would go for a one-hour walk, and then it would be my turn. Finally, I told my pediatrician that I absolutely had to get some sleep, and he offered me sleeping pills. I turned them down and said I could sleep with no trouble if only my baby would sleep. He gave me some drops for her and said to use them with caution. We faithfully followed his instructions except for one day when Mohammed invited Syrian friends for dinner. In order to be able to cook a meal and make the place presentable for our guests, we gave Susu a few more drops than usual, and she slept for eight hours. Every photograph we took of her that day shows a peacefully sleeping baby, but I never dared to do that again. Actually, I didn't have to. When she finished her third month. the crying magically stopped, and we found ourselves the exhausted but proud parents of a delightful baby.

We had everything we needed to make us happy except money. Mohammed's stipend from his government was never meant to support three people so I needed to get a job. Mohammed scheduled all his classes at night in order to take care of Susu during the day while I worked. He thought he could combine baby-sitting with studying. I found an office job with a small family company not too far from our apartment. When I came home at five thirty and Mohammed went to his classes, Susu would cry for her "Baba," the name Syrian children call their fathers. This was fine for several months, but then Mohammed said it wasn't working out. He found his baby daughter so entertaining and he had such fun taking care of her that he couldn't study.

I looked into child-care facilities available in the city and was told we didn't qualify for low income day-care. However, they added, if I left my husband (and wasn't he some kind of foreigner, anyway?), Susu would be eligible for free day-care. I couldn't believe my ears. I told them it was disgraceful that the welfare department of the city was encouraging the break-up of families and walked out, saying I had *no* intention of leaving my husband.

It was then, when there seemed to be no way for me to continue working, that Mohammed began talking of sending Susu to his family in Damascus with friends of ours who would soon be flying to Syria. I was appalled. Of course, we looked at this from completely different perspectives. Mohammed would be sending his daughter to his loving mother and sisters, but I would be sending her to people I had never met, to strangers in a strange country, and I could never agree to that.

At this time, Mother had two jobs and worked more than forty hours a week. She was a full-time secretary at Lamont Geological Observatory and worked several evenings a week and Saturday afternoons as the town librarian. I knew she could not take care of Susu, but I was confident she would find a solution. She did.

Constance Lieval Price was the answer to our prayers. Connie and my mother were childhood friends who attended the local elementary school together. After Connie's seven children were grown, she said she missed having little ones under foot so she established a child care center in her spacious home down the hill from our house. Mother appealed to Connie to take Susu, and although she did not usually board her charges, she made an exception in our case. So it was that our daughter became one of the fortunate ones to be cared for by Connie. Susu spent five days a week at the Prices for seven months, and Mother paid the nominal fees. Weekends, Susu would go home to her "Mommy" as she persisted in calling her grandmother, and we would come up from the city. We always had tears in our eyes when we stole out Sunday nights to take the bus, but Susu shed no tears when we left. Mother said she would stand by the window Monday mornings, watching for Connie's car, and would get in, waving a cheerful goodbye.

We missed Susu greatly, but it did give us a little more time together, time that we needed to strengthen our marriage. Our first year together put our love to the test. We had become parents before our first wedding anniversary, had lived through the stress of Susu's colic and were burdened with constant worries about money. In addition, there was always the pressure on Mohammed to succeed in his studies. We had some spectacular fights, and after one particularly stormy one I left our apartment in a rage, slamming the door behind me and swearing I would never return. That memorable time, Mohammed came running after me all the way to the subway entrance in his pajamas and slippers, and we went back hand in hand. We fought over everything and nothing, but, in the end, love always won out.

One serious source of dissension was my objection to keeping our marriage a secret. Mohammed wrote to his parents faithfully every week, omitting, however, the crucial news that he had married an American and had a daughter. Much depended upon Mohammed successfully completing his studies, and he was afraid that his family would think he had abandoned them and his goals if they knew he had married. Even Mother was concerned that, burdened with a wife and a child, Mohammed might fail his studies and go home defeated.

Good Arabs postpone telling "bad" news as long as they possibly can. Mohammed had his "bad" news that he kept from the family–and the family had theirs. They decided that Mohammed should not be told anything upsetting while he was studying in America, so they never wrote him about the stroke his father had in 1958. By the time Mohammed got around to writing about our marriage–when he was thinking of sending Susu to Syria–the stroke had left his father partially paralyzed. Mohammed's letter was read to him, and he seemed to understand and to be pleased. Only one sister was upset about our marriage, and she soon got over it. My brother-in-law wrote me a charming letter welcoming me into the family. It was addressed, in his inimitable English, to "Dear Wife-Brother". The family also sent me a gold and pearl bracelet. It seemed to me that all Mohammed's fears had been for nothing.

My father-in-law died nine months after his stroke, and once again Mohammed was not told. Months after his father's death, Mohammed heard the news from a Syrian student he hardly knew. It was a terrible shock to him and convinced us–Mohammed, Mother and me–that it is wrong, even cruel, to postpone telling bad news in this way.

Mohammed soon was able to prove that marriage had helped, not impeded, his studies. He finished all the courses for his doctorate in the time his scholarship allotted for the master's, and then got permission from his government to stay on until he finished writing his doctoral thesis. When Susu was almost two-and-a-half, Mohammed was notified he had passed his oral exams, the last remaining step for his doctorate. When Mohammed came home with the good news, Susu (well-coached by my sister and me) ran to him shouting, "Dr. Baba, Dr. Baba!" There was even more good news. He was informed that he had won the Founders Day Award of New York University. This "mark of special honor" was for having achieved "a place in the highest bracket of scholastic preferment recognized by the University." How proud we were of him!

With this good news, we began packing for Syria. There was never any question about Mohammed's returning to Syria because the terms of his scholarship obliged him to work for his government for eight years, two years for every year of his scholarship, or forfeit the family house.

Mother loved Mohammed dearly but felt he loved his country too much to be objective about what Susu and I would face there. As she herself wrote, "I was haunted with fears of all kinds of wildly improbable dangers which my son-in-law wasn't able to allay."

In her usual way, she looked around among her large network of friends and acquaintances for someone who could help prepare me for life in Syria and settled on her good friends and neighbors, the Haagensens. Dr. Cushman Haagensen was a renowned breast cancer specialist and a good friend of Dr. MacDonald, Dean of the Medical School in the American University of Beirut. Over the years, Dr. MacDonald had sent Dr. Haagensen many young Arab doctors whom he took under his wing at New York Medical Center. Also, the Haagensens were world travelers and were familiar with quite a few Arab countries, including Syria.

Of course, Mother insisted that we visit the Haagensens before we left, and we were glad we did for their information and advice proved very helpful. Dr. Haagensen talked at length about his favorable impressions of the Middle East, which helped Mother and me view the upcoming trip to Damascus with less trepidation. He also handed us several packets of a medicine which he said would be very useful in dealing with diarrhea from unaccustomed bacteria. (It was.) Both Dr. Haagensen and his wife were very positive and enthusiastic about our trip and almost seemed to wish they were coming with us. Our friendship with these good people was enduring. As the years went by in Damascus, we were to turn to our distant friend, Dr. Haagensen, for his advice in more than one medical crisis.

Since I was afraid of flying, Mohammed agreed we could travel by sea and booked passage on a Greek freighter leaving New York for Beirut on February 7, 1960. A few days before we left, Mother invited friends and relatives to a big farewell party. Of course my sister, Jo, with her fiancé, Dave, came as well as my younger sister, Jan, and her husband, Bob, plus many Arab friends. My Danish friend, Anna Maria, was there with Haidar, her Syrian husband, as well as my friend, Jill. Jill had gone with Adel, her Syrian husband, and their children to Syria the year before. She had only stayed a few months in Damascus before leaving her husband and coming home with her two boys. During Jill's stay in Damascus, she had gone to visit Mohammed's family "to check them out" for me. Her report was very negative, but, knowing Jill, I took it with a grain of salt.

Although Mother was worried about an ear infection Susu had before our departure and the fact that our ship had no doctor, she tried to put a brave face on our leaving. It didn't make her feel any better when Jill told me, "Take a good look at the Statute of Liberty when you leave the harbor because you'll have no liberty from then on."

At the same time, Anna Maria kept assuring Mother that she shouldn't feel so unhappy because we would certainly see each other again before very long.

We spent our first night on board while the *Hellenic Sailor* was still docked. I thought we would be too excited to sleep, but we slept soundly. Around ten thirty the next morning, we got under way. We all went up on deck and watched the tugboat push us out of the harbor. After it tooted a farewell and our ship replied with a deep blast, Mohammed took Susu inside since it was getting quite cold. I stayed on and watched first Manhattan, then the Statute of Liberty and finally even Long

Island disappear from sight. Although it was rather hazy, you could see the Statute of Liberty for the longest time. It shone in the feeble sun with an almost phosphorescent green light.

I remembered Jill's remark as the Statute of Liberty receded into the horizon, and I also thought of all the thousands of immigrants whose first glimpse of that same statute must have been such a joyful moment. Although I was sailing in the opposite direction, I felt some of the same anticipation they surely felt. A new world lay ahead for me, and, like those immigrants, I looked forward to it with hope. My father had told Mohammed that I would "do fine in Syria" because I came of "good pioneer stock." Now here I was, a pioneer in reverse, and the months ahead would put his claim to the test.

Although the ship began to pitch and roll as soon as we were out of the harbor, not a one of us was ever seasick. But the ship's sideways motion really unnerved me. The nearer you got to the center of the ship, the less noticeable it was, but since we were in an outside cabin, it was as though we were on the end of a seesaw. We tipped toward the water at such an alarming angle I feared the ship would never right herself and the first few nights I was too worried to sleep.

The ship seemed much larger after it was emptied of the visitors who came to wish us *bon voyage,* and we seven passengers just rattled around in it. When it wasn't too rough, the enclosed top deck was a nice place for Susu to run around and for us to get some exercise. We would often be joined there by the only other English-speaking passengers, a retired school teacher and his wife, Sam and Anne Glass from Seattle. We kept a lookout for other ships, but didn't see a one after the luxury liner, *Empress of Britain,* passed us our second day out.

Anne Glass, who was about the age of my mother, soon became "My Lady" to Susu. Before long, Susu made friends with practically every one aboard ship. The cabin boy played with her and the steward gave her rice pudding now and then as a treat. Abdullah, one of the passengers, gave her chocolates. The captain's wife played games with her, and the captain drew her pictures of boats. Anne read to her, and Sam–now "Unca' Sam"–danced with her. Susu loved the attention. I don't suppose a freighter like this often has young children as passengers, so she probably was a welcome novelty to everyone.

After eight long days at sea, we were in the middle of the Atlantic. I felt we were a solitary dot on an endless ocean, and time passed slowly. For six days we hadn't seen another ship, and we felt alone on the planet. Every day the three of us went up on the upper deck and looked in vain for any sign of life. Above was the sky. and all around us was the vast indifferent ocean in perpetual motion. Sometimes it seemed peaceful and sometimes menacing. I never realized before how brave the first explorers must have been crossing the Atlantic in their tiny sailing ships.

To help pass the time, Mohammed tried to teach me some useful basic phrases in Arabic like *hello, goodbye, please, thank you, how are you, I'm pleased to meet you,* etc. It was hard going, and I began to realize I should have started studying Arabic much earlier.

On February 24th, the captain told us we were to pass Gibraltar at about noon. Only someone who has not seen land for fourteen days can imagine how excited we were. We all dashed up to the top deck, and there, to the south, we saw the dark craggy mountains of Morocco and, to the north, was Spain. Africa and Europe in one view! We were closer to the European coast, close enough to see the waves dashing up on the sea walls of a little fishing village through the field glasses. Africa's coast looked grim and forbidding, truly the Dark Continent.

Finally Gibraltar came into view. There were at least ten other ships in sight, one a huge British liner. Dolphins, neat and black, were jumping the waves. The sun was sparkling on the water which lay in different colored bands, green, green-blue, bright blue and dark blue. Gibraltar reared up out of the water exactly like the logo of the Prudential Life Insurance Company ("solid as the rock of Gibraltar"). The Straits of Gibraltar are ten miles wide at its narrowest point so we weren't right next to the rock, but we were quite near enough for an exciting eyeful.

That afternoon we began sailing along the North African coast, about six to ten miles off shore. Our visibility from the ship on a clear day was around fourteen miles in any direction. At about five p.m., the city of Algiers came into view. Mohammed and I stood together on the top deck and, as it grew darker, we watched the lights of the city flick on. There were three lighthouses winking with a sharp bright light and, along the coast, the softer blurred lights of houses and street lights.

Earlier this same day, Mohammed had sent his family a wire so that someone would meet us. I could hardly believe we would be in Damascus by the end of the week. Now that we were going along the coast of Algeria, I couldn't shake off the feeling we were on the Hudson River.

Two days into the Mediterranean, the weather turned perfectly beautiful, the best weather of the entire trip. The sun was bright, and there was no wind. The sea was like a lake or a river with nothing more than little ripples on the water. The sea gulls were cawing, and everything was very peaceful. Susu was taking a nap and Mohammed was translating his thesis into Arabic while I was up on the top deck enjoying the lovely day.

That night, we played canasta with Sam and Anne as we often did, and the nice day ended badly. When we won, Sam criticized his wife for the way she played and she almost cried. Sam was getting on my nerves. However, the next morning he was debonair and charming again as if nothing had happened. He asked for Mother's address and promised to write her, and I didn't doubt he would write a lovely letter. We were all a little touchy after being cooped up together for almost three weeks.

Two nights later, on our way to the Syrian port of Latakia, we had a terrible storm with very rough seas. It was the worst weather of our voyage, and I was frightened to death. We had only one more night to spend aboard ship before reaching Beirut, but now it seemed we would never get there. The ship rolled and pitched far more than she ever had on the Atlantic, and for the first time, the waves splashed on our portholes. Although Susu never stirred, we spent most of the night peering out to be sure we were still afloat or climbing up to check with the captain. Mohammed was far braver than I, but even he was worried.

The lower deck of our ship was covered with cars that were lashed down and–we had never understood why–smeared thickly with some kind of grease. Standing on the bridge with the captain, we finally realized the purpose of the grease as the entire lower deck would be momentarily submerged under the salty water when the ship pitched forward. What a terrifying sight this was! The boat would shudder and groan as it struggled to pull up the prow from the tremendous weight of the water. It was so easy to imagine a monster wave crashing over the bow and defeating the efforts of the captain to right the ship. It occurred to me during this raging storm that perhaps flying isn't such a bad way to travel, after all. At least it, is over quickly!

We finally fell asleep. When we awoke, the storm had passed, and we were pulling into Latakia. We were anchored off Latakia about eight hours and spent the day watching dock workers unload cars and other cargo onto big wooden barges. Mohammed said Syria was trying to increase the volume of shipping in this harbor and therefore refused to accept goods imported indirectly by way of Beirut. I could see the houses of Latakia and, in the far horizon, green mountains rising against the blue sky, my first tantalizing glimpse of Syria. The Glasses disembarked and did some sightseeing, but we did not since, as a Syrian citizen, Mohammed would have needed an exit visa to get back on ship.

By nine o'clock the next morning, our small ship was finally riding at anchor in Beirut harbor. We stood on deck, enjoying the hot Mediterranean sunshine while all around us in the harbor shifted a colorful kaleidoscope of ships. A crude-looking barge near our ship caught my eye. It had no visible means of locomotion, and the waves gently rocked its sleeping occupants, who were dressed in baggy trousers and head cloths. I stared down disapprovingly.

"What's the matter with them? Why aren't they working?" I asked Mohammed. After all, I thought to myself, it was nine thirty in the morning.

Mohammed said, "It's the first day of Ramadan. They're fasting. They probably were up by three to eat and pray before beginning the fast. Working in the hot sun makes you thirsty and tired," he said, "and besides, you know it takes time to adjust to fasting. The first day is always the hardest"

Remembering how Mohammed and I had gone right on with our usual schedules in Ramadan, making no concessions because we were fasting, I was not convinced, but I held my tongue.

This was only the first encounter between my native directness and impatience and the maddening patience and circumvention of the Middle East. Over the years, I would grumble to myself that the famous patience of the East is often a vice, not a virtue, and a good excuse for laziness.

We weren't sure there would be anyone to meet us, but suddenly a porter, who came aboard by harbor launch, told us that someone was waiting for us below. Susu hugged "My Lady" and "Unca' Sam" goodbye while Mohammed and I shook their hands and wished them well. Then, we went down to the lower deck.

I recognized Mohammed's brother, Abdulgani, instantly. Jill had described him as looking like the actor, Ricardo Montalban, an apt description. First, the brothers hugged and kissed while Susu stared at her new uncle wide-eyed. Then it was her turn, and she didn't resist at all when Abdulgani swept her up in his arms. Still holding Susu, he turned to me saying, "Well-COME, well-COME!" He was about five feet eight with quite a dark complexion and dark hair and eyes. He had a lovely smile, nice features, not a bit like Mohammed, but handsome in his own way. Almost a year younger than I, he somehow looked older, more Mohammed's age. Actually, there are five years between the brothers. As he shook my hand, I remembered the letter he had written to me welcoming me into the family which began, "Dear Wife-Brother", and I felt he was a friend.

The porters stowed us and all our baggage into the launch, and as we sped towards shore, I turned and took a last fond look at the *Hellenic Sailor*, which had brought us safely so many miles from home.

3.

The Road to Damascus-by Taxi

No brass band or fanfare greeted our arrival in the Middle East. Instead, Susu and I spent our first half hour in Lebanon sitting in the Customs Building while the brothers settled things. Actually, with all the Arabic spoken around us and the oddly dressed people passing by us, it was quite entertaining.

After the formalities at customs, our bags were stuffed into a taxi, and we took them to Abdulgani's hotel. The weather was balmy and quite like May in New York so we were glad to leave our coats in the hotel. Mohammed went off to see about having our crated household goods sent to Damascus while Abdulgani took us for a walk in the city.

We walked along the corniche, the broad street that runs along the Mediterranean, and Susu and I marveled at the palm trees–the first we'd ever seen–that marched down the center of the avenue. Sunlight glinted off the small waves whipped up by the fresh westerly breeze blowing steadily over the bay, over Homer's "wine dark" sea. Lime green, I thought, would be more accurate today but less poetic. I fleetingly remembered my last view of the oily, turgid, khaki-colored water of New York harbor.

We ended up in a dusty, high-ceilinged coffee shop on the corniche. The place had an air of faded elegance and sunlight filtered through latticed windows while a ceiling fan turned languidly. Travelers are exempt from fasting during Ramadan so Abdulgani ordered sandwiches and then coffee for us and soda pop for Susu. As we ate, Abdulgani talked in his own inimitable, halting and heavily accented English. He was the only one in the family besides Mohammed who could speak English, and this helped Susu and me feel at ease with him from the beginning.

He spoke of his university studies and of the family, and I surprised him with my store of information about the many family members. Finally, we went back to the hotel, and Mohammed came within minutes. It's all arranged," he said with satisfaction. "We can get under way."

Although we had a letter of introduction from Dr. Haagensen to the Dean of the AUB Medical School, we didn't look him up. Mohammed was very eager to get to Damascus since he was supposed to report to work this day, March first, and would already be a day late. I decided to send the Dean a postcard and hoped that we could see him some other time. After five hours in Beirut, we were starting out on the road to Damascus.

I had no idea what to expect at the end of this journey. Most of my life had been spent in rural Rockland County within commuting distance of New York City. I was definitely un-traveled and provincial, but since my "province" included New York, I was both naïve and sophisticated. There is a humorous *New Yorker* magazine cover representing a New Yorker's view of the United States: New York City and Long Island take up about half of the picture; New Jersey, Connecticut and Pennsylvania another fourth; and, telescoped all around the three sides of the picture, are the remaining states with only a few, like California, Florida and Texas, clearly visible. This not only accurately represented my national view, but also my world view. In New York City, I felt I was a citizen of the cultural and even the political center of the universe. After all, isn't the UN Headquarters in New York? Now I felt I had slipped off the edge of the page. Yet, at the same time, I was eager to see what lay ahead. Maybe I had landed on another interesting page.

Even Mohammed was probably wondering what lay at the end of our journey. Four years earlier, he had left the Syrian Arab Republic and was now returning to a "new" country, the United Arab Republic, the result of a union between Syria and Egypt. He had left a proud capital city with many embassies and was returning to the provincial capital of the "Northern Region" where only consulates remained. His father had died while he was away, and now, as the oldest son, he would be head of the family. He had come to New York as a young, unmarried graduate of Damascus University and now was returning with a doctorate in economics, a foreign wife and a daughter. I am sure he must have wondered how his family would receive me and how I would adjust, as well as what impact all the other changes would have on our future.

We got into our *service* (serVEECE) taxi after an improbable quantity of luggage had been packed in and on the vehicle, and off we went down the real, not the Biblical, "road to Damascus". Whatever I expected this legendary road to be, it was something altogether different. In no time, we were ascending the hairpin turns above Beirut. Abdulgani, in front with the driver, sat sideways and talked away in Arabic to Mohammed while the car radio played some exotic music–or so I thought.

I remarked it was the first time I had heard Arabic music on the radio, and Abdulgani turned completely around with a shocked look on his face. "That's not music," he said, "it's the Qur'an!" I had never heard the Qur'an recited like this before and felt I had made a terrible *faux pas.*

Meanwhile, the driver guessed this was my first visit to Lebanon and was determined I get a good look at the scenery. We came to a place where the mountain road ran close to a sheer drop-off with green valleys and picturesque towns far below. The driver steered the car close to the edge and swiveled around to face me. With only one hand on the steering wheel, he flamboyantly swept his other hand to indicate the view:

"Look, Madame!" he shouted.

I almost screamed. I closed my eyes, cringed away from the cliff and, holding Susu tightly, waited for the moment we went over. I was sure we would never see Damascus but would end up a flaming wreck in the valley far below. Mohammed saw my terrified face and told the driver to stop, but Abdulgani almost had to physically restrain him. From then on, he ignored us all in disgust and thankfully directed his attention to the driving.

The drive takes about three hours counting stops on both sides of the Syrian/Lebanese border and crosses the Lebanon and Anti-Lebanon mountain ranges. In places, the road reaches the clouds, and you are surrounded by what looks like fog. Yet you can look down on sun-drenched hills and valleys. The first range we crossed was quite green almost to the top and dotted with houses and villages and "summer resorts". The second range reminded me of the barren, reddish brown hills in Western movies: no trees, in fact, little or no vegetation of any sort. The few buildings we saw were border posts or served some governmental function.

The day I arrived in Syria was a day marked by an unusual convergence of the solar month and the lunar month; it was the first of March and also the first of Ramadan. We arrived at the border just at sundown, and our way was expedited by Mohammed's official passport and also because of the day and the hour. The border guards and officials were just about to break the first fast of Ramadan and were far more interested in eating than in detaining anyone or inspecting any luggage. Not a suitcase of ours was opened.

After crossing the border, it got quite cold because of the altitude and the fact that we were moving inland. The rest of the drive was in total darkness except for the stars above which were brighter than I had ever seen them. No streetlights lined the highway, and there were no restaurants, no motels, no gas stations, nothing. We seemed to be driving through a wasteland, a lunar landscape. We hardly passed another car on our two-lane highway, and I began to get the same feeling I'd had on the *Hellenic Sailor* when we seemed to be alone on the planet.

The radio was turned off now, and no one found anything to say. The dark and the quiet were unnerving. As we passed mile after mile of barren empty land, I tried to resist a growing feeling of apprehension. After all, I told myself, Mohammed was by my side, and it was his family who awaited us.

By the time we reached the outskirts of the city, it was about six o'clock. We turned onto a broad street with a row of palm trees planted in the central divide. The street was lined with three-story apartment buildings, each with its patch of greenery around it. As we drove down this broad avenue, ahead rose the dark mass of the mountain of Damascus, Jebel Qassioun, rearing up protectively over the city. The district we were driving through was clean and modern, and I began to think Damascus was not at all the insignificant city I had imagined.

Our car headed north, and ahead of us the city seemed to climb part way up the mountain. Soon the streets narrowed and the buildings were set side-by-side. Mohammed said this was the district of Mohajareen, and now we were almost home. We turned a corner to a street running horizontally along the slope of the mountain and heard a voice shouting, "*Ahlan, ahlan. Al hamdila asalamay*!" (Welcome, welcome. Thank God for your safe return!) A short little man was running alongside of our car, waving madly at us.

The car slowed, down and Mohammed smiled and said something in reply and then explained that this was Shasho, the dwarf, who sold vegetables and fruit from a sidewalk stand on their street. I would never forget he was the first person I saw in Damascus.

We came to a stop halfway down the block in front of a four-story building. It was the tallest building on the block and much larger and more attractive than I had expected. Here we were. I took a deep breath to calm myself, but my heart pounded as I got out of the car.

On entering the building, we plunged into abysmal darkness for three flights of rough unfinished concrete stairs. I remembered Jill warning me that the building was being remodeled and was like a "bombed-out site". Mohammed, Abdulgani and I hauled our luggage and Susu, who was asleep by this time, up the very steep stairs. Finally, on the third landing, a door was flung open, and we were suddenly ushered blinking into blinding light and unceremoniously set upon by what seemed to be hordes of people who passed us among them, talking incessantly, and kissing us right and left.

I sorted out my diminutive mother-in-law from the confusion, and she smiled up at me, then pulled my face down to kiss me and said, with Mohammed translating, "One hundred welcomes! Thank God for your safe arrival. Our home is your home, my daughter."

We embraced, and I stammered some inadequate words about how happy I was to finally meet her. I will never forget her heartwarming, welcoming words to me, a total stranger.

In the midst of this warm reception, I couldn't help noticing that the hallway where we stood was cold, stark and anything but cozy. Very high ceilings, blank walls and cold tiles underfoot did not make for a homey look. However, we were quickly ushered into a heated room with a beautiful carpet covering the floor. "This," Mohammed whispered, "is the best room in the home, what we call the salon or the guest room."

Back home we'd call it a parlor. There were large, stiff armchairs lining all the walls of this good-sized rectangular room and, hanging from the lofty ceiling by a chain, an odd glass chandelier with its light bulbs screwed into rather grotesque, blown-glass flowers. It was an impersonal room as the walls were bare of pictures and there were no books, magazines or whatnots, but the Persian carpet was lovely and the heater was warming the room nicely.

I impressed everyone by picking out Mohammed's sisters and naming them correctly and even asking after the missing, youngest sister. Poor Inayat. I learned that shortly before we arrived, she broke a tall glass jar filled with at least three quarts of olives in olive oil. I guess all the sisters were running around cleaning up the kitchen after their Ramadan meal, hoping to have everything shipshape before our arrival, when the unlucky Inayat dropped the jar. The mess must have been unspeakable: broken glass and olives swimming in a pool of olive oil all over the kitchen floor. It took Inayat more than two hours to put the kitchen to rights and another hour to bathe and clean herself up. When she finally appeared, she looked exhausted but was touched when I kissed her and called her by name. I think my sisters-in-law were more nervous about meeting me than I was about meeting them.

The first thing I noticed about the sisters was that none of them were tall, which proves Mohammed was not very observant. He always said I was "short" and that some of his sisters were my height and some were taller, but I looked around for the "tall" sisters and found that I towered over everyone except Abdulgani, who was a few inches taller than I. Not one of the sisters was my height. They were all between five feet one and five feet three and had the smallest hands and feet. I wondered who my tall Mohammed took after.

The moment I saw Mohammed's mother, my heart sank when I thought of the size sixteen coat we bought for her. She was even shorter than her daughters and barely reached five feet. Her wavy hair, which she wore back in a soft bun, was a lovely white. She had a very sweet, wrinkled face with nice features; her voice was gentle, her smile warm; and she had a quiet dignity. She looked much older than her sixty-two years, but her daughters told us she hadn't been this happy or this well since Mohammed left four years ago.

Kawsar, at thirty-eight, was the oldest sibling and was around eight years older than Mohammed. She was the big sister in every sense of the word. She was the cook, the hostess, the family seamstress and the one who kept the household running smoothly. Everyone in the family relied on her, as I, too, shortly would. She was sturdily built and had a pleasant, open face with apple cheeks and smiling green eyes.

Next were the two married sisters, Lamat and Bara'at. Lamat, at five feet one, was the shortest sister and was plump and fair. Bara'at, who was the tallest, had brown hair and green eyes. She had recently come down with some kind of malady and was left with a slight paralysis on one side of her face. Mohammed told me she had been the prettiest sister so this must have been hard for her. She put on a brave show of not caring, and, of course, no one mentioned it in front of her. Both the married sisters taught school and had their own homes. Riad, the fourth sister, was elegant and sophisticated. Like Bara'at, she had brown hair and green eyes. She was also a schoolteacher but was studying nights for her university degree and hoped to get a job as a government official when she graduated. She spoke French to me, and I was sorry I couldn't answer her.

Finally, there was Inayat who was slim and fair with light auburn hair and blue eyes. She and Riad were about five feet three. She worked at the Ministry of Finance and was one year older than Mohammed. However, since she was still unmarried, the family maintained the fiction that she was a few years younger than her brother. Finally there was Abdulgani, the youngest.

After all these years, that first night, with all its impressions, good and bad, is as clear in my mind as yesterday. My worst shock was catching a glimpse of a young girl, a child of no more than nine, carrying a heavy pail of water into the hallway where, bending over from the waist, she began to wash the floor. This, I learned, was Amira, who worked for Lamat, my sister-in-law, one of the young, far too young, servant girls who lived with and worked for Damascene families back in the sixties. Nothing and no one had prepared me for this, and I was really taken aback.

Mohammed *had* tried to prepare me for the Arabic toilet–the small closet with the hole in the floor over which you squatted. I delayed using it as long as I could, but in the end there was no escape. It was worse than I imagined. You were expected to take off your shoes and wear wooden clogs because the floor was always wet. Someone was always throwing a pail of water over the floor since I was the only one who ever seemed to use the flush chain. Squatting does not come easily to Westerners, especially when you are desperately trying to keep your clothes off a wet floor. Even worse, Mohammed neglected to tell me that Arabic toilets do not come equipped with toilet paper. There was a hose, but then how to dry oneself? With great relief I found some tissues in my pocket. Did I mention the cold? The water in the hose was frigid. The room was probably the same temperature as outside, and there was no hot water in the bathroom next door to wash your hands. The mild weather we had enjoyed in Beirut only a few hours earlier seemed an unreal dream in the biting cold of Damascus.

That night the three of us slept in an unheated bedroom huddled together under a heavy wool quilt and between the family's best embroidered sheets. I had no idea, as we tumbled gratefully into that bed, that we had put my mother-in-law out of her room.

It seemed I'd been asleep no more than a few minutes when I heard loud shouting and what seemed to be the sound of someone beating a drum on the street below. I sat up with no idea where I was, completely befuddled with sleep and the emotional overload of our arrival. I saw Susu sound asleep beside me and Mohammed getting out of bed. Then I became aware of someone knocking on our door.

Bewildered and half-asleep, I said, "What's going on?"

"*Suhoor*," said Mohammed, opening the door.

Kawsar came in smiling broadly and carrying a tray with two small cups of coffee. It came back to me then as I struggled awake–Ramadan, *suhoor*. Before going to bed, I had agreed to join the family for *suhoor*, the pre-dawn breakfast, and Kawsar promised to wake us. This was my fifth Ramadan, but the first time I'd ever heard of *suhoor*. When we fasted in New York, we used to have our second meal before going to sleep.

I gulped down the hot, sweet coffee, ran a comb through my hair, made sure Susu was covered and trailed down the hall after Mohammed to the sitting room. How cold the floor tiles were to my bare feet! However, the sitting room was carpeted. and through the window in the potbellied heater you could see blue flames dancing, making the room pleasantly warm. There, on the floor, seated cross-legged in a circle around a large brass tray, were Mohammed's mother, brother and three sisters, waiting for us to join them. Spread out on the tray, were all kinds of unfamiliar dishes, a pile of flat bread, a steaming pot of tea and small tea glasses. "*Ya meet ahlan wa sahlan*"–"A hundred welcomes"–they all said and made room for us. Kawsar handed me a rolled up sandwich of white cheese with homemade apricot jam, the best I'd ever tasted, and Inayat poured me a glass of tea and passed me the sugar. I told them both *shukran* (thank you), and they smiled and said *afwan* (you're welcome). I thought I was too sleepy to eat a bite, but everything was so tasty that I found I had an appetite.

"What was all that noise down in the street just before we got up?" I asked Mohammed. "I even thought I heard someone shouting and beating a drum."

"That was the *musaher* (moo-SA-hair), beating his drum. He walks the streets before dawn calling for people to wake for *suhoor*."

"Does he get paid? Is it a job?"

"Not really. But neighbors take turns giving him *suhoor.* They sit him down on the stairs of their building with a plate of food and some tea. Generous housewives send him away with food for his family."

How interesting, I thought, and I determined to wake up the next night and look for the *musaher.*

After our meal, the sisters whisked everything into the kitchen, and everyone took turns to wash (in the frigid water) for the Morning Prayer. I wasn't asked to do a thing so I gratefully went back to bed, and Mohammed soon followed. I gasped with shock when he snuggled up to me with his icy hands and feet.

I woke up to bright sunshine pouring in on the bed, sat up, careful not to disturb Mohammed and Susu, and looked around the strange room. I guessed the ceiling must be at least fourteen feet high, which in the large salon was rather nice but was quite another thing in this small room. The night before I had noticed that voices echoed off the high ceilings, especially in places like the halls, where there were no carpets. It would take some getting used to.

The room was dominated by a large wardrobe. The floor was tiled like all the rooms in the apartment, and instead of indoor window shades, there were wooden blinds outside the glass which were hand cranked up or down. In addition to the door to the hallway, the room had another door with a window. I got out of bed, opened it and found myself outside on a narrow balcony that ran the length of the front of the building. Before me was a sweeping view of the city, and below was the street. The sun and the view lifted my spirits. My first day in Damascus had begun.

4.

First Days

After Mohammed went to report to his ministry, Kawsar and my mother-in-law watched me unpack my clothes with great interest. I learned later that they were quite disappointed in my wardrobe. What I considered my best outfit, an expensive tailored suit I had bought especially for Damascus, they rejected as completely inappropriate to wear in front of the guests they were expecting that night. I was Mohammed's American "bride" as they insisted on calling me, whom they planned to show off to one and all, and I should be dressed to suit the role. I believe they expected me to arrive with a trousseau–a trunk full of fashionable outfits and jewelry such as every Damascene bride had as a matter of course.

I quickly learned Damascene women not only wore western dress, they were very fashion conscious. As Kawsar looked at my clothes, she told me the hems of my skirts were too long, and she said, with Abdulgani translating, she would take them up to the middle of the knee in accordance with the latest fashion. But, as I later found out, not all Paris fashions were acceptable. Sleeveless dresses, low cut dresses or trousers might be worn at home but were not considered respectable street wear in Damascus in the sixties.

Kawsar finally smiled as she came across the dress I had worn at my sister Jan's wedding the year before and an old prom dress Mohammed had insisted I bring with me. I had wanted to leave these fluffy, pastel creations behind, but now I found I was expected to wear them every evening when guests came calling–so said my helpful translator.

After unpacking, five little cousins were brought to meet Susu. I sat on the floor of our bedroom with them and broke the ice by getting out the bottles of bubble water I had handy for just such an occasion. Susu showed them how to blow bubbles, and soon some were waving streams of bubbles from their plastic wands and others were trying to catch the fragile, iridescent spheres. By the time we used up all the bottles and there were wet splotches covering us and the carpet, we were all laughing and comfortable together.

I already knew their names from the photos that had been sent to New York and now Susu learned their names. Also, to my surprise, I found that Susu and I had acquired new names. The children called Susu "Sawsan"[1] and me "Mart Khalo" which Abdulgani said meant "wife of my maternal uncle." Oh dear, I thought, every possible relationship here probably has its own specific name – all of which I will have to learn! (I was right). The good news was that Abdulgani said I could call him "Abdo", a shorter easier version of his name.

As soon as Mohammed came home, he took Susu and me down to the third floor apartment that was to be ours as soon as the workmen finished painting it. We walked through the empty rooms marveling at how big and inviting they looked after our tiny apartment in New York. The sun poured through the windows and everything – wood, tiles, plaster and paint - smelled new. There were two men plastering the walls, and Mohammed told me that his family had waited for us to arrive before the final coat of paint went on the walls so we could choose the colors.

The U-shaped apartment had two rooms in the front, one big, one small, and two large rooms about the same size in the back. A hall connected the front and back rooms, and off the hall was the kitchen. The bathroom–with a real toilet!–and the closet for the Arabic toilet were off a smaller hall next to one of the back rooms.

Our fourth day in Damascus was a Friday, the Syrian weekend, and Wahid Beyk[2], Lamat's husband and the only member of the family who owned a car, offered to take us for a ride outside the city. His car was a tiny little Fiat into which we crammed four adults and five children.

Wahid Beyk, small and compact like his car, held the important job of Director of the Damascus Airport. He had a boyish figure, a full head of wavy hair and a neat little mustache. He was always perfectly turned out with a sharp crease in his trousers, an immaculate shirt and a shine on his shoes. Like many short men, he was very self-confident and opinionated. Strange to say, in all these respects, he reminded me of my grandfather.

Also, again like my grandfather, I was told he was an authoritarian father and husband. However, he could be very charming, and this is the side of him I knew.

As we started off, Mohammed said we were going to the Ghouta to see the fruit trees in blossom. The Ghouta, I knew, was the green belt of orchards and woods around the city, but I was surprised that the fruit trees could be in blossom so early.

1 "Sawsan" is Arabic for Susan. Everyone soon called our daughter by her nickname, "Susu."

2 His name was Wahid al-Hawasli, but he was always called "Wahid Beyk". "Beyk"is a term of respect dating from the days of the Ottoman Empire.

However, cold as the March nights were, the daytime sun could take the temperature up to the seventies. I was told that the almond blossoms bloomed even earlier, in February.

Mohammed said on Fridays in the spring everyone wants to escape the city and picnic under the blossoming fruit trees. It seems the farmers don't mind city folk on their land as long as no one picks their blossoms.

Sad to say, at first sight, I was not at all impressed by the fabled Ghouta, which some Syrians insist is the original Garden of Eden. There had been a drought in Damascus for the last few years and, as we drove along the narrow country roads, dust billowed up on both sides of the car. Instead of proper fences, the boundaries between the different farms were marked with crumbling mud brick walls. It was all very strange and different. The orchards of blooming trees, mostly apricot, were lovely, but I was fixated on the parched, dusty state of the land which was very unlike the lush countryside I was used to. Already I felt homesick.

Fat-tailed sheep crowded the narrow road, and sometimes our car had to stop while young boys or girls shepherded their flocks across the road. Even the sheep looked odd. Their coats were dingy from the ever-present dust and had large red, orange or black ownership splotches on them. As they trotted along, their enormous fat tails waggled absurdly to and fro. Susu hung out the car window, staring and probably thinking that these dirty animals couldn't possibly have any relation to Little Bo-Peep's sheep or Mary's little lamb.

Wahid Beyk chose a field and parked the car. We got out and put up folding chairs under the trees and had what Lamat called a "dry picnic," meaning that, it being Ramadan, only the children would eat or drink. After they had eaten their sandwiches, they had a great time running around, exploring and trying to pat the little lambs.

I could hardly believe that Lamat went on this picnic wearing a good suit, stockings and high heeled shoes. Her heels sunk in the plowed furrows between the trees, but she didn't seem to mind. From what I'd seen so far, there wasn't anything called "casual clothes" here. It was either pajamas and nightgowns, which all the family members put on the moment they walked in the door, or outdoor attire, which was always suits and elegant outfits. However, to my surprise, that morning I had seen several men going past our building to the mosque in their pajamas! Not Mohammed, of course.

Finally, we called the children and got back into the car. Soon it would be time to start preparing the sunset meal. We drove slowly, but again the dust billowed up from the dry earth. In places, we had to roll up the windows and could hardly see the orchards in bloom through the clouds of dust.

About two years would pass with good rainy seasons before I was able to truly appreciate the Ghouta in the spring. Then I saw it at its glorious best: field after field of fruit trees whose blossoms were so thick you could scarcely see their branches. Then the trees were truly like–as the Syrian poets say–thousands of brides in their wedding finery. I never again saw the Ghouta as dusty and forlorn as it was that first spring.

Driving back from our aptly named dry picnic, Wahid Beyk took us past part of the old city wall. It didn't seem much like a wall to me since houses were incorporated into it. Curtained windows looked out from the wall, and lines of laundry hung out to dry on top of it. Maybe at one time it had served as a bulwark, but now it was a tamed, domesticated fortification. We also passed two of the old gates of the city, one with enormous metal doors.

As we rode through the modern part of the city, I saw mostly three-story stucco buildings in beige, brown or gray enlivened with the bright colors of wooden shutters and painted flowerpots filled with flowers. These pots adorned most of the balconies, and no building was without a balcony. Finally, we drove up to our building which was quite typical except for the color, which was the rarely seen coral with cheerful fire-engine red wooden shutters.

Starting our second night in Damascus, we had guests pour in every evening after *iftar,* the big sunset meal that breaks the fast. The people came to welcome Mohammed home, to welcome Susu and me into the family, and most of all, to get a good look at these curiosities, an American "bride", as they insisted on calling me, and her daughter. We were put on display as prize exhibits number one and two. Susu wore her Sunday best and I was feeling foolish in a cloud of tulle as I received visitors in my bridesmaid's dress. I met all Mohammed's extended family and said *marhaba* (hello) to dozens of friends, relatives and neighbors and I smiled and smiled until my facial muscles were tired. This is how Queen Elizabeth must sometimes feel, I thought.

Since I couldn't speak Arabic, I had a lot of opportunity to study everyone's behavior, and I began to see that these welcoming visits adhered to a well-understood formula, being almost a choreographed event. As the weeks passed, I would gradually become aware that many social situations had an elaborate code of etiquette which I would learn bit by bit, day by day, but now I sat clueless in the salon and looked around me.

When the guests came in, they were first welcomed by Kawsar, and then, before sitting down, the visitors went round the room and greeted every one in the room. As the guest approached, each person rose to welcome the newcomer, and women even stood for men. I looked around and followed the example. Women kissed each other on both cheeks and shook hands with the men while the men mostly shook hands, but some men also kissed each other. Each visitor asked everyone in the room in turn about their health and the health of their relatives and then was asked the same questions in return. All this had to transpire before any other topic could be broached.

How very, very strange, I thought. They hear all the others asking the questions, and they hear the answers. Yet. they go ahead and ask the same questions themselves. Kawsar was the official hostess, and she deftly stage-managed who sat where and whose turn it was for juice or coffee. Her round face beamed a welcoming smile at each guest, and then, lips pressed together, she became seriously intent as she made certain no one was forgotten or served out of turn, with older guests taking precedent. She and Inayat brought in tray after tray of fresh orange juice, large sesame seed cookies and small pistachio baklava pastries, always followed by the thick, strong, cardamom-flavored coffee that was served in dainty little cups. On their way out, callers were offered wrapped chocolates in a silver dish. People came and went, but there was never an empty chair. I think Kawsar directed the overflow to the sitting room until there was a place in the salon.

The evenings went slowly for me. When someone came, I stood, shook hands (if a man) or kissed (if a woman). Then I said, in Arabic, "Hello, how are you," and depending upon the day, "It's warm (or cold) today." Then I sat and smiled and said in Arabic, "I understand" or (mostly) "I don't understand" at the appropriate times. Finally, when someone left, I said, "Goodbye, God be with you." More standing up, more handshaking or kissing. I was picking up words fast, and people were impressed by my Arabic efforts.

Some of the visitors were very amusing once the barrier of rote questions was overcome. One evening, a jolly gentleman married to a cousin of Mohammed's, kept us entertained for hours. He wore an old-fashioned *tarboosh* or fez and was a great story teller. Mohammed sat beside me and translated all his tales so I wouldn't feel left out when everyone burst into gales of laughter.

Sometimes the voices of two or three guests would rise, their faces would look agitated, and they would gesture excitably. I would be sure they were furious with each other or that something was wrong and would worriedly ask Mohammed what was the matter. He would laugh and explain that it was nothing, that Syrians were simply more vehement, fiery and emotional than Americans. Perhaps, I thought. But Mohammed was not like that at all. He always spoke quietly and calmly.

After five nights of an endless stream of guests, we were worn out and needed a rest. I think it was Abdo's idea that we turn out all the lights in the apartment and not answer the door. Quite a few people rang the bell over and over, but we sat in the dark like naughty children, whispering and smothering our laughter until at last they gave up and went away. We finally got to bed early that night.

The next day, to our great surprise, Sam and Anne Glass came to visit us. They were on their way from Jerusalem to Turkey, where their son was teaching. They had a terrible time finding us because we had no phone, and although they had our address with the name of our street and the number of our building, Syrians are accustomed to a different way of locating places, what I call "the landmark method". A Damascene would give directions to our home by saying: "The Imady building is one street up from the tram street in Mohajareen. Walk up one block from Abu Saoud's drugstore at Shutta Street, and then turn left. It's the tallest building on the block."

As it was, it took Sam and Anne more than two hours of bus riding, walking and asking dozens of people to find us. I hope the welcome we gave them made up for their trouble. Susu was delighted to see "Unca'Sam" and "My Lady" again and ran to hug them. We took them downstairs and showed them through our new apartment, with Susu holding Anne's hand and chattering away with her about Khali ("Auntie") Kawsar and Tete[3] ("Grandma"), the two newly important people in her life.

Sam and Anne arrived in the afternoon, and we insisted they share our *iftar* meal and spend the evening with us. When Kawsar heard they were staying, she suddenly disappeared. A while later, I looked in the kitchen and found her presiding over the stove with a satisfied look on her face. Her sleeves were rolled up and a lock of hair kept falling over one eye as she put the finishing touches to the six or seven dishes she had whipped up with no fuss and little help from anyone.

I am sure the Glasses were impressed by the splendid feast she prepared and perhaps a little overwhelmed not only by the huge meal, but also by our usual onslaught of evening guests. A friend of Mohammed's showed up that night who could speak English, and he and Sam enjoyed talking about Jerusalem and Damascus. Sam had many nice things to say about the Palestinians and said he was strongly in favor of the Arabs' claim to Jerusalem. Needless to say, this went down very well.

Before they left, Sam told me he would write Mother and tell her of their visit. In fact, he told me their visit was to keep a promise they had made to Mother on board the *Hellenic Sailor* before we sailed: to check up on Susu and me in Damascus and to write her the truth of our situation. I found Sam's letter among Mother's papers after her death (she was a first-rate hoarder), and thirty-five years after it was written, I read it for the first time. I was touched and felt guilty for my long-ago criticism of him.

Here is part of his letter:

"Since there were only seven passengers aboard ship, we became very close-knit, and I had the opportunity to study Mohammed quite closely. My conclusion before we reached landfall was, 'Here is an exceptionally fine young man.'

"I am being very frank with you when I say we worried about Elaine's reception and her ability to adapt herself to the Mohammedan way of family life. However, she said herself this first week she wasn't asked to do one chore around the house but

3 Pronounced TAY tay, like MAY day.

feed Susu. The mother is just the picture of your son-in-law, utterly gracious and thoughtful.

"Before the evening ended, Anne and I can reassure you we felt your daughter should be proud to be part of such a fine family. The change in faith, the distance from home, living with one's in-laws in the same four-story building–none of these seemed to be insurmountable problems."

Mohammed's friend offered to take the Glasses back to their hotel and, as I watched them walk down the stairs, I thought, now the last slender thread that connected me to New York has snapped...

The next morning Abdo took Susu and me for a walk, and on our way back, he promised to take us up to the roof of our building. It was a strenuous climb of eighty-two steps (I counted) from the street, and the first flight of twenty steps was unreasonably steep. But it was worth it. When we finally got to the top, there was Jebel Qassioun rising starkly behind our building with the city and its green Ghouta and brown desert stretching out spectacularly on the other three sides as far as the eye could see. Looking north to the mountain, we saw houses on the steep slope climbing perhaps a quarter of the way up where they abruptly stopped, and above there was nothing but barren rock: no trees, no grass, no buildings, just rock. It was an odd sight to someone used to the gentle, green hills of the Hudson. Looking south, we saw the entire city with the three minarets of the Umayyad Mosque dominating the skyline. East was the Ghouta and west, desert.

The roof was perfectly flat and tiled, and the wall around it came up to my chest so I didn't need to worry about Susu falling off. Of course, like our apartment, it was U-shaped, the inside of the "U" being the courtyard. There were electrical outlets and water spigots, and it was more like a penthouse terrace than any roof back home; a marvelous place for summer parties under the stars or a place for children to play. In fact, in the years to come, we would have dozens of children's birthdays and grown-up parties on this roof.

Since my arrival, I had been alarmed by a strange noise that no one seemed able to explain to me. I would hear it and ask nervously, "What was that?" and everyone one would look at me blankly. Finally, up on the roof this day I heard the noise again, and Abdo laughed and said, "Oh, *that* noise. It's just the neighbor's peacock." Apparently, a peacock was kept on a roof nearby us, and its screeching was the noise I couldn't identify. Who would expect a peacock on a city roof? And that was not all. You could find sheep, goats and chickens right in the heart of the city. Across the street, the neighbors had a sheep pen with several sheep and a lamb in it. Pigeons were raised on the rooftops, as well as rabbits. And chickens! There were more roosters on our block in Mohajareen than there were in all of Palisades, and every one of them crowed madly in the early morning. What a strange city this was.

There was great excitement when the truck arrived bringing our household goods from Beirut. Every member of our family and practically the entire neighborhood turned out for the event. Our street was filled with people gaping and shouting advice as to how the heavy crated appliances should be manhandled up our steep stairs. Finally, with much grunting, sweating and calling on *Allah*, three rather small, wiry men got everything into our apartment. The neighbors across the street brought us flowers in honor of the occasion.

It was not surprising that the whole neighborhood considered the arrival of our kitchen appliances an occasion to celebrate. My electric refrigerator was the first one on the block, and my gas stove with its big oven and my large electric wringer washing machine were just as novel. I knew after I had been a day or two in Damascus that my in-laws had no refrigerator, and I marveled at how they managed without one. Now I learned they would be sharing mine, an arrangement that lasted successfully for six years, until they bought their first refrigerator.

Kawsar showed me what they had used to put their food in: the *nemliya*, or "ant-proof food keeper" which was a screened cupboard where cooked dishes were put to protect them from flies, ants, cockroaches or mice. However, in the heat of the summer, you could not count on anything lasting very long. Consequently, Damascenes, from necessity, were ingenious at preserving food. Many staples could be kept for months in olive oil. Various kinds of cheeses, artichokes and grape leaves were preserved in salt water and even cooked meat could be kept for weeks if covered with *semnay*, a kind of ghee. In addition, some vegetables and herbs were dried.

5.

Ramadan

All through the month of Ramadan, Kawsar and my mother-in-law set a table like something out of the *Arabian Nights* for the sunset meal. At first I thought my new family always ate like royalty, and then I realized that Ramadan meals are unique, with many special dishes, something like our Christmas holiday fare. But even for Ramadan, the meals we had when we first arrived were unusually grand. The family wanted to celebrate Mohammed's return, as well as Susu's and my arrival, and food is the favorite Syrian way of showing how much you care for people. Although almost everything was new to me, I was willing to try anything, and luckily I seemed to have a cast iron stomach. Many foreign wives lose weight the first few weeks they are in Syria, but I actually gained a pound or two.

The long days of Ramadan passed slowly, filled with the new rhythm of our lives. There was so much to learn, so much to absorb, so much to do that I didn't find time to be homesick. Every day Mohammed and I worked on getting our new apartment ready. With the help of a cleaning lady Kawsar hired for a few days–not one of the child maids–I washed windows, scraped paint off floors and scrubbed floors.

We didn't have much furniture but gradually were getting what we needed. "Gradually" is an understatement. There was no such thing as ready-made furniture back then. You had to go to a carpenter, choose a style you liked from a catalogue or, better yet, from completed samples, then decide what kind of wood you wanted and finally order it. The whole process took months. The family ordered a bedroom suite for us as a wedding present three months before we came, but when we arrived only the bed had been delivered. We already had a dining room table, another present from the family, but needed a china closet, bookcases and living room furniture.

One of the things that arrived with our household goods, was Susu's crib, which we immediately set up. Fortunately, it was still large enough for her. And still there were dishes, cooking pots, towels, sheets, blankets, carpets, curtains to buy. The list was endless.

* * *

My first weeks in Damascus, I found any and every excuse to sit on the balcony adjoining our bedroom, writing letters, reading, watching the street action below or, best of all, just looking at the city. I knew this sight was one thing I would miss when we moved downstairs because there, the house across the street blocked most of the view.

The balconies on our building were enclosed by a stone wall about three feet high and were, in typical fashion, surmounted by another foot or more of wrought iron, artfully twisted and bent into arabesque patterns. Some balconies were generously built and could seat a large family and visiting friends. However, even smaller balconies, like ours, were crowded with potted flowers - geraniums, rose bushes, jasmine, climbing vines and one or two caged songbirds.

Balcony floors were tiled and had a drain at one end. Mornings I would find Kawsar and other industrious housewives sluicing them down with pails of water and afterwards, bent double over their handle-less brooms, sweeping the water down the drain. Then, watch out below! The dirty water spurted out of a spout down on the street or onto any unlucky passerby. The balcony was also where Kawsar pinned up the larger pieces of the weekly wash which quickly flapped dry in the sun and where she hung pungent garlic bundles and ropes of dried okra.

One day that first week, I asked my mother-in-law, through Abdo, if I could help her with the time-consuming preparations for *iftar*. She handed me a tray and some lentils to pick clean, and I carried them out to the balcony. I sat down and turned my face up to the delightful and surprisingly hot rays of the March sun.

"What bliss," I thought, "after the cold of last night! Why do they build their homes as though hot weather was all they ever expected?"

Characteristically for desert weather, the temperature could drop twenty-five degrees Fahrenheit or more from noon to midnight, and the tile floors, high ceilings and drafty windows meant bone-chilling rooms at night. I had never been so cold indoors before: no central heating, and only one room of my in-law's five-room apartment had a heater. Oh yes, the salon also had one, but it was only lit when guests were expected. I could see my breath in the kitchen and bathroom at night. The water heater in the bathroom was only lit for the weekly wash and the Friday once-a-week family baths.

But if some creature comforts were lacking, there were the more important plusses of life in this strange place. First and foremost, there was my new family who had welcomed me with open arms. Many foreign wives, so I had heard back in New York, received an icy reception from their husband's family, but I found only the apartment cold.

And then there was the city. I stared out at the sunlit city pinned to a cloudless blue sky by its pointed minarets and could not get my fill of the sight. The fourth-floor balcony where I sat gave a commanding view of Damascus, from the east where the newer districts of Tejara and Kasaa' spilled over the ancient city walls, to the south where the district of Midan sprawled towards the horizon and finally, to the west past the extensive fields of cactus fruit where one desert road led, beyond my range of vision, to the small village of Mezze and another to the International Airport. The clear air gave almost a supernatural sharpness and clarity to the scene.

Of course, none of the districts of the city had names to me yet. What I saw was an enigmatic panorama: unfamiliar flat-roofed buildings with balconies interspersed with domes and tall minarets. All around me were unfamiliar noises and smells I couldn't identify. It was strange, stimulating and exciting.

Suddenly, my attention was drawn to the narrow street below by a raucous motorcycle roaring by, followed by an ear-splitting sound I didn't recognize. Rounding the corner appeared a *fellah*, a peasant, leading a braying donkey, its saddlebags overflowing with vegetables for sale. I had never heard a donkey bray before and was astonished at the sound. The peasant seemed to be competing with his animal as he chanted in a loud carrying sing-song, advertising his wares. Together, they were making almost as much noise as the motorcycle had.

The peasant's *sharwal* (baggy pants) and *keffiyeh* (headdress) and the laden donkey were still novelties to me, and I had a good opportunity to observe them when a neighbor, dressed in her flannel nightgown, but with a scarf on her head, called out to the *fellah* from her balcony. A lively exchange between them ended with the woman sending a little girl down with a large pot and a handful of coins. The *fellah* weighed out the vegetables–was it cabbage and eggplant?–with a hand-held scale under the watchful eye of the woman on the balcony. Then he dumped the vegetables into the pot and took the change the girl counted into his hand.

The girl, no more than a wisp of a child, I knew was a servant. I could spot these little housemaids after only a few days in Damascus. Like Amira, my sister-in-law's servant girl, they were invariably dressed in ill-fitting clothes, wore slippers on their bare legs, and, unlike the spotlessly turned out children of the city, had an unkempt, but often capable and cheerful, look about them. I felt a pang when I saw this child. Perhaps, as I had been told, these girls were better fed by the families they worked for and lived with than they would have been at home, and possibly they were learning skills they might not have acquired back in their villages, but surely even the poorest child would prefer to be with her own family.

Mohammed assured me that issues like schooling and playtime for these girls were not relevant. If they were at home, their parents would have them hard at work and would certainly not send them to school. It went to show how far from home I was and what a different a world I had stepped into.

I looked down at the lentils I was supposed to be picking clean. There were small stones and twigs to be removed before they could be cooked. However, as I looked closer, some of the lentils seemed to move. To my horror, little insects, brought to life by the warm sun, were wriggling their way out of the lentils and flying away. I quickly put these lentils in the discard bowl which reduced the pile on my tray drastically.

Suddenly Abdo and my mother-in-law appeared at the door of the balcony. She looked at me anxiously and said something in her sweet voice. Abdo explained, "My mother says the sun can kill. You shouldn't sit too long in the sun."

"How funny," I thought. "They worry about this lovely sun and not about the frigid bathroom at night."

My mother-in-law noticed the large pile of discarded lentils on my tray and smiled. She gestured for me to hand her the tray and scooped up the rejected lentils and added them back to the pile. I decided I'd lost my appetite for lentil soup that day.

The balcony was my lookout and my first "classroom". It was there I discovered our neighbors raised chickens on their balcony and that a troop of black, nimble-footed goats passed by our building every morning on their way to pasture and back again every evening, chased by a skinny, little goatherd.

Then, there was Shasho the dwarf, who sold fruit and vegetables on our street. I was told he was a fixture in our neighborhood, that all the housewives bought from him. Mohammed told me he did a good business because you got your money's worth from him.

Every day I saw him from my balcony setting up his wares on the corner of our block. He arranged his fruit and vegetables artistically on an oilcloth spread over the sidewalk and sometimes his much taller, pretty young wife could be seen helping him.

A close neighbor raised pigeons on his roof, and around sunset I would watch him, mesmerized, as he stood on the rooftop and directed his flock with a rag-topped stick. The birds flew in the sky swooping in circles, now left, now right, now higher, now lower, perfectly matching the motions of their owner's stick which he wielded like the baton of a symphony conductor. The swirling and wheeling of these birds through the twilight sky seemed a kind of mute music to me. I was disappointed to learn the ulterior purpose of all this. Mohammed said pigeon fanciers try to steal valuable birds from their neighbors, that when the pigeons wheel in the sky close to a neighbor's flock, some birds may desert their owner and join the neighbor's birds.

Maybe so, but still it was lovely to watch the birds flying graceful arabesques in the darkening sky.

Waiting with Mohammed on the balcony for the daylong fast to end, I saw all the minarets simultaneously illuminated as the sunset call to prayer floated over the city. Before this call, both a summons to prayer and a signal to break the fast, the whole city seemed hushed, holding its breath, a city full of fasting people like ourselves, lightheaded with hunger and thirst, almost ready to see visions, hear voices.

The days passed in this strange city with its extremes of temperature and its volatile people. Sometimes I could hardly believe where I was and would awake disoriented in the morning, blinking in the bright morning sun and thirsty from the dry air of Damascus. The neighbor's peacock screeched on its rooftop, the voices of Kawsar and her sisters could be heard in the kitchen, and far above my head was the ceiling of this unfamiliar room. Where was I? To reassure myself, I would reach out for Mohammed; without him it all would have been too alien. Some of the foreign wives I came to know in Damascus had visited the city and their in-laws before deciding to start a new life in Syria. I found this odd. For me, all that mattered was Mohammed.

* * *

There was a quaint little electric streetcar that clanged along on the street below ours to the center of the city for the equivalent of pennies. The driver would ring his bell and shout, "*Yalla, yalla*," which seemed to mean, "Out of my way fast or else." Susu fell in love with this trolley–called the *tramwye* (from the British, *tramway*)-at first sight and asked daily to be taken for a ride on it. One day Riad found she needed more yarn for the sweater she was knitting, and Kawsar said she would buy it. She told Susu and me to come along since she was taking the *tramwye*.

I still remember the names of all the tram stops in Mohajareen: Shora, Bashkatib, Shamsiya, Mustabay, Shutta, Murabbet, and the Akher Khut or the "last stop". We crossed the street to our stop, Shutta, and in no time the trolley made its dramatic appearance; its wheels clattering and clanking along the tracks, its bell ringing insistently and sparks spitting and hissing from the overhead cable.

The trolley was small and could only seat about thirty-two people, but besides the driver, there was the ticket seller–grandly called the *commissionaire*–who came around to take your money and give you a numbered ticket which he then punched. Every so often there would also be an inspector on the train checking to be sure that all passengers had a punched ticket. Kawsar, Susu and I sat in the rear of the tram in the tiny "ladies only" compartment. As we barreled along, children recklessly jumped on the back of the tram and off at the next corner, and young boys on bicycles grabbed on for a free ride. I kept expecting them all to be killed. At least we were downtown in no time.

Along the way, I saw few private cars on the road, but plenty of taxis and busses. There were no traffic lights in the entire city, but down by the Victoria (pronounced "Fiktoria") Bridge in the center of town, a lone policeman stood on a round platform directing traffic. At all other intersections, the traffic moved freely and chaotically with a great blaring of horns, shouts and gestures from the drivers. On the way back, I made up my mind to take Susu for a ride on the tram one day soon, just the two of us.

Every day we thought of something we absolutely had to have for our apartment, so before long I had been all over the city on shopping trips. My first trip down to the souk, or market, was with Mohammed and Susu in search of pots and pans and other kitchen things. We went through several of the covered markets, but the most impressive was Souk Hamadiyeh. Its arched roof, which was probably forty feet above street level, gave a spacious open feel to the place–at least if you looked up. At ground level it was as crowded and raucous as New York's Times Square on New Year's Eve. The metal arcade was pierced in many places with holes which, Mohammed told me, came from the bombardment of the city when Syria was fighting France for its independence. Through these holes the light sifted down, flecked with dust motes, on the dim and crowded street.

As my eyes adjusted to the subdued light, I found the main thoroughfare lined cheek to jowl with small shops. Most had some of their merchandise on display outside, either piled up on the sidewalk or hanging above the shops on "clothes lines". But the merchants didn't stop there. They sent young boys out into the crowds to entice you into their dens with insistent cries of "*Tafuddily*!"(Come in!)

Our fellow shoppers were wearing every sort of costume from the baggy trousers of the typical peasant garb to the Arab sheikh outfit with flowing robe and head cloth–plus everything in-between. Women were sandaled, wearing high heels, veiled and bare headed and a few were even tattooed on their faces like the women pictured in that first book I read about Syria. On the other hand, some stylishly dressed men and women would not have looked amiss on Fifth Avenue in New York.

Mohammed told me that Kawsar could name the village of many peasant women just by the color, pattern and style of their distinctive clothes and head coverings. For example, orange cloaks with black stripes were worn by the women of Mezze, and the women from Jobar wore cloaks with the three colors of blue, indigo and black.

In ten minutes of walking in the souk, we saw for sale wooden clogs, slippers, children's clothes, underwear, perfume, head coverings for men and women, brass trays, gold and silver jewelry, chess boards, lutes, rugs, prayer carpets and rolls of fabric of all kinds–but no pots and pans. Beguiling and exotic smells wafted through the air. There were fragrant scents from the perfume and attar shops, pungent odors coming from the spice market and the distinctive smell of tanned skins from the leather souk.

Every so often, we came across the arched entrance of an old stone khan with its huge, embossed metal door. Most of these buildings originally had domed courtyards, but over the centuries the domes had collapsed and now the courtyards were open to the sky. Mohammed said these khans once played an important part in the caravan trade of the Middle East as resting places for traveling merchants and their animals, as well as warehouses for their goods. Although the last caravan had crossed the desert perhaps sixty years earlier, the khans, far from being abandoned ruins, were bustling with workshops and business offices.

We had a hard time finding pots with handles. All the pots we found were *tanajers* (tan-NA-jers), the big round metal pots without handles, like the ones Kawsar used. Only the frying pans had handles. At last we found one store that had what they called "foreign pots," and we bought several along with lots of other items for the kitchen.

The next day Susu and I ventured forth alone for the first time. We took the tram to the park behind the Parliament building, and Susu was overjoyed to find there were swings and a slide. Everyone knew we were foreigners, and we created a sensation. Mothers stopped talking and came closer to listen to us speak English, children stared wide-eyed, and two ladies were very interested in Susu's wool knit hat with the rabbit fur pompon. They gestured that they wanted to see it and passed it between them, carefully counting stitches. I guess they planned to knit one like it.

Finally, although all the attention was friendly enough, we got tired of being stared at and left the park. Coming home on the trolley, no one collected a fare from me, and Mohammed said later that in all his twenty-nine years that had never happened to him. Maybe they thought I didn't have any Syrian money. I heard the conductor call out, "Shutta," and we got off.

As we walked around the corner to our street, there was Kawsar leaning anxiously out of the window. What relief on her face when she saw us! They were all afraid I wouldn't be able to find the way home by myself. Mohammed was proud of me when he heard of our adventure.

* * *

From my first week in Damascus, I kept hearing the word "eid" (it rhymes approximately with "feed"); "eid" this and "eid" that, people would say. Intrigued, I asked Mohammed what the word meant. He told me it was short for Eid al-Sagheer (sa-GHEER)[1] the Small Feast which is the three-day holiday that comes at the end of Ramadan. Two months and eleven days after the Small Feast comes the Eid al-Kabeer, the Big Feast, a four-day holiday which celebrates the end of Pilgrimage. Unlike Christmas and Easter which fall on fixed days and in two different seasons, the two Muslim Feasts are close together and move backwards through "our" solar calendar

1 The pronunciation of the Arabic "gh" is similar to the French "r".

months. They can and do fall on every month of the year. Also, Damascenes commonly refer to both Feasts as "the Eid" without any distinction. More and more odd facts to conjure with!

All Ramadan, Kawsar spent every free moment sewing Feast dresses for Susu and her cousin, May. With the emphasis on new clothes, the Eid seemed to be sort of a Muslim Easter to me.

I looked forward eagerly to this holiday and imagined that, as wonderful as Ramadan was, the Eid must be even better. I was wrong. The day arrived, and we all woke very early, happy to be able to have breakfast after one month of fasting. Everyone had a bath, and Susu put on one of her two new dresses. Like all the children whose parents could afford it, she also had new socks and shoes. Her grandmother gave her a gold locket on a chain with a tiny Qur'an inside, and every relative who came visiting us gave Susu some money–her Eid money. Mohammed bought me a pretty blouse, and the family gave me baroque pearl earrings to match the pearl bracelet they sent me when they heard of our marriage.

Then came the let down. In the Eid, I soon found out, everyone went their separate ways. The men called on all their friends and male relatives. The women were cooped up in the kitchen serving coffee and sweets to the male visitors, and the children were down in the streets where, at several places in the city, temporary children's street fairs had been set up. These fairs had swings, hand-pushed merry-go-rounds and other rides, as well as little booths selling fire crackers, sweets and snacks. Young peasant boys brought their horses, grandly decorated with feather plumes, blue beads and bells and charged the braver children for rides. One of these fairs was set up in our block, and the noise of children shouting and singing as well as the endless crack and bang of firecrackers was deafening to me but thrilling to Susu. She could look down on all this exciting activity from the balcony and cried inconsolably to join the fun.

Finally, her oldest cousins came and took her down into the thick of it with her hands clutching her Eid money. I kept an eagle eye on her from the balcony as she went from booth to booth and ride to ride with her cousins. That took care of Susu, but I was now left to myself and not at all pleased.

After two days of this, I was seething. "What kind of holiday is this," I said to Mohammed. "Where I come from, families spend their holidays together!"

"*Habeebti* (my love), I'm so sorry. I had no idea you were upset."

"Of course! You've hardly been home since this so-called holiday began."

He was truly contrite and promised we'd spend the remainder of the Eid together, and we did. We visited many of the relatives, with Susu in tow, and took the family out to eat in a restaurant. This set the pattern for the future, and Mohammed never again left me alone on a holiday.

6.

A Different World

As soon as the Eid ended, the postman showed up with a letter and several photographs from my mother of their unusual March snow storm. Susu and I looked long and hard at the photo of Mother and Jo standing next to the car almost buried in snow. We could hardly believe there was snow anywhere, let alone a blizzard. It was now April first, and the temperature on our balcony was around seventy-six degrees Fahrenheit. Susu hugged and kissed the picture. Both of us missed all our dear Palisades people

Mother was worrying about Susu not being able to speak with the children, but that didn't seem to be a problem. In fact, Susu was beginning to pick up phrases from her cousins. Lamat had a girl and two boys, and Bara'at had three boys, and all were close in age with the two oldest both six years old. The cousins regarded Susu as an exotic and fascinating being because she spoke a foreign tongue with her strange mother and had more toys and books than they had ever seen. They all competed for her attention, but Susu predictably had the most fun with her only girl cousin, May, who was just a year older than her.

In Ramadan, it seemed the only fixed thing was our sunset meal and the hordes of people who came to see us every night. But after Ramadan, life settled into a more regular routine. Our day began when Kawsar knocked on our bedroom door at seven with a tray of Arabic coffee–such a nice way to wake up. "Good morning!" she would say cheerfully. "*In sha' Allah* (I hope) you slept well?"

She would have a cup for herself, and as we three sipped the sweet, scalding hot coffee, Mohammed would inquire about Tete's night. The sun would light up

Kawsar's smile if the answer was favorable, and then she and Mohammed told each other of their plans for the day and would ask me if I had anything special in mind.

Every morning I made Susu French toast. No sliced bread existed in the city, so we bought rolls, somewhat like fat hot dog rolls, which I sliced lengthwise. These rolls were called *khubbiz efrenjouni*, or "foreign bread," because the usual bread was a round, flat disk about the size of a dinner plate ("pita" bread). We found a small grocery store which specialized in imported foodstuffs where we could buy corn flakes, powdered milk, and peanut butter, all of which we kept on hand for Susu. Other than these few things, she happily ate Syrian food.

Kawsar and her sisters helped to prepare breakfast, and we all gathered to eat at about seven o'clock. Mother would have fainted to see the odd things consumed here for breakfast, particularly *makdous* which are small pickled eggplants, no longer than a finger, stuffed with walnuts, red peppers and garlic and preserved in olive oil. Another odd item was *zaatar*, a powdered spice blend made from thyme and other herbs which we ate by dipping bits of bread in olive oil and then in the *zaatar.* We also ate white cheese, creamy yogurt, and olives, all of which were scooped up with torn off pieces of bread and washed down with strong, sweet tea.

After breakfast, Inayat and Riad went to work, and Abdullah, Bara'at's husband, showed up with baby Amer. Mohammed's mother and Kawsar took care of the baby while Bara'at taught school.

Mohammed usually had some errands to do in the morning, either for the apartment or for his impending decree. After all his anxiety about getting back to Syria in order to report to work on the first of March, he hadn't begun working yet although now it was April. I soon learned how typical this delay was. The government decided to transfer Mohammed from the Ministry of Finance to the newly established Ministry of Planning, and because of all the red tape involved, Mohammed was asked to wait until his transfer decree went through before reporting to work. The good news was that, along with the transfer, came a rise in rank and, consequently, a higher salary. His title would be "Director of the Department of Commodities Balances," which sounded very grand to me.

Abdo usually hung about the whole morning, ostensibly studying, but actually talking to me. Easygoing Abdo was the exact opposite of his conscientious and hardworking brother. He admitted his ambition was just to enjoy himself and avoid hard work. However, he patiently entertained Susu and was always ready to translate for me.

Kawsar spent her mornings cleaning the apartment and then buying, preparing and cooking the food for dinner. Cooking was a daunting chore that took forever because everything was made from scratch and Syrian cookery involves lots of cutting, coring, peeling, slicing and pounding in a mortar and pestle. My mother-in-law did the sitting down jobs like feeding baby Amer, and Kawsar did the back-breaking ones, like sweeping the carpets. She swept the carpets bent almost double over a broom without a handle and washed the tile floors bent over a floor cloth. All Syrian women cleaned their rugs and floors like this although brooms and mops with handles *were* available, and Mohammed bought them for me to clean our bedroom. I handed Kawsar my mop with a handle one day, but she just laughed and went on using her own method.

Susu tagged about after me or Abdo or went with Kawsar on her expeditions outside. At noon, Bara'at and her two boys arrived, and the children ate lunch while their mother nursed Amer. Since our arrival, I hadn't seen anyone feed a baby with a bottle. Babies were breast-fed until they were toddlers. A two-year old would walk over to his mother and ask to nurse and not be refused.

Sometimes Lamat and her three children would drop in, but by 1:00 they all left. Around 2:30, Inayat and Riad arrived home from work, Mohammed would show up, and we had our big meal. Afternoons, Susu usually had a nap, and sometimes Mohammed and I went shopping for the new apartment with Kawsar. Evenings were still mostly taken up with guests, and by eleven we collapsed in bed.

One of the hardest things for me to get used to was the Syrian week. What had once been a concrete, tangible thing became a jumble in my mind. Syria was on a six-day week, and since Friday was the one-day week-end, Saturday was "Monday", the first working day of the week, Sunday was "Tuesday" and so on. Because of this strange setup, I couldn't keep track of time or think of the past or future in terms of neat weeks or months. My sense of time was completely thrown out of kilter.

To further complicate matters, instead of the second Sunday in May, March 21st, turned out to be Syrian Mother's Day. Now, I would have to keep track of both dates, one for my mother and one for my mother-in-law. I was baffled by these cock-eyed days and weeks, but hoped that eventually, I would hammer them into some kind of shape and pattern.

Mealtime was also unsettling. Since working hours were from eight-fifteen to two-fifteen, breakfast and dinner were more than seven hours apart, and by two thirty I was famished. For months, my rumbling stomach continued to alert me that it was twelve noon and time for lunch. Supper was very unimportant because people were so full after the big meal. Some people ate nothing at all, and many would just have fruit. The evening meal had no fixed time and was never a proper sit-down affair, unless we were invited out. Then, an elaborate dinner would be served, sometimes as late as eleven-thirty at night.

It was the second week of April before Mohammed started working at the Ministry of Planning. He was happy to finally begin working after the long delay and was pleased to find his director was a knowledgeable and experienced Egyptian economist.

A few days later, we moved into our apartment. The painters still had two more coats of paint to go, but we moved in anyway. For some ungodly reason, they put eight or so layers of plaster and paint on these cement walls, and we got tired of waiting. Whenever they got to the final coat, I was ready to tell them the colors I had chosen. Eventually, all the rooms turned out nicely, and my cheerful pale yellow *salon* looked exceptionally fine. Actually, I refused to shut up the best room in the house and save it only for visitors. My *salon* immediately became the living room.

One good result of moving into our own apartment was to finally escape the family's tallying up our baths. In order to keep the fast in Ramadan or to pray, if you have marital relations you must take a bath the next morning. How embarrassing these baths were for me!

There was only one bathroom in the apartment, and the water heater was only routinely lit twice a week, on laundry day and Friday, the family bath day. Baths on any other day could not fail to be noticed since heating the water was a major production. Although no one ever commented, I was sensitive and knew what they were thinking.

Several old ladies who came to welcome us the first weeks, had patted my stomach and asked, "*Fee shee*?" meaning, "Is there anything?" I didn't need to be told that they wanted to know if I was pregnant. The family would never have done anything like that, but they knew we had been married three and a half years and had only one child, a girl. I imagined, probably correctly, that they were very hopeful that all our baths would eventually produce a little Imady son.

In a corner of the bathroom, extending from floor to ceiling stood the fearsome water heater, a large, shiny, metal cylinder. Attached to its side and somewhat smaller than a basketball, was a round aluminum container for the *mazote*, the fuel oil, and from it ran a pipe down to the combustion chamber at the foot of the cylinder. You turned a round screw at the top of the fuel container to start the oil dripping. One small section of the pipe was clear plastic so you could see how fast it dripped and adjust the speed accordingly with the screw–the same principle as an intravenous drip in a hospital.

First someone, usually Kawsar, had to fill the *mazote* container through a small round hole at the top with a can with a long spout. Then the wretched thing had to be lit, not by pressing a pilot light–that would be too easy. First, you started the *mazote* dripping into the combustion chamber, and then, when you hoped there was enough oil there to light, but not to explode, you would risk throwing in a lit match as you quickly moved back. It would ignite with a frightening whoosh, and, as it got going, there was a constant, ominous roaring of burning fuel. For months, every time I took a bath, I was afraid the entire contraption would blow up, bringing me and the house down with it.

Since we still needed a water tank for the "Western" toilet, we temporarily had to flush with a pail of water, but I didn't mind. It was a joy to have a proper toilet after one month of using a hole in the floor.

Mohammed decided to install an electric buzzer by the bathtub so you could ring for a towel, for someone to scrub your back or for a cup of coffee. Many bathrooms here had such a bell, and people did ring for all sorts of things. It was a throwback to the fairly recent days when houses did not have bathrooms and everyone bathed in the *hammam*, the public bath. There were special days for ladies and it was a very jolly all-day outing to hear my mother-in-law describe it: women took picnics along, prospective brides for sons were checked out head to toe, henna was applied to hair and hands, some women had massages and a good time was had by all. Now, in the apartment, no one but Mohammed, Abdo and I took solitary baths. Everyone else bathed together, dressed in their underwear. Otherwise, who would scrub their backs or help apply the henna or the sugar taffy used to remove unwanted hair?

Mohammed gave me a free hand to choose whatever furniture I wanted for the living room. He said since I was so far from home, I should at least feel comfortable in my own apartment. However, I had trouble finding a style I liked, because the current fashion in Damascus consisted of ugly couches and chairs with flimsy-looking pencil legs. In the meantime, Bara'at and her husband loaned us a set of living room furniture. Eventually, we saw some couches and armchairs we liked at a friend's house and had them copied.

How pleasant our new apartment was. We could lie in bed and hear the small Damascene pigeons cooing and see the blue cloudless sky overhead. Sunshine poured into our room in the morning, and Susu would come and snuggle between us. No more tearful weekend goodbyes to Susu. Finally, in our own apartment, we three were all together.

April 16th arrived, my first birthday in Syria. All day long I kept thinking of my sister Jo, who was marrying her David the very same day. I hoped their weather was as pleasant as the mild spring day we were having, just perfect for a wedding. I also wished I were there to see Jo walk down the aisle and share her happiness. I pointed out Dave and Jo's Caribbean honeymoon island to Mohammed's family on a map, and they were all very interested and asked me to send their best wishes. It was clever of Jo to get married on my birthday. Now I'd never have an excuse to forget her anniversary.

Mohammed brought home a gigantic birthday cake for me with "H. B. My Love Lulu" written on it. When he ordered the cake, he asked the bakery to write "Happy Birthday", but they couldn't spell it so they abbreviated it. It even had candles, six instead of twenty-six. Susu and Mohammed helped me blow out my candles, and my wish was that Jo and Dave would be as happy as Mohammed and I.

It took me more than a month and a half, but I finally settled on what to call Mohammed's mother. From the first day, Susu had called her "Tete", or "Grandma", just like all the other little cousins. Now I began calling her "Tete", too. It was easy to pronounce, and she said she didn't mind having her daughter-in-law call her "Grandma". Had I been a Syrian daughter-in-law, I would have called her by her proper title, "Mart Amo". "Mart Amo", means both (paternal) uncle's wife and mother-in-law, reflecting the traditional belief that cousin marriage is the ideal. However, no one suggested that I call my mother-in-law "Mart Amo". Even stranger, no one ever told me to kiss her hand to show my respect. My foreign friends found this hard to believe since many of them had been expected to do this. Some fell in line, and others rebelled. In fact, Tete did not like anyone kissing her hand. Sometimes her children would try. She would laughingly push them away, and they would end up kissing her cheeks. She was an extraordinary mother-in-law in a land where most women, when they rise to this position of power, are glad for the chance to assert themselves and control–and often oppress–their daughters-in-law.

One April morning, Susu and I went upstairs to see Tete and Kawsar. As usual, we found them sitting on the floor. Kawsar did all her sewing on an antique manual Singer sewing machine sitting cross legged on a padded cloth on the floor. I got the impression that while chairs and tables were always found in the salons and dining rooms, they were a fairly recent innovation. For everyday, many people still preferred to sit on cushions on the floor.

Kawsar was expertly spinning the wheel of the sewing machine while running up a seam on a new dress for Lamat while Tete was stringing beans. Her feet were stretched out in front of her, and baby Amer was lying cradled lengthwise on her legs with his head supported by her feet. Amer was tightly swaddled into a neat bundle, like all Syrian babies, and fitted perfectly in the indentation between her legs. While her nimble fingers made short work of the beans, she gently rocked Amer by slightly tipping her legs left and right. I made no comment, but privately admired this ingenious solution for soothing a cranky baby while getting on with the preparations for dinner.

Both Kawsar and Tete truly enjoyed children, and children sensed this and were drawn to them. Tete, so I was told, had never struck a child, and I only saw her provoked to anger by a grandchild once. She often said there were no naughty children–just tired, hungry or sick children. Babies stopped crying when she picked them up, and she had dozens of ways to distract an impatient or mischievous child.

She kept a supply of pistachios or *bizer* (pumpkin or watermelon seeds) under her pillow ready to crack open for a hungry child. There were finger plays for very young children, and she had a fund of stories and games for entertaining older, bored children. I loved watching Tete and the aunties play *barjeez* with the children. This game, which is the origin of our "Parcheesi", was played like a life or death affair, with the players shouting in triumph or moaning in despair. Everyone sat on the floor and instead of a board, *barjeez* was played on a green satin cloth embroidered with the markings of the game and, in place of dice, shells were used. Even stranger, the players used Persian numbers for counting in the game. Susu soon learned this game and played it very competitively with her aunts or grandmother.

I can't say I liked everything about raising children Syrian-style. Tete told me that in the old days a spot of opium paste was sometimes put between a colicky baby's eyes "to help the baby sleep." She assured me that this was no longer done. Thank goodness! Like most mothers in Damascus, she had nursed her babies for two years (Mohammed even longer), which certainly seemed excessive to me. On the other hand, toilet training was started far too early, often at nine months. I heard mothers brag about how their tiny babies were "toilet trained." Of course, it was the mother who was trained and rushed to put the little one on a potty.

Another practice that I'm happy to say was dying out was the use of threats to discourage accidents during toilet training. Some mothers would say "*ih ih*"–baby talk for fire–to their young children while holding up an imaginary or an unlit (I hope, unlit) match near their bare bottoms. Maybe, as a result of too much emphasis on early toilet training, bed-wetting seemed common in Damascus. I would often hear mothers discussing with each other how to cope with this problem.

Children in Syria are encouraged to feel dependent upon their parents, which helps to knit the family together in a way Americans might envy on the one hand and find stifling on the other hand. First Susu, and then my other two children, were to walk a tight rope between the expectations of two very different cultures. Upstairs with their Syrian grandmother, uncle and aunties they would fit in seamlessly, accepting the dependent role unquestioningly. Downstairs, with me, they would be independent, assertive and self-reliant. As they switched from Arabic to English effortlessly, so they seemed to adjust their behavior automatically.

Before we left Palisades, David, my sister's fiancé, told Susu she could not go to Syria until she had learned to tie her own shoes. Although she was only two years and seven months old, she worked hard at it, and before we left could tie her shoes as well as any adult. If anyone tried to help her, she would wave them off. "By myself," she would insist. How proud of her independence we were.

David would have been very surprised if he had been told that Susu was going to a place where no one would even appreciate this accomplishment. Susu's six year-old cousin thought nothing of sticking out his feet for the little servant, Amira, to put on his shoes, in addition to tying them. Before long, Susu was willing to have her uncle or aunts help her tie her shoes while in her own house she continued to do it by herself.

* * *

Reading my letters to Mother, you might think my life had changed little. Much of the news I wrote her was about other foreign wives who were my friends, American movies we saw and the things Susu said and did. Actually, I lived in a drastically different world. It is true that we moved downstairs after only a little over six weeks in Syria, but our apartment was not really that "apart." The bell rang constantly as the "upstairs" people came down to put dishes in or take dishes out of our shared refrigerator, to get ice, to invite me up for a cup of coffee or to ask me to try on a skirt Kawsar was sewing for me. Finally, fed up with the endless bell ringing and door opening, I passed out keys to one and all and told them to just walk in.

Some of my friends found this lack of privacy unbelievable and said they couldn't imagine how I could live like this. One explanation is that I became good at tuning out, but also I truly felt we were one family and the traffic on our stairs ran both ways. Tete's door was never shut, and Susu and I were always welcome. Mohammed worked long hours, and when we were lonely, company was just a flight of stairs away. Whenever I had a problem, I ran upstairs and asked Kawsar for help. She was the guide who steered me through this unfamiliar world. People came to my door for one incomprehensible reason or another: a man bringing the electricity or water bill, someone begging or someone selling things. Kawsar coped with them all. When a cousin triumphantly presented me with a dead chicken with all its feathers intact, it was my sister-in-law who sent the bird off to the butcher to be plucked. Kawsar was the dragon who guarded my door, ran my interference, and excused and explained all my outlandish ways to critical relatives and neighbors.

When I unknowingly blundered, Kawsar would tell people, "Lulu's a foreigner, she doesn't understand," and then whisper to me what I should do. Somehow, even in the beginning, I always understood her.

This different world that entranced me could also leave me painfully homesick. To me, New York was the center of the world; in Syria, there were days I felt I had moved to the very outer rim. I ached for my mother and my sisters; I longed for Mother's library, for newspapers and radio broadcasts. I missed hearing English and understanding all the chatter around me; I got tired of having to explain myself and not being understood.

The first months I was in Syria I had no idea what was going on in the larger world since I never saw an English newspaper or heard an English radio station. It was a happy day when Mohammed came home with a short wave radio for me. I found that by putting it on top of the refrigerator, I could get the one-hour broadcast of the BBC in the morning. In addition to the news, there were musical programs, book reviews and discussions, all in English.

Best of all was Alistair Cooke who gave his chatty and insightful commentary "Letter from America" once every week. The family soon learned that as long as the BBC was on, I might as well have been in London for all the response they could get from me. I drank in every word. The BBC was my lifeline to the world I had left, and, sometimes, I think, it helped save my sanity.

Some of the things I did when alone sound wildly bizarre to me now. I remember playing Al Jolson records (I must have brought them with me) and singing along as loudly as I could while dancing all over the living room–including on top of the couches. Mother's music cabinet had been full of old sheet music of popular songs from the twenties and thirties, and they were as familiar to me as the fifties music from my high school years. What could be more evocative of Broadway, of New York, of America, than Al Jolson and his renditions of *Swanee; California, Here I Come;* and *Toot. Toot, Tootsie, Good Bye*! Sometimes I would be singing through my tears.

Reading, however, was my greatest escape. I always managed to have a good book handy. Mother sent me books, I borrowed books from all my English-speaking friends, and I bought them whenever I could. I propped up a book over the sink while I did the dishes and on top of the washing machine when I did the laundry–and ended up with many a water-soaked book. All my children were nursed or given their bottles with a book in my hand.

After I had been in Damascus for several years, I overheard Kawsar saying to Riad that Lulu had become a much better housewife now that she didn't read as much as before. Actually, I simply had become more discreet in my reading when I realized it was considered a time-wasting vice by my new family.

Many Syrians had an odd attitude about books. Books were something onerous that you had to study–in fact, practically memorize-in order to get through school. Few people read for enjoyment, and many, after they finished school, never again opened a book. They might read magazines or newspapers, but not a book.

When we first arrived in Damascus, Tete was taken aback by the great pile of books we brought for two-year old Susu. "Poor little thing," she exclaimed, "her books weigh more than she does!" Tete could not imagine what a joy they were to Susu. She only saw them as a heavy burden for a little child.

My new family did not share my love for many of the things that I valued most, and the reverse was also true. Books and music were my loves, while they cared greatly about clothes and doing things by what I called privately "the Damascus Code." In this city, there was a right way to do everything and a right phrase to say for every occasion, and you were judged by how well you conformed. It was my great good fortune to have married into a family where the rules were always suspended or bent for me. I was never measured by the general yardstick, and excuses were made for me when I broke the rules. I hope I was as tolerant of them as they were of me. I did try to be.

One day I spent the morning doing a huge wash. I must have carried five or six loads of wet, heavy laundry up two flights of stairs to the roof and filled all the clothes lines there. After lunch, Mohammed and I went shopping and when we got back, I found all the laundry piled on our bed, still quite damp. Kawsar heard us come back and called to me that she had taken my wash down and it was ready to iron. To iron! There were sheets, towels, undershirts, underpants and pajamas–none of which I would ever dream of ironing. Not to mention that after spending the morning washing, I had no intention of ironing all evening. I was tired and really cross with Kawsar about this, and I groaned as I thought how I'd have to carry it all back upstairs to hang again.

Mohammed put his arms around me and said that Kawsar had done it out of the goodness of her heart, which I knew, and said, "You will always have to go more than half way with my family in things like this. You can understand them, but they will never really understand you." It was true, and I never forgot this–and incidentally Mohammed helped me carry the wash back to the roof.

I later thanked Kawsar and explained to her that I always waited until my laundry was completely dry to take it down and then, when I was ready to iron it, I sprinkled it. I didn't add that, in my opinion, none of the items I'd washed that day needed ironing.

Several years were to pass before I had a name to put to this misunderstanding. "Culture shock" was not the buzz phrase in 1960 that it has become today. In fact, by the time I heard of "culture shock," I was surprised to learn that what I considered an intensely personal and unique reaction was a common phenomenon.

7.

Summer

We were beginning to make a modest splash in the social life here. One night we were invited to dinner by Mohammed's mentor, Dr. Homad, the Minister of Finance, and his wife. Dr. Homad was a family friend and the man who had arranged for Mohammed's scholarship to America. At the dinner, I met Lillian from Kentucky, who was married to a friend of Mohammed's. She had been here eight years and spoke Arabic fluently. I was impressed and wondered if I would ever speak as well as she did.

Two weeks later, Lillian and her husband had a small party in our honor. There were five American women counting me, and all the husbands were Syrians who were friends and colleagues of Mohammed's. We seemed to be thrown in a great deal with the Syrians who had foreign wives, which, I suppose, was only natural. The evening was pleasant, and I was especially glad to meet Dolores, a lively Cajun from Lousiana.

Around this time, I also met a young Englishwoman, Rita, whose husband, Rafik, worked with Mohammed. Rita, like me, was a reader, and we had fun borrowing each others books. Rita and Dolores were the first two of a revolving sisterhood of close friends I would make over the years. Someone was always leaving, and new wives were always arriving. We were not all Americans, and we did not all speak English. However, we all were far from home and family, and we helped each other cope with the strangeness and difficulties of life in Damascus as foreign wives. We gave each other advice and comfort, exchanged recipes from our mothers and Syrian mothers-in-law, and even learned some Arabic words and customs from each other. We celebrated Thanksgiving and Christmas together with baked turkeys and held birthday parties for our children and tea parties for ourselves. We were what is called today a support group, and some of the friendships forged then have lasted decades.

There were no concert halls in Damascus in the sixties and few theaters and of course any plays were in Arabic. Also, most of the movie theaters in town catered to *shabab* (young men) and showed only garish Indian films with scantily clad singers and dancers. There was only one family movie theater, and it specialized in American films. We had to settle for whatever was being offered, and as a result, we saw quite a few bad films. One truly dreadful film happened to be Susu's first. Usually we left her with Kawsar, but this time Kawsar and Susu came with us. The film was *Hannibal* with Victor Mature, and with its bloody battles it was most inappropriate for children. But all Susu saw were the "heffalumps" climbing the Alps in the snow before she went to sleep. Quite a few soldiers fell screaming from one precipice or another and were gnawed by wolves, and we were afraid Susu would be upset. We needn't have worried. Her one concern was for the "heffalumps". She had two tense moments, one when an elephant slipped on a piece of ice (it got up) and another when an elephant had to be urged along with a stick whereupon Susu said in an anxious voice that could be heard from one end of the theater to the other, "But why the bad man hit my heffalump?"

Susu's favorite book was Beatrix Potter's *The Tale of Mrs. Tittlemouse.* Half the time she *was* Mrs. Tittlemouse, and Mohammed had to be Mr. Jackson, the obnoxious frog who invited himself in, ate up all her honey and left dirty footprints in her clean house. Since Mr. Jackson was toothless, Susu would remind her father to cover his teeth with his lips. We re-enacted this story endlessly.

This book, in the way books can, became part of the mythology of our family. There was a man who worked in the Ministry of Planning with Mohammed who had a habit of visiting us at the most awkward times–before breakfast or after the big afternoon meal when most people were napping. He not only picked the worst times to come calling, but he also only came when he wanted some favor or other. He had a round stomach, prominent eyes, long arms and short legs. His neck was almost nonexistent so that his head seemed to rest on his shoulders. In short, he was remarkably like a frog. It wasn't long before Susu picked up on his physical resemblance to Mr. Jackson, the frog, as well as his similar behaviour. She began calling this unfortunate man "Baba's Frog." As the years went by, all Mohammed's inopportune colleagues–and there were many–acquired the collective name of "frog" with our children. They would say, "Mama has friends, but poor Baba has frogs." Like the frog in the fairy tale who became a prince, there even was the case of a "frog" who, by strenuous efforts on his part and demonstrated loyalty to Mohammed, transformed himself into a friend, even in the eyes of our critical children.

Susu was growing like a weed. After three months in Damascus, she was taller than all the five-year-olds and was now aiming for the six-year-olds although she was not yet three. She had also passed me as far as Arabic goes. She not only understood more, but also could say more. One day I was with a new English friend who was quite fluent in Arabic, and she remarked on how well Susu spoke Arabic. I said, "Good heavens, was that Arabic? I thought she was just speaking gibberish!"

As the month of June wore on, I began to understand why Mohammed has always hated the sun. With the arrival of summer, the sun became relentless during the day, but, as is typical for desert areas, it was pleasantly cool most nights. The streets were deserted between two thirty and four-thirty in the afternoon.

One cloudless sunshiny day followed another, and I had to admit the dry heat of Damascus was far more pleasant than the sticky humidity of New York. Also, now the full benefit of our high ceilings, tiled floors and thick walls was clear. Often, it would be more than ten degrees cooler in the apartment than outside.

In the late summer afternoons, as the air cooled, our balconies with their perfumed jasmine and warbling song birds were a pleasant place to end the long, hot days. We would gravitate there to catch a breeze, enjoy a sunset or watch the crescent moon rising in the summer sky attended by *ibn amo*, its "cousin", as Tete called the evening star.

I close my eyes and see us again on Lamat's balcony: the old folks, Mohammed's mother and Wahid Beyk's Auntie, sitting quietly, content to watch the world go by in the street below; the young women, Lamat, Kawsar and I, socializing and gossiping, happy to have the chores of the day behind us; the men, Wahid Beyk, Abdo and Mohammed, heatedly discussing the latest political news while Susu and her cousins squabble underfoot and bid for attention by leaning recklessly over the balcony wall.

I began to miss rain. Every morning we woke up to a perfectly cloudless blue sky, the kind of day I would have exclaimed about back home; the kind I used to pray for when I was planning a picnic or any kind of outing. But when you've had two months of such days, you begin to long for a change: a thunderstorm, an overcast day, anything.

With all this hot weather, I thought a lot about swimming. I had heard there was a pool which was mostly for foreigners, but I had no idea where it was. At last, thanks to my friend, Rita, Susu and I actually went swimming. Rita came over one day and announced that we were going swimming at the so-called American Consulate pool, that the lunch was packed, her friend, Pauline, was driving us and she would accept no excuses. She was so insistent–to the point of loaning me a swim suit–that I said if Mohammed agreed, I'd go. I phoned him at work from Rita's house, and he said fine.

The pool was lovely, and the place could have been anywhere in America except for the baggy-trousered workers. The sun was fierce. I got a bad burn, but Susu didn't even get pink. I kept her hat and beach robe on her when she was in the sun and slathered lotion on all exposed parts. She had a wonderful time in the wading pool, the sand box and floating in the big pool in a rubber tube with me.

Our lovely day ended abruptly when Pauline let us out in front of our building. There was Abdo waiting for us, his usually pleasant face dark with anger. He must have learned from Kawsar and Tete where we had gone since I certainly had made no secret of it. Before Pauline and Rita drove off, Abdo began shouting at me.

"Shame on you! Going swimming and showing your body in front of strange men and taking your daughter with you. It is disgraceful, a scandal. You have blackened the family name!"

Actually, his sentences were a lot more incoherent, but this is the gist of what he said. I could hardly believe this furious person was my friend, the easygoing Abdo I thought I knew.

What could I say? Susu and I went upstairs in silence, thoroughly deflated. I don't know what Susu made of this outburst, but I held her close and told her everything would be all right.

Then Mohammed came home. I told him the story and cried on his shoulder. He said, "Pay no attention to Abdo. I said it was all right for you to swim, and that is that. I'll see to it that he won't interfere again."

Ten days passed, and Abdo and I started speaking again. Abdo never referred to his fit of anger, and although he never said he was sorry–Arabs don't apologize–we became friends again. Also, I went swimming that summer many more times, sometimes with girlfriends and a troop of children and sometimes on Fridays with Mohammed and Susu. Abdo studiously ignored our swimming excursions.

For Susu's third birthday party we had twelve children plus all the mothers. The children were too young for games, but Susu's toys kept them happy as did the present-opening. To my surprise, there were no gift-wrapped presents. Some presents were wrapped in newspaper and tied with string, and some were in paper bags. We played the birthday record Mother sent about a thousand times, and finally the party was over. One child had to be dragged away bodily.

Among the children at the party were two little servant girls. One was Lamat's Amira and the other was Najah, who began working for my in-laws the day before Susu's birthday. Her father deposited her bare-footed and with only the red cotton dress and head scarf she was wearing. This little nine-year old helped me clean my apartment and then joined in playing with the other children at the party.

I swore I wouldn't have one of these little girls cleaning my house, but every one of the foreign wives said I'd come around and I did. Of course, these girls should have been in school, but if you sent them home they'd be taken to another house to work or kept home ragged and hungry. Tete sewed a pretty dress for Najah, and we bought her shoes, but since she wouldn't wear them in the house, we also got her some house slippers. She and Susu got along very well, and Susu taught her to say "Come!" in English. It sounded so funny to hear Najah calling "Come, Susu!" Kawsar sent her down to wash my floors about three times a week.

July 22nd, the day of the Egyptian Revolution, was a big holiday in Syria and was also the inaugural day for Syrian television. Weeks before, Mohammed had come home with a new twenty-one inch set and put it in our living room with its big blank screen waiting for the day when broadcasting would begin.

The day came and Mohammed's family, who had never seen television, was very excited. There was one channel which was on from six p.m. until midnight, and broadcasting began with a fifteen-minute children's program. We saw a lot of Egyptian movies, which Tete and my sisters-in-law loved, as well as musical programs featuring Arab singers. Mohammed always translated the international news for me, and it helped me feel more in touch with the world I'd left behind.

Since Syrian television was Government sponsored, instead of commercials between programs, they showed scenes from around the country and played bland "elevator" music. However, as I was to learn, whenever there was a coup d'etat, they would switch to military marches, and many foreigners were amused at this socialist government's selections. Two of the favorites, which were played over and over, were *The Stars and Stripes Forever* and *Rule Britannia*. Even I enjoyed the joke for a while, but finally, I told Mohammed who notified the television people, and that was the end of it. I hated to see Syria a laughingstock in the foreign community.

* * *

One day, after washing all my floors and doing the breakfast dishes, Kawsar, Susu and I went downtown to buy material for Susu's bedroom curtains. In the sixties, no one bought anything at the first quoted price. Bargaining was an art, and both sides clearly enjoyed the give and take. As I listened to Kawsar and the shopkeeper, I wondered if I'd ever be able to bargain like her. It went something like this:

Kawsar: *Ya akhi* (My brother), how much is an arm's length of this curtain material? [In the sixties, fabric was often sold by the salesman holding the cloth in his hand and measuring it to his elbow. Although some people bought and sold in meters, the *dra'*, or arm's length, was still widely used.]

Shop owner: Whatever you like, Khanum.[1]

1 "Khanum" is a term of respect for women dating from the days of the Ottoman Empire. It was often used in Damascus in the sixties.

Kawsar: I'll give you fifty piasters [half a Syrian pound].

Shop owner: Fifty piasters! No, no, *ya* Khanum. That's less than the price it cost me. Here, take it for free!

Kawsar: So, how much do you want for it?

Shop owner: You want the truth? Three pounds, *ya* Khanum, a very reasonable price.

Kawsar: Three pounds! You must be joking. I could buy imported French material for that price. *Ya akhi,* favor us with a discount. I'll give you one pound. We need fifteen arm's lengths. Don't you want us to return here? Don't you want us to become your customers?

Shop owner: One pound? Do you want my family to starve? However, for your sake, I'll give you the special price of two pounds, seventy-five...

Of course Kawsar protested vehemently and this went on with smiles and frowns and raised voices for several minutes. At times, I was convinced they were really angry at each other, but no. With satisfied expressions on their faces, they settled on a price of two pounds a *dra'*.

The shop owner picked up his scissors to cut the cloth and said as he cut it, "In the name of God."

Kawsar counted out the money they had agreed upon, which he took and said to her, "May God return to you what you have spent."

Then he wrapped the cloth in a newspaper, tied it with string and handed it to Kawsar saying, "*Mabruk* [Congratulations], and be careful not to tell anyone the special price you paid for this fabric or I'll be ruined."

* * *

One evening near the end of July, Rita and Rafik, had an enormous party in honor of the Egyptian Secretary-General of the Ministry of Planning, where both Rafik and Mohammed worked. There were about fifty people invited, including the American vice-consul and his wife. We talked to the vice-consul about the American School for Susu, and he dashed our hopes. He said it was only for children of foreign diplomats and if an exception were made for Susu, he would be besieged by the parents of "children of mixed parentage". What a way to describe our daughter, I thought.

The vice-consul's wife mentioned she had just had her third baby in Beirut. I casually said I knew a doctor in Beirut, and it turned out her doctor actually was Dr. Williamson, Mother's gynecologist, who was temporarily working in Beirut. Another woman I met said her husband was an archeologist working for the summer in Shechem, and she was driving there the next day. Another surprise! My sister Jan's brother-in-law, Stanley, was at the same dig and was actually planning to visit us at the end of the summer. I told her this and asked her to say hello to Stanley. It was a small world here as far as we foreigners were concerned. Everyone seemed to be connected in one way or another.

In August, Mohammed and I went to the gala opening of the International Fair of Damascus. Damascenes looked forward all year to the Fair which was the biggest commercial, social and cultural event of the summer at this time. It was held in the center of the city on the banks of the Barada River and during its three weeks it attracted not just businessmen, but all Damascenes and nearby villagers. Around thirty countries participated in 1960, and each had its own pavilion.

The most popular attraction of the Fair was the nightly entertainment at the outdoor theater presented by the various participating countries. We heard the Americans were planning to put on an ice show this year although how they could in this heat was beyond me.

8.

Damascus without Mohammed

Everything happened at once. Five days after the Fair opened, my sister's brother-in-law, Stanley, had come and gone, and Mohammed was in Moscow. The Fair opened Monday, Stanley arrived Wednesday, Mohammed left Thursday, and Stanley left Friday morning. Mohammed's trip, as usual, came up with no forewarning. He was sent in a group of twenty, headed by the Vice President, to work out details of several economic projects the Soviet Union would finance, and it was an honor for him to be chosen. He said he'd be gone between fifteen and twenty days.

With Stanley's arrival, Riad and Abdo were pressed into service as guides since Mohammed was busy getting ready for his trip. Wednesday afternoon, Abdo and I took Stanley to the International Fair, the Street Called Straight, the old city wall, the souk, and the Umayyad Mosque. It was my very first visit to this famous mosque in the heart of the old city.

We set out walking down Souk Hamadiyeh and there, at the end of the souk, we suddenly saw two rows of enormous pillars and a triumphal arch rising up as high as a house. These majestic ruins marked the spot where the entrance to the vanished Roman Temple of Jupiter once stood. Shabby little shops clustered around these noble columns with their impossibly godlike girth and height, and the contrast was startling. One of the columns was integrated into the wall of a shop selling rugs and Oriental antiques. Syrians don't have the American reverence for the past, probably because their country is flooded with ancient relics, and they often casually appropriate historic ruins for their own purposes.

The confusion of shops almost concealed the massive wall of the mosque, but suddenly there it was, with groups of people removing their shoes and stepping into the marble entry of the main entrance. However, we did not join them, but turned left to the tourist entrance. There, a nominal fee was charged for Stanley as the non-Muslim among us, and I put on the long hooded robe provided for women who are not "suitably dressed"–that is, those whose heads, arms and legs are not covered. We handed our shoes over to the guard at the entrance and stepped into a very large courtyard, surrounded on three sides by an arcade formed of rows of columns and arches. The sun was blinding as it reflected off the vast expanse of white marble tiles that paved the courtyard.

Some of the huge Roman temple stones still stand at the bottom of the walls, and traces remain of the Byzantine church this mosque once was. Also, over the centuries, different Islamic rulers have added their own touches, and, as a result, the mosque is a synthesis of many styles of architecture. For example, there are three minarets, each with its own name and its own distinctive style. In the southeastern corner rises the slim Jesus Minaret where some believe that Jesus will descend at the end of time to defeat the Antichrist before the Last Judgment. The odd-looking Minaret of the Bride is in the middle of the north wall. It is a four-sided tower with a square wooden platform halfway up. Above the platform, the minaret continues in a narrower version of the lower part and, near the top, it becomes octagonal. Finally, there is the Western Minaret, decorated with geometric marble designs. Abdo said it was unusual in Syria for a mosque to have more than one minaret, let alone three completely different ones.

Beautiful green and gold mosaic murals of gardens, palaces and rivers, what some say is an Islamic version of Paradise, cover part of the outer wall of the courtyard and the main entrance to the mosque. Abdo told us that originally every inch of these walls was decorated with mosaic pictures or marble in geometric patterns and that all the columns were once sheathed in marble. The mosque has survived fire, earthquake and more than one invasion, but is still magnificent.

We crossed the courtyard, the tiles hot to our bare feet, and stepped into the cool, dim mosque. Unlike a church where the altar facing you attracts your attention, in the mosque our eyes were drawn to the left and the right, down the long columned prayer hall. Mosques are laid out horizontally to accommodate long lines of people praying towards Mecca.

The soft light and the respectful hush of the carpeted hall were in great contrast to the blazing sun of the courtyard and the raucous confusion of the souk just outside its walls. Everyone instinctively lowered their voice in this huge building with its soaring central dome and strange marble mausoleum which is said to contain the head of John the Baptist. Some of the ceiling is covered with elaborately painted and decorated wood paneling. In the center of the south wall is a carved niche that marks the direction of Mecca and of prayer. We saw people praying, students sitting cross-legged in a circle around a turbaned old man giving a religious lesson and awe-struck children looking up at the light filtering through the stained glass windows high above their heads. There were many people, but the mosque was so large their number seemed insignificant. I think Stanley was impressed; I know I was.

That night we gave Stanley our bedroom and we three went upstairs and turned Abdo out of his room. I'm not sure where Abdo ended up, but guests always come first in Syria.

The next morning, Riad and I took Stanley to the National Museum. Stanley was most interested in the Ancient Syrian wing in the museum and amazed us all by his ability to read the cuneiform tablets. Of course, this was his field, but it still seemed astonishing. The museum is stuffed with a bewildering collection of weird and outlandish statutes, glorious mosaics and all kinds of odd artifacts. Sadly, most of the exhibits had no more than little index cards of explanation in Arabic and French, but Stanley was a knowledgeable guide. Many people left their mark in Syria: the Mesopotamians, Phoenicians, Hittites, Arameans, Assyrians, Egyptians, Greeks, Romans, Persians and, of course, the Arabs. Unlike Egypt, where one monolithic civilization arose, wave after wave of different people swept into Syria bringing their languages, religions and culture with them. Some stayed and some vanished, but all left behind relics that are strange and unique. I love Syria's wild archeological diversity.

That afternoon, Abdo, Riad and I took Stanley to the disappointing and quite modern church of St. Paul which is supposedly on the site where Paul was let down in a basket. We then went to the ancient Chapel of St. Ananias near the Eastern Gate. This small, below-ground chapel is at the street level of Roman Damascus and has been a Christian place of worship since the lst century AD. Oral tradition holds that St. Paul was taken to this building, then the home of a man named Ananais, after he was struck blind. Few Westerners visit this simple sanctuary without being moved by its aura of quiet holiness.

In the evening, we left Stanley watching TV while we took Mohammed to the Airport. Susu was apprehensive about the airplanes and afraid that she would have to get on one of those big monsters, but when we told her that only Baba was going to travel, she felt better. She certainly sensed my fear and, when I said in a hollow voice, "I love airplanes," Susu answered very seriously, "No, you don't, Mama, and I don't either." So much for trying to fool Susu.

I blinked back tears as Mohammed boarded the plane and still didn't quite believe it. I didn't realize until he was gone that he wouldn't be here to celebrate our fourth wedding anniversary. I wondered how I would get through the next two or three weeks without him.

The next morning, Mohammed's brother-in-law, Wahid Beyk, drove Stanley to the Beirut taxi station and off he went. When Wahid came back, he announced we were going to spend the day at a "coffee shop" outside Damascus. Tete, Susu and I squeezed into the Fiat with Wahid Beyk, Lamat, their three children and Lutfia Khanum (Wahid Beyk's old auntie) while Abdo, Kawsar and Riad took a taxi. Unlike the real coffee shops in the city, the "coffee shops" outside the city were actually outdoor restaurants with playgrounds for the children so the adults could relax and after shepherding Stanley all over Damascus we were more than ready to take it easy.

With Mohammed away, I had a lot of time to take stock and I realized I was beginning to feel at home. We had our comfortable apartment and although we still had no car, and buying one seemed very unlikely, that didn't bother me. None of our friends had cars and the only relative who did was Wahid Beyk. We also had no telephone, but again, neither did most of the people we knew. We were on a waiting list for a phone and had been told it could be several years because they were laying down new lines. I could wait, I thought. There was no rush.

Somewhere, buried deep in my mind, I sensed that I would spend the rest of my life in Syria, although on a conscious level, I could not yet accept this. We were here, I told myself, until Mohammed worked off his obligation to the government for his scholarship and for as long as Tete lived. Now that I had come to know and love Tete, I prayed as fervently as her children for her health and I would never want to leave while she was alive. However, someday, somehow, we would end up in America.

In the meantime, there was much to enjoy and much to learn – such as Syrian cooking. I spent hours in the kitchen, watching and helping Kawsar cook. She taught me a new way of preparing food with handfuls of this, pinches of that and never a cookbook, a recipe, a measuring spoon or measuring cup in evidence. We used vegetables, herbs, spices and condiments I had never used before and some I had never seen before. There was okra, Swiss chard, *meloukhia*, mallow, fava beans, chick peas, coriander, purslane, cardamom, cumin, turmeric, *zaatar*, sesame seed oil, yogurt, pine nuts, tamarind syrup and pomegranate molasses. As Kawsar competently moved about her small kitchen, her contented face reflecting how much she enjoyed cooking, she kept up a running commentary about what we were preparing: how this dish should only be cooked over a low fire, how the onions for this dish should be fried until they were brown and crisp, but not burned and how cooked yogurt should be stabilized with an egg and some cornstarch dissolved in water and then constantly stirred until thickened so it wouldn't separate. She would remind me to never cover a pot of cooking yogurt. She put up with my endless questions and everything I know about Syrian cuisine I learned from her. How she praised me when I did something successfully! She was a gifted cook and a patient teacher.

We were having the hottest weather of the summer now. Temperatures hovered around 100 degrees Fahrenheit and higher for more than a week and afternoons were not fit for anything but sleeping. We all were glad it hadn't been this hot when Stanley was here and said Mohammed was lucky to be in Moscow. Nights, we escaped our hot apartments by going up to the roof where it was always cooler and there was sometimes a bit of a breeze. Some settled down on the *ahteh* (a low outdoor couch) and others on garden chairs. Kawsar would bring up a pot of tea and a good supply of *bizer*, the favorite Syrian snack, and we all sat around drinking tea and cracking *bizer* between our teeth – at least they did. They were experts and could crack these toasted seeds and pop the tiny kernel in their mouths in one motion. I usually failed in my attempts and had to pry them open with both hands.

The sky was amazingly clear and there appeared to be many thousands more stars than at home. It almost seemed you could pick out individual stars from the great stain of the Milky Way. However, the constellations were the same, only easier to see.

We would stay on the roof until it actually began to get cool, reluctant to go down to our hot bedrooms. Still we lingered on until Susu was fast asleep and we were almost too tired ourselves to move. Finally, Kawsar took Tete's arm and they descended one stair at a time and then Abdo picked up Susu and carried her down to my apartment where he deposited her in my big empty bed. At last, too tired to mind the heat, I curled up beside Susu and went to sleep.

The beginning of September was the height of the tomato season and housewives all over the city were buying vast quantities of ruby-red tomatoes, boiling them, straining them and setting the sauce to thicken in the sun. Large, round, gauze-covered trays of tomato paste could be seen on all the rooftops in Mohajareen and the tangy smell of ripe tomatoes filled the air.

Mohammed had been gone two weeks and I missed him although I had Susu for company and the members of Mohammed's family went out of their way to keep me happy and busy. They took me to the movies several times and one night Abdo took Tete, Susu and me to see "Holiday on Ice", the ice skating show put on by the Americans at the Fair. How they managed to freeze ice when the temperature was in the nineties, I can't imagine, but it must have cost a fortune. The first number featured an enormous cardboard birthday cake and chorus girls with birthday cakes for dresses. At the finale, all the candles lit up and Susu puffed mightily trying to put them out. Another number had the skaters dressed like children's storybook characters and probably Susu was the only child in the audience who identified all the different characters. She gleefully picked out the three little pigs, the big bad wolf and Little Red Riding Hood. She loved the performance and so did we grown-ups. It was the first time any of us, including me, had seen an ice skating show and, of all places, to see it in Damascus!

When the weather cooled off a bit, we spent many nights watching TV together. We saw a few American westerns with Arabic subtitles, American cartoons and some old silent Chaplin movies, in addition to the inevitable Egyptian movies, many of whose plots were lifted from well-known classics, such as *Jane Eyre*. At least this made them easier for me to follow.

We were thrilled one day to find Mohammed's picture on the front page of a Lebanese newspaper along with Mikoyan and some Egyptian VIP's. The article didn't mention his name, it just said "some United Arab Republic economic experts". We were hoping to see him on TV when they reported on the Soviet/UAR meetings, but never did.

Each day I missed Mohammed more, but it was in his absence that I really started speaking Arabic. Mohammed had been told his trip would last from fifteen to twenty days, so when fifteen days were up, we began expecting some word that he would be home soon, but time passed and there was no news. It would be over a month before he returned and in this time, I spent almost all my waking hours with his family hearing nothing but Arabic from everyone, except Abdo and Susu. I did my halting best to take part in the conversations and, with all this practice, my Arabic was improving.

After all these years, I still remember the first Arabic word I learned in Damascus. Sometime during the first days, I washed a load of Susu's clothes and took them to my sister-in-law, Kawsar, and asked her with pantomime where I should hang them to dry. Pointing up, she said, "*Foe, foe*." Of course! Up, up. I remembered seeing a clothes line on the roof of the building.

Without doubt, learning Arabic was the hardest thing I have ever done. With Arabic, you face a completely unfamiliar alphabet containing at least eight letters with sounds that don't exist in English. In addition, you read Arabic from right to left – backwards for any Westerner. Furthermore, every one of the twenty-eight letters is written in three different ways depending on whether it is the first letter of a word, the last letter or in the middle of the word. Even worse, modern Arabic is written without the *teshkeel*, that is, without the short vowels and grammatical endings of the words. You must know enough Arabic to supply them yourself.

While we were still in New York, Mohammed told me that there were actually two versions of Arabic I should master, the "formal" or standard language and the Syrian dialect which everyone spoke. That was the last straw. I decided I wasn't interested in studying Arabic, but would pick up the dialect by hearing it.

And I did. I learned Arabic the way children learn their mother tongue and one of my best teachers was Tete. Most people I met in my early days in Damascus trotted out their formal Arabic for me; I was a college girl, after all. But dear Tete knew better and treated me like the clueless beginner I was. She called upon all her ingenuity to communicate; her expressive face, gestures, body language. Using the same simple words with me she used with my two-year-old, she patiently repeated everything over and over. The difference between my daughter and me, however, was that Susu acquired the language effortlessly, while I struggled. Susu gobbled up chunks of Arabic, processed them and spit them out, perfectly pronounced, whenever she wanted. Oh, how I envied her!

Learning Arabic was a battle. There were days – many days – I cried in frustration and often when I was struggling to make myself understood, I felt I had returned to my helpless infancy. Had it been almost any European language, I could have looked up words in the dictionary, but I didn't know one Arabic letter from another. Every day I had a list of words to ask Mohammed about when he came home from work. Since I wrote them down transliterated into English as I thought they sounded, they often didn't mean anything to him. He'd tell me, "That's not an Arabic word," and I would despair.

One initial help, was that Arabic is filled with polite formulas: set answers to set phrases. I first came across this during my first days in Damascus when we had visitors every night. I learned these phrases by rote, often not having a clue as to what they literally meant word for word. I only knew that this is the correct answer to that, and when to say it. In fact, in some cases, it was years before I discovered the precise meaning of some of these phrases I used so glibly. I would learn that in such and such a situation - when someone has recovered from an illness, taken a bath, done you a favor or just finished a meal - you say thus and so and will receive the expected reply.

I would say to a friend who had just given birth, "*Imbarak ma ijakon*" and receive the reply, *Allah ya barak feeki* – which exchange means, "Blessings on what you have received," with the reply: "May God bless you."

I learned these formulas so fast and so well that early on people were fooled into thinking I could really speak Arabic. But once they began talking to me, they found out that I could not carry on a conversation past the polite preliminaries.

Yet another plus in my learning Arabic, although perhaps I did not see it as such at the time, was the fact that in my husband's family, only Abdo, could speak any English and his was colorful, but rudimentary. I could either learn Arabic or be excluded from all the family life. Particularly while Mohammed was away on this first long trip, I was totally immersed in this impossible language and I began to understand it in spite of myself.

As my Arabic improved, I became closer to the family and, as they drew me into their circle and began to think of me as a true member of the family, they started telling me stories of their family: of Mohammed's mother and father, Yisra and Jowdat, and their long, loving but difficult marriage; of Jowdat's brother, Uncle Hamdi, and Jowdat's six sisters, the spinster aunts who cheated Jowdat of his rightful inheritance. They told me of Tete's brother, Ghaleb, who loved women and married six or seven, of Mohammed's grandfather who presided over the Garden Coffee Shop in the center of Damascus and of rich Uncle Ezzat who lived like a king in Beirut.

They also told me something of the history of Damascus, the city where the Imadys had made their home for hundreds of years. The al-Imady family, they said, had once been one of the eminent families of the city, part of the class of religious scholars, but after a glorious two hundred years, the family's importance waned.

Listening to Tete, Abdo and my sisters-in-law, I sensed they dreamed that our Mohammed might be the one who would once again burnish the family name.

I. Tales of a Family and a City

I first heard some of these stories more than fifty years ago in English from the homesick Syrian student at NYU who became my husband. He told me tales about his family and his city; of strange customs and universal joys and woes; the welcome arrival of children and the sadness when they died; of people struck by the evil eye and dying of broken hearts; of the "forty Imady muftis" and a pure bred Arabian horse sold to a king; of a lost inheritance and a family tree that goes back 600 years in one city.

Later, in Damascus, I heard the same stories and others in colorful English from his brother and in Arabic from his mother and sisters. When I had learned enough to understand conversational Arabic, the stories I heard gained a new dimension. My understanding of my Damascene family grew as I listened to Tete, Kawsar and other family members. As they reminisced, they drew me into their world and made me one of them. Listening to the family legends and the stories of old Damascus improved my Arabic, but even more importantly it helped me feel I belonged to this Syrian family and was part of this old world that was so new to me.

The stories that follow were told to me by different family members; mostly Tete, Mohammed, his brother Abdo and his sisters, Kawsar and Lamat. Occasionally, I would be intrigued by some information they told me about Damascus and would hunt around for a book that would add to the story.

When I began to understand a little Arabic, the first stories I could make sense of were Tete's. She spoke simply, adjusting her language to my limited understanding and she told her tales over and over again. Each time I heard them, I understood a bit more.

Some of these stories were of her little adventures, the highlights of her long life, some told of the trials and the losses she endured over the years and some were memories of her childhood. They were a window into my new family and into the disappearing past of Damascus and I listened gladly. Tete's children were bored with her recollections, having heard them many times, but I was a willing listener. One of her favorite stories was of a frightful event she witnessed in her father's coffee shop when she was a child. I call it:

The Lady and the Tiger

We are together, Tete and I, in her bedroom. I am sitting on a bentwood cane chair next to her bed on which she is sitting cross-legged. Her wavy white hair is in a loose bun with an aureole of wispy hairs framing her head. She is wearing a cotton nightgown so it must be one of her bad days when she isn't well enough to get up. The sun shines outside in a blue sky and, in the bedroom, Tete's blue eyes shine. Her delicate face, crisscrossed with wrinkles, is smiling and animated. From the courtyard we can hear Susu imperiously ordering her protesting cousins around, and from the next room comes a whirring sound as Kawsar turns the wheel of her old Singer sewing machine. Although more than forty-five years have passed, I hear it all clearly and see Tete's expressive face as she leans forward and begins:

"*Ya* Lulu, when I was a little girl, Abi, [my father] had a big coffee shop in the center of the city near Marjay Square. This coffee shop was special because, unlike all the other coffee shops in town, it provided entertainment. There were singers and dancers – foreign women dancers! – who amused the customers while they drank their coffee or tea. Once in a while, Abi would hire a circus with clever acrobats and strange big animals and then he would take my sisters, my brother and me to see the show.

"One day, a famous circus troupe arrived at the coffee shop – *ya Allah*, I will never forget it in my life! Abi told my mother to get us children ready to go with him to see the circus. We were happy as we put on our good clothes and impatient as Immi [my mother] saw to it that our hands and faces were clean and our hair neatly combed.

" '*Yalla, yalla*' [Hurry, hurry], said Abi and off we went, walking the short distance from our home in Bahsa to the coffee shop; Aisha holding our big brother's hand, Abi holding my sister Bahira's and my hand. The sun was shining and my heart beat fast as Bahira and I skipped to keep up with Abi's long steps. In a short time we stepped into the cool shade of the coffee shop. It was so large it always made me feel very small. Left and right, tables of men filled the room as far as my eye could see. We pressed tight against Abi as he led us to the front of the room, winding our way between the crowded tables. This took some time because one man after the other got to his feet and saluted Abi as he walked past them.

" '*Ya meet marhaba* [One hundred hellos], Adeeb Agha,'[1] they called out. Some shook his hand, some pressed their right hand to their heart in greeting, others pulled him close and kissed him on both cheeks.

1 His name was Adeeb al-Hawasli. "Agha" is another term of respect dating from Ottoman Empire days.

" 'Welcome, welcome, one hundred hellos', said Abi in answer to each one.

"Finally we came to our reserved table. On a raised platform in front of us, the show had already begun. We truly saw wonders that day. I remember it all - snake charmers who bewitched black serpents out of a basket with their piping music, jugglers whose hands moved like lightening, acrobats who twisted their arms and legs like rubber and a magician who pulled coins from his ears and then made them disappear. Some of his tricks amazed us and some made us laugh.

"When it seemed there could not possibly be any more surprises, a beautiful young woman came out leading a large golden tiger with black stripes. *Ya Allah!* Our words stopped in mid-sentence. The smokers stopped puffing on their *argheelays* [water pipes], the coffee drinkers put down their cups and the hands of the backgammon players froze. There was complete silence as everyone stared at the young woman and the huge beast. The woman's left hand was on the tiger's back and in her right hand she held a short stick. Her face was calm and fearless, but the tiger swished its tail restlessly and swung its big head from side to side, looking at everyone sitting very still. Abi whispered to us that the woman was going to put her head into the tiger's mouth. I stared at the fragile woman and the powerful tiger and my heart fell.

"Slowly, the woman turned and faced us all. She smiled, waved the stick in the air and said some strange words we couldn't understand. Then she turned to the tiger. She spoke to it in her foreign tongue and tapped it gently on its head with the stick. The tiger obediently sat and opened its mouth wide, showing all its cruel, sharp teeth. I was very frightened. I reached for Bahira's hand and whispered '*A oothu b'illa*' [I seek refuge in God]. I wanted to hide my head in Abi's lap, but couldn't stop staring at the woman and the tiger. My sisters and I moved closer together and we all held hands tightly. No one in the coffee shop breathed. Then, very slowly the woman bent down and, still smiling, put her head in the tiger's open mouth. *Ou lee!* Suddenly the tiger lashed its tail and with a dreadful roar bit down on the woman's neck!"

Tete paused, her eyes widened with remembered shock. Then she said in a hushed voice: "*Ya miskeenay*, [Oh the poor thing] how young and beautiful she was! *Ya Allah*, I will never forget them - the huge tiger and the beautiful young woman ... *Allah yer hama* [May God bless her soul]."

* * *

The old photographs of Tete's father, Adeeb Agha al-Hawasli, show a spare, straight man with a fair complexion, light eyes – Tete says they were blue - and the usual impressive mustache of all the Damascene men of his generation. His granddaughter, my sister-in-law, Lamat, remembers him as a kindly father and grandfather, but told me that like many well-to-do men of his milieu he had a Jewish *petite amie* on the side so it seems he was *not* an ideal husband. Above all, Adeeb Agha was a man of property who owned extensive farmland in the river village, Souk Wadi Barada. In addition, around the turn of the twentieth century, he was the proprietor of the Garden Coffee Shop.

Coffee shops in Damascus, then as now, were strictly male havens where men escaped from their women, drank cup after cup of Turkish coffee or tiny glasses of strong sweet tea, played *tawlay* (backgammon), smoked water pipes and talked endlessly. Adeeb Agha ensconced himself in a room near the entrance to his coffee shop from which he presided like a potentate over this unusual and slightly disreputable establishment that took up an entire city block and was very strategically situated near the Horse Market, just off Marjay Square.

As Tete said, this coffee shop differed from other coffee shops because its customers were entertained by itinerant dance and circus troupes. My sisters-in-law have said the dancers were probably from the far borders of the Ottoman Empire, perhaps Albania or Bosnia. Wherever they were from, the very idea of women dancing in public at this time, was scandalous. Seventy years later, my husband and Abu Rateb, a distinguished old merchant who was head of the Syrian Chamber of Commerce for many years, were sitting together at a dinner and Abu Rateb, who was at least thirty years older than Mohammed, began reminiscing about Damascus in "the old days". Mohammed happened to mention his grandfather and the Garden Coffee Shop. Abu Rateb looked shocked. "Your *grandfather* was the owner of that coffee shop?" he asked disbelievingly.

Tete never told us what happened to the rogue tiger and I never thought to ask her. She always ended the story with the tiger's deadly attack. Most likely that is all she glimpsed before her father rushed his young children away from this dreadful sight, but surely a customer or one of the circus troupe shot the tiger before it turned on anyone else. And what of the coffee shop itself? Was it perhaps closed by the government after this fatal accident? The story remains intriguingly incomplete.

I would expect the tiger's vicious killing of its trainer must have been a huge sensation, the gossip of the city for weeks. I read somewhere that Damascus got its first Arabic language newspaper in 1897. It is my dream to find an archive of old papers and locate in them an article about the lady and the tiger that would answer all my questions.

* * *

Tete's parents named her "Misirra", which means "she who creates happiness", a very appropriate name. But since one of her husband's sisters had the same name, after her marriage, her in-laws insisted on changing her name. Although my mother-in-law was unhappy about losing her name, her new name, "Yisra"[2], which means

2 From now on the young Tete will be referred to as "Yisra".

"the conciliatory one", also suited her and, in fact, would come to exactly characterize her marital role. To my children and me she was always "Tete," the affectionate name for "Grandma" in Damascus.

She was born in 1898, the third child in the well-to-do Hawasli family. Her brother Ghaleb was the oldest and then came the girls; Aisha, Yisra, Bahira and Yezda. All the children were fair with the light hair and blue eyes of their parents. Yisra was not tall, hardly an inch above five feet, but was slim and graceful and had the blonde wavy hair and the delicate features of a little Dresden doll. She certainly looked nothing like what Westerners expect Arabs to look like. No photograph exists of her as a child or young woman, but although she was in her sixties when I met her, I could imagine her young. My mother-in-law had a perfect oval face with a high forehead from which her wavy white hair was brushed back into a loose bun. The fair skin of her face was cross hatched with fine wrinkles. Her nose was delicate and slightly turned up, her lips were full and her large blue eyes were usually sparkling with fun. She had a girlish, almost flirtatious manner of speaking that instantly charmed and won you over. Take away the wrinkles and the white hair and it was clear that she had been a beautiful young woman. The femininity of many women becomes blunted with age, but this was not true of my mother-in-law. The little girl, young wife and young mother she had been still lived in her love of fun, her graceful gestures and her winsome manner.

Her gentle and unselfish nature was in sharp contrast to the personalities of her brother and sisters. Aisha, the oldest, is remembered by Lamat, as a *sitt salon*, an elegant, intelligent woman whose friends were the elite women of the city. *Sitt salon* is the Damascene expression for "lady of the salon", in contrast to *sitt bait*, or housewife. Surprisingly, Lamat also claims that although Aisha was the oldest sister she could read and write, quite an accomplishment for a woman of her generation. Aisha was fated to be the young bride of a rich, elderly cousin. Shortly after their son was born, she was widowed and went home to her parents with her son, Anwar. A few years later, she lost her son and not long afterwards, Aisha herself died of cancer. She was still a young woman and the first of her siblings to die. Tete must have been close to Aisha. She spoke often of her older sister to me and would say with regret that Aisha had deserved a better fate than wife of a doddering, old husband and an early death. Although he left her a rich widow, neither she nor little Anwar lived to enjoy their wealth.

Ghaleb, the only Hawasli son, was a charmer, a ladies' man, and a selfish, self-centered person; while Yezda, who was almost a generation younger than her siblings, was spoiled, lazy, and fond of getting her own way. Bahira, who was only a year younger than Yisra, was strong-willed and out-spoken. I just missed meeting Bahira, since she died while we were crossing the Atlantic on the *Hellenic Sailor*.

Jowdat, my father-in-law, first had his eye on Bahira as a prospective bride and, years later, the family used to say that that these two, the overbearing Bahira and the difficult Jowdat, deserved each other. They would go on and say that the sweet-tempered Yisra should have married her sister's quiet, mild-mannered husband, Mahmoud al-Idilbi. On the other hand, they would laugh and admit that a match between Bahira and Jowdat might have started a war!

Of course Ghaleb was sent to school, and of the four Hawasli sisters, only my mother-in-law failed to get an education. Aisha was taught at home and Bahira and Yezda, attended school for a while.

At different times, Lamat, Riad, Abdo and Mohammed told me how their parents met and married. Each one had some bits of information the others didn't know about or didn't mention, but pieced together they tell the story. They all agree that their father first caught sight of his future wife in her father's coffee shop. This is a reasonable scenario since Jowdat raised horses and the Garden Coffee Shop was near the Horse Market. He is said to have glimpsed two of the blond Hawasli sisters, Bahira and Yisra, while passing their father's coffee shop – for it was not the kind of establishment he would frequent – and first set his sights on the younger, Bahira.

Ordinarily, a man's mother and sisters would be delegated to call on the family of a prospective bride, but Jowdat was not your ordinary prospective bridegroom and asked neither his mother nor any of his six sisters to make this visit. Instead, he dispatched his aunts to ask for Bahira's hand. He probably was fonder of his aunts and their brother, Uncle Abu Ismaeel, than he was of his immediate family members - and he had his good reasons for this, as will be seen.

His aunts duly called on the Hawasli family and both Bahira and Yisra were presented to them for their inspection. At the end of their visit, they sized Bahira up as a bossy little spitfire and were certain she would be a terrible choice of wife for their opinionated, short-tempered nephew. They loved their nephew, but knew his faults very well. On the other hand, the aunts were charmed by Yisra. The two sisters, who were only a year apart, were both golden-haired blue-eyed beauties, but Yisra had a more appealing personality. The aunts decided it was premature to make a marriage offer and ended their visit with a promise to return. Then they reported back to Jowdat that Bahira wouldn't put up with him for a day whereas Yisra with her gentle ways was a far better choice. Jowdat was captivated by what his aunts told him about Yisra and decided his search for a bride was over. It would be Yisra Hawasli or no one. Neither family was enthusiastic about the marriage, but Jowdat prevailed.

In fact, the Hawasli family and the Imady family were poles apart. Jowdat Imady was descended from an old, eminent, scholarly family whose members considered themselves better than the rich and successful Hawaslis with their rather shady, but very successful, coffee shop. The Hawaslis were a family of *aghas*, but the Imadys were a family of muftis. *Agha* is a Turkish title which originally referred to a paramilitary chieftain; with time, it had come to designate a high ranking notable in Damascene society. The *aghas* were merchants, administrators and financiers and only the pashas outranked them. However, the muftis, as scholars and interpreters of Islamic law, trumped even the pashas.

Both families owned large tracts of land, but Adeeb Agha Hawasli also had his profitable coffee shop. On the other hand, the Imadys were justifiably proud of their respected lineage and a family tree that could be traced back six hundred years in Damascus.

The Imadys kept their hand-written family tree rolled up in a leather cylinder inside a large tin container along with other documents. The container was stored up on a *s'eefay* (a loft used for storage) where it gathered dust. My sisters-in-law firmly believed that every time it was taken down, someone in the family would die. Since no one has been able to locate the family tree after Kawsar died, we suspect that certain family members may have disposed of it because of the superstition they attribute to it. Fortunately, we still have several copies of the original.

A member of the family who has researched the family origins traces the Imadys back to Abu Bekr, the first Caliph. According to this version, a number of Abu Bekr's descendents traveled to central Asia, to what is modern-day Uzbekistan. There, in Samarkand, and later in Bukhara, members of the family became important scholars; one of them, in fact, was the chief scholar in the kingdom of Timur Lenk (Tamerlane). During the 14th Century, members of the family migrated to Damascus. Two of the earliest ancestors of the Imady family whose presence in Damascus can be documented are Muhabedeen Imady who was a judge in the late 15th and early 16th centuries and Imad ad-Deen, (1530-1578), a respected scholar whose son became the first Imady mufti.

It was part of the family lore that the Imady family had produced "forty muftis". I first heard this in New York from Mohammed and, after arriving in Damascus, it had been repeated many times by different members of the family.

Of course, Mohammed had to explain to me exactly what a mufti was. Muftis, I learned, were the highest legal authorities in the Ottoman Empire. They interpreted religious law and could issue binding legal decisions called *fatwas*. The Mufti of Damascus was appointed by the Sultan in Istanbul and was chosen from among the *'ulama,* the most eminent Islamic scholars of the day. The mufti was an elite, highly respected official of the governing class during the Ottoman rule and was appointed for life.

A long time passed before I discovered that the claim of "forty Imady muftis" was not to be taken literally. The historical records show that over a period of one hundred and eighty-eight years, the Imady family produced seven muftis who held this post in Damascus for a total of ninety years. The first mufti of Damascus from the Imady family was Abdul Rahman Imady, who held the post from 1570 to 1621 and the last one, Hamid Ibn Ali Imady, was mufti from 1723 to 1758.

However, Mohammed says if you count all the outstanding Imady scholars including muftis, judges, teachers, writers and *khatibs* (preachers in the Umayyad Mosque) they number about forty and he thinks this is how the myth of the forty muftis arose. He believes the family began by saying "There were forty Imady muftis, scholars, judges, teachers, writers and *khatibs*," and with repetition over time this was shortened to "There were forty Imady muftis."

Many of these ancestors left behind learned tomes, mostly on their legal decisions, but they also wrote books of poetry, history and one Imady even produced a book on earthquakes. It must be said that the last of these distinguished forebears died two hundred and fifty years ago and, since then, the family had been content to coast on its long-past achievements – until my husband came along.

Shortly after I arrived in Damascus, Mohammed told me about another feature of the family's history, the Imady *waqf*, or endowment, established by a wealthy and eminent ancestor, Judge Muhabedeen Imady in the year 1505.

In the past, rich Muslims often left part of their property in a family trust for their descendants 'in perpetuity'. This legacy is called a family *waqf* and in Syria there is a Ministry of Endowments that administers these philanthropic and family trusts. Over the years, since many of the Imady notables were from the *ulama'*, grateful students would present them with gifts of land or money which added to the extent and value of the Imady *waqf*. For centuries, the heads of each Imady household would go to the designated office every year to collect their share of the proceeds from the *waqf* until the 1950s when the Syrian government began to sell off these family trusts. The red tape involved in administering these endowments to an ever increasing number of people finally became too much of a burden for the government. Around the time I arrived in Damascus, the last *waqf* payments were made to the Imady family.

The Massacre of 1860

Jowdat, unlike Yisra, had few family stories to tell, but when he was in the mood, it was often his son, Mohammed, whom he singled out to be his audience. One of Jowdat's tales concerns the terrible 1860 massacre of Christians in Damascus. When I first heard about this shocking event, I found it so upsetting that I investigated the subject and read several versions of the event, trying to understand how and why it occurred. Before recounting Jowdat's story, a glimpse at what I learned about the factors that led up to this tragedy will help set the scene.

For hundreds of years, the Druzes, and the Maronite Christians lived in Mount Lebanon as neighbors with the Druzes as the dominant sect. However, in the nineteenth century the balance began to tilt towards the Maronites with the arrival of European powers and the Ottoman Empire's enactment of the *tanzimat,* a series of reform policies. The European merchants gave preferential treatment to local Christians and the Muslims and Druzes believed the *tanzimat* benefited the Christians.

As the Maronites prospered and grew rich, relations between the two groups deteriorated and, in May 1860, civil war broke out. The Druzes were better prepared for battle and quickly overwhelmed the Christians. Before the Ottoman authorities interfered, thousands of Christians had been killed.

When this news reached Damascus, the Christians there feared the worst because divisive economic and political factors, similar to those in Lebanon, existed in their city. As in Lebanon, European merchants in Damascus preferred to trade with Christians. Furthermore, the Ottoman government created sectarian friction with the so-called "capitulations". These were agreements which gave citizens of certain European countries special privileges and immunities. In time, a large number of Damascene Christians were made "honorary citizens" and came under the protection of the capitulations. While they grew wealthy, many Muslim merchants and textile workers sank into poverty.

Both Leila Tarazi Fawaz in her book, *An Occasion for War,* and Linda Silcher in her book, *Families in Politics* strongly insist this massacre was no "holy war". These two scholars point out that Christians and Muslims had lived peaceably in Damascus for centuries. Also, when the killing began, only Christians of the walled city, where economic friction between the sects was strong, were attacked. Outside the city walls, where Christians held no economic advantage over their Muslim neighbors, they were unharmed. Furthermore, in the old city itself, only some Muslims joined the mayhem while others gave shelter to the Christians. The primary motives behind the mob's fury were economic, not religious.

None of this is to excuse the appalling bloodshed that began in the city on July 9th, 1860. The rioters attacked the Christian quarter and no effective attempt was made by the Turkish Governor to stop their killing and looting spree which lasted more than a week. The quarter was burned to the ground and although it never will be known how many died, estimates of the dead run anywhere from 2,000 to 5,000 or more.

Afterwards, the Sultan sent a special envoy, Fuad Pasha, to restore order. He oversaw the trial and sentencing of the guilty and many were punished for their part in the massacre, including the Governor of Damascus who was executed by firing squad. Some officers received sentences of life imprisonment. As for the mob, some were hanged, some imprisoned and some exiled. Fuad Pasha ordered stolen property returned and levied taxes to help rebuild the Christian quarter.

Jowdat was born in 1882, twenty-two years after the massacre, and *his* father was only five years old in 1860, so it was Jowdat's grandfather, Mohammed's great grandfather who was the eye witness to this tragedy. The story was passed down the generations to Jowdat as part of the family history and Jowdat, in turn, retold it to his son. He said:

"*Ya* ibni, [Oh, my son], This was a terrible time in the history of our city. They say a small incident sparked the anger of the mob, but no one really knows what or who started it. What I do know is that one morning the streets suddenly filled with angry, shouting people running towards the Christian quarter with murder in their hearts.

"*Ya Allah,* if only the Turkish Governor had acted quickly and stopped them – but he did not. The authorities lost all control and looting, burning and killing continued for eight days and nights. In the end, the Christian quarter was destroyed and hundreds - no thousands of Christians were dead.

"*Ya* ibni, there were not many heroes in this shameful event, but Abd al-Qadir al-Jaza'iri[3] was truly one of them. He and his troops saved more Christians than anyone else. Some other notables - although they had no soldiers to help them like Abd al-Qadir - also rescued Christians and Abdullah Effendi Imady, my grandfather's cousin, and Mohammed Imady, my grandfather were among them. Many Christians were given shelter in their home until calm and quiet returned to the city. I am proud our family acted as true Muslims should."

So ended my father-in-law's story, but Mohammed added a bit more to it. He said that when he was around two years old, his sister, Riad, accidentally dropped him and his leg was broken. His mother took him to the best doctor in Damascus, a Christian, to set the bone. After the leg was put in a cast, she tried to pay the doctor, but he refused the money. She was puzzled and asked him why.

The doctor said, "It is to keep a promise I made to my father, may God bless his soul. My grandparents took refuge in the home of the Imady family during the massacre of 1860. Grandmother was pregnant at the time and my father was actually born in the Imady home. Because of this merciful act, when I became a doctor, my father made me promise that I would never take money for medical treatment from any member of the Imady family for as long as I practiced medicine."

Lest the story of this dreadful event that happened almost one hundred and fifty years ago give a false impression of relations between Christians and Muslims

3 Abd al-Qadir al-Jaza'iri was a greatly respected Algerian Prince who had been exiled to Damascus by the French. He and his armed men are credited with saving around 11,000 Christians.

today in Damascus, I would like to add this little vignette. On Christmas Eve, 2006, Syrian television broadcast a joint concert of an ensemble composed of a local Sufi order and a Christian choir with singers from several of the churches in the city. The Muslims and the Christians took turns singing some of their respective hymns and finally the two groups sang several religious hymns together. It was beautiful and very moving and I seriously doubt in these polarized times if there is any other Muslim country where such an ecumenical performance would be possible.

* * *

How little I knew of this city when I met Mohammed! To begin with, I quickly learned that "Damascus" or "Dimashq" in Arabic is a name almost never used by Damascenes. They call their city "Sham", and themselves, "Shwam", and actually the ancient name for what is now Syria, Lebanon, Palestine, Jordan and Israel is "Belad Esh-Sham", the country of "Sham" or Greater Syria as it is usually translated.

Damascus, which claims to be the oldest continuously inhabited city in the world, owes its existence to the Barada River, a surprisingly small river. In fact, by American standards it is no more than a brook. It begins as a spring in the green Zebadani valley northwest of the city, fed by snow melt from the surrounding mountains, and flows southeast through a bleak landscape of craggy gorges and rocky mountains. As it nears the foot of Jebel Qassioun, the river branches into seven tributaries - small canals really - and the inhospitable desert gives way to the Ghouta, a lush area of trees, orchards and farmland, all made possible by this miniature, ancient river. Nestled below the mountain, in the midst of all this fertile, blooming land, is Damascus. If the city had to depend upon rainfall it would be a barren place, indeed.

Damascus has been called an oasis along with its Ghouta, the green belt that stretches thirty kilometers to the east of the city, but it is too vast for an oasis and where is the sand and where are the groves of palm trees? It has been called a "port of the desert" which was true when it was the axis of caravan routes running south, east and north. What is certain, Damascus with its green Ghouta is a surprising and welcome anomaly in a harsh climate and consequently has been greedily eyed by conquerors for thousands of years.

When Jowdat was born in 1882, the Ottoman Turks, fellow Muslims, but not Arabs, were the most recent conquerors of Damascus. After defeating the Mamelukes, they had been ruling not only Damascus, but Greater Syria for more than 350 years. All the religious, political and cultural ties of Syria were linked to the central government in Istanbul. A Turkish Governor appointed by the Sultan ruled Damascus and the entire social system was based on Ottoman laws, culture and tradition. The elite sent their sons to study in Istanbul and the most fortunate Damascene notables were given government positions in the Ottoman administration.

At the end of the nineteenth century, Damascus was a sleepy provincial capital. It must have seemed a secure and stable time to Damascenes living then, but its stability was an illusion. A cascade of events would shortly change the map of the Middle East and the lives of its people drastically. The first of these events occurred in 1909, when the Ottoman Sultan, Abdul Hamid II, was overthrown by a group of Turkish military officers and officials who called themselves the "Young Turks". The Young Turks promoted the idea of a Turkish nation as opposed to the Ottoman caliphate. Rachad V became the next Sultan, but power was now really in the hands of the Young Turks who alienated their non-Turkish subjects with their policy of "Turkification". Some Arabs no longer considered the sultan with his reduced powers as the Caliph of Islam. As a result, a tiny Arab nationalist movement, which had arisen at the end of the nineteenth century, gained momentum.

So it was that the world into which Yisra Hawasli and Jowdat Imady were born was a world on the cusp, a world about to undergo vast political, economic and social change. Some individuals thrive during these times of intense change; Jowdat was not one of them. He was born in 1882 in Qaymaria, behind the Umayyad Mosque, to Sa'eed al-Imady and Kulthum al-Mardini, the oldest of eight children. There were two brothers, Jowdat and Hamdi, who were eighteen years apart and, sandwiched between them, were five sisters. The youngest child was a sixth daughter who was always called by her nickname, "Bahjay".

Jowdat began his education when he was about six years old in a small school, a *kittab,* where he was taught his letters and to read the Qur'an. When he was around thirteen, he was sent for further education to Maktab Anbar, a school in a building of such extraordinary beauty that tourists today are taken on tours to view its three courtyards and carved stone arcade, its rooms with intricately painted wood paneling, and the elaborately carved stonework over its doorways and windows.

It was built by a wealthy Syrian Jew named Yusef Effendi Anbar who wanted to create the most beautiful home in Damascus for his family and he almost succeeded. He started work on the building in 1867, but spent such huge sums in the process that he went bankrupt. Poor man, he lost his dream house before it was even finished. The building was confiscated in lieu of the large debt he owed the Ottoman government for unpaid taxes. The government completed the work on the building and then decided it would make a fine school.

In 1887, the building was opened as the first public (boys only) school in Damascus and was called Maktab (meaning school) Anbar after the name of its first owner. It was regarded as the most prestigious school in the city and provided a more modern, secular alternative to the many private, religious schools in the city. Like most of the boys in Maktab Anbar, Jowdat was a day student and attended free of charge. The school consisted of a six-year course of studies which Jowdat completed at about the age of eighteen.

I learned from Abdo that Maktab Anbar was not only his father's school, but that Riad and Bara'at had also studied there when it became a girl's school in the twentieth century.

9.

Settling In

When Mohammed returned from the Soviet Union, he immediately commented on my Arabic. He was surprised and pleased to hear me actually carrying on conversations with his mother and sisters. It was Tete's stories, I told him, that and hearing Arabic morning, noon and night.

He also noticed other changes. When I first arrived in Damascus I would almost knock pedestrians down with my New Yorker's stride, but now, Mohammed said, I seemed to have slowed down.

True enough. After seven months in Syria, I was imperceptibly slipping into a slower-paced rhythm, not just while walking the city streets, but everywhere. I was getting accustomed to the outlook reflected in three of the most commonly used words and expressions in Damascus: *malaysh*, (it doesn't matter), *bukra* (tomorrow) and *in sha' Allah* (God willing).

Susu had adjusted almost overnight. She was completely at home with her Syrian relatives and spoke Arabic now as fluently as her cousins. At the same time, she continued to speak English with me and her father.

October in Damascus was perfect; clear, blue skies, a slight tang in the air hinting of a seasonal change and some leaves turning yellow or brown, but although the days were getting cooler, we were still comfortable in summer clothes. The temperature hovered around a pleasant seventy-two Fahrenheit at noon and no rain fell.

Mohammed began teaching at Damascus University five nights a week in addition to his job at the Ministry of Planning. He temporarily took over several classes for Adel and another friend who were sent to Washington D.C. for training courses with the World Bank. Mohammed had always dreamed of being a professor at his old university and, although it meant a lot of extra work, he enjoyed it.

Around this time, Najah, our child maid, left us very suddenly. Her father came unannounced one day and took her away and we never saw her again. We suspected he had found her a higher paying job. She was such a bright little girl; everyone missed her, particularly Susu. We all hoped she was with a nice family.

The big news back home in November 1960, was the surprise election of John Kennedy and all my family voted for him like the good Democrats they were. Our exciting news in Damascus was that it finally rained quite hard for three days. Everyone was happy and maintained that winter had arrived and actually there were some chilly days. However, the cloudless, sunny days returned and the weather turned glorious, like early September in Palisades. It seemed incredible that Christmas was only a month away.

Of course, cold weather eventually arrived and I was determined to keep our apartment warmer than my in-laws' had been last March. I saw to it that we bought two *sobas* or heaters for our apartment. I hoped if they were kept lit all day, they would pretty well heat the entire apartment. Like the water heater, *sobas* run on *mazote* and a barrel of this fuel oil stood in our Arabic toilet, which we had turned into a storage closet.

It was my job to fill the tanks of the *sobas* with *mazote* every day. First you filled a can - like a watering can, but without a sprinkler - from the barrel with a dipper and then, holding a rag under the dripping can, you carried it to the *soba* and started pouring into the funnel you had placed over the opening. There was no indicator to show when the tank was full, so *mazote* often overflowed onto the floor. I hated these heaters because they were messy and such a lot of trouble. Even lighting them wasn't that easy. However, as Mohammed said, everyone had them and the alternative was a cold apartment.

I put away all our summer clothes, but there were days I wished I hadn't. The houses retained cold and warm clothes were usually welcome inside, but outside in the middle of the day even the November sun could be too hot for winter clothes.

One Friday in November, Mohammed, Abdo, Susu and I walked up one of the mountains to the northwest of Damascus. We then walked down the other side through a wasteland, carrying Susu part of the way. Not a soul was in sight. We were alone with the sky and the rocky slope. The mountains around Damascus, really hills, are all convoluted limestone and made me wish I knew more geology. Since they are almost bare of vegetation, the rock formations are in plain view. Mother's geologists at Lamont Geological Observatory would have a field day here, I thought. We finally arrived at Dimmar, a small town west of Damascus, and ate at a "coffee shop" on the banks of the Barada. We took the bus back to Damascus and arrived home exhausted, but happy. It was one of the nicest things we had done since coming here. Little did any of us guess then that forty-five years later the village of Dimmar would have grown into a huge suburb of Damascus with perhaps 200,000 people living there, including Susu and her family.

We celebrated Mohammed's thirtieth birthday two days late, on December 3rd. Mohammed thought I'd forgotten it completely and was very surprised to come home to a birthday cake after his university classes. Abdo helped me pick out a suede leather jacket for his present. Tete said a funny thing when she realized the cake was for Mohammed's birthday. She looked very puzzled and said, "But it was hot when he was born!"

I didn't comment, but thought to myself - even if I had ten children I would remember when each child was born.

Actually, they didn't really celebrate birthdays here at all. I was starting a new tradition in the family with my cakes, candles and presents. However, everyone fell in with my new ways and got into the party spirit. Susu helped her Baba blow out his candles and sang "Happy Birthday" with me. No doubt, I thought, after a few more birthdays, my in-laws will all learn how to sing it with us – and they did.

Twelve years would pass before I discovered that Tete was right about Mohammed's birthday. What we had been celebrating was the date that Jowdat Imady had registered his son's birth: December 1st. This was the "official" date of his birth that appeared on all his papers and passport. However, several years after Tete died, Susu found a notebook of her grandfather's in which he had written: "Today my son, Mohammed, was born on the 31st of August, 1930."

Dear Tete, of course it had been hot. How could I have doubted her? I was sorry I could never tell her she had been right, after all.

As my first Christmas in Syria neared, I confess I felt very homesick. Christmas here is called "Eid al-Melad" in Arabic which simply means "Feast of The Birthday". Muslims revere Mohammed and Jesus as the two greatest prophets and the birthdays of both are official holidays in Syria, but only Christians actually celebrate Christmas. Back home, I knew there was excitement and anticipation in the air as my mother and sisters dashed about buying presents, baking Christmas cookies and practicing carols for the Christmas Eve service. Here, there was no holiday spirit and the days were quiet and ordinary. I thought longingly of the old, familiar Christmas songs and wished I had a piano to play them. I remembered the wonderful holiday smells: the piney, outdoorsy odor of Christmas trees, the pungent scent of cloved oranges, the cinnamony fragrance of baking pies and the mouthwatering aroma of a stuffed turkey browning in the oven. I also missed snow although shortly before Christmas our weather finally turned bitterly cold. I taught Susu to sing *Jingle Bell*s and *I Wish You a Merry Christmas* and that cheered me up a bit until I thought of my last Christmas in Palisades when Susu had helped decorate Mother's tree sitting on Uncle David's shoulders. That had been a bittersweet holiday since we all knew our ship would sail on February 7th.

When Christmas finally arrived, friends and family came to my rescue and, thanks to them, my first holiday season in Damascus turned out much better than I expected. New friends, Holly and Fuad, had us over for dinner Christmas day along with Rita and Rafik. They had a big Christmas tree which Susu and I thoroughly enjoyed. Holly was from Oklahoma and had arrived in Damascus shortly before me. She and Fuad - "Fred" she called him - had been married two years, but had no children.

That same night, Wahid Beyk and Lamat invited us to the very fancy Airport Restaurant for yet another Christmas dinner. Going out on Christmas was not something they ordinarily did, but they guessed I was feeling homesick and thoughtfully wanted to cheer me up. There was a dance band, but Mohammed said it wasn't proper for him to dance "in public" although the dance floor was filled with people who didn't have his scruples.

New Years Eve we were invited to a big party whose guests included many foreign wives with Syrian husbands. Ruta, a tall, blonde, attractive Latvian American and her husband, Suheil, a high school friend of Mohammed's, held the party in their spacious apartment. I wore my black dress with the spaghetti straps and, since the party was in a home, Mohammed and I danced the night away and had a wonderful time. The new year also brought exciting news from Mother. She wrote that she was coming to Damascus around the middle of August for a month. We all were delighted and the first thing I did was to cut out a picture of a bed from a Sears catalogue and give it to a carpenter for him to copy. It would be Susu's bed, but since it was a full length, three-quarter bed, it would be large enough for Mother to sleep in when she came.

Not long after this, we visited the couple next door – a Syrian man and his young Italian wife. She was only twenty-two, but had been married six years and had a little boy about Susu's age. After studying music in Italy for seven years her husband returned to Damascus with Bianca and their son. Although I arrived four months before Bianca, she spoke Arabic almost as well as I did, probably because she lived with her in-laws and not one spoke a word of Italian. We managed to communicate quite well in broken Arabic to the amusement of our husbands. It was nice to have a fellow foreign wife nearby and we soon became friends. One day Bianca and I were walking together on our street speaking our fractured Arabic when two little girls behind us overheard us and started laughing.

In between giggles they said, "Listen to the poor foreigners speaking Arabic together – they must have forgotten their own language!"

* * *

Our trip to Egypt came about very suddenly. First, without any warning, one of the Vice Presidents of the UAR, Noureddine Kahale, transferred Mohammed to the Presidential Palace to be his planning adviser. Mohammed hadn't been there more than two days when the VP announced he was taking him to Cairo for a conference at the ministerial level with Nasser. Mohammed wanted to take me with him, but was told he'd be flying with the VP on a special plane. He also realized, what with meetings and such, he would be too busy to spend much time with me so he decided that Riad, Abdo and I should go to Cairo together. Abdo had been to Egypt before and could take us around.

Mohammed flew off on January 23rd on his official plane and we three left the same day, on Syrian Airlines, Riad's and my very first plane trip. I was still terrified of flying, but had decided I would never go anywhere if I gave into my fear.

Once in Cairo, I phoned Mohammed at the Hilton from our modest hotel and he said Mr. Kahale had taken the Presidential suite for the two of them. It had two bedrooms and a connecting living room which would make it awkward for me to stay there. We were both disappointed. That night I slept in the same room with Abdo and Riad in a Spartan, dormitory-like room with three single beds. At least it was clean.

The next morning we had breakfast with Mohammed at the Hilton and afterwards he took us up to his room. One wall was mostly glass and had a sliding door which opened onto a balcony with a panoramic view of the pyramids in the distance and the Nile directly below. Palm trees lined the river banks and, on the river *feluccas* darted around the bigger, slower ships.

Mohammed went to his meetings and we went off to Giza to see the three great pyramids and the sphinx. It is unsettling to see those massive structures rising out of the sand after all the pictures and films you have seen of them – none of which do them justice. They look incredibly old and unbelievably huge. It is easy to see why some superstitious Arabs believe the jinn built them.

Abdo had the movie camera Mohammed bought in Russia and, without telling me, decided to get action shots. We hired a camel for me to pose on and I passed myself off as a Syrian so we wouldn't be overcharged. My Arabic was improving and I could really get away with it provided I didn't try to say too much.

I handed Riad my camera and the moment she took my picture on the camel, Abdo gave the beast a hard smack. Off it dashed in a burst of speed heading into the desert with me hanging on for dear life, the owner swearing as he chased after us and Abdo gleefully filming away. Finally the angry camel driver caught up with us and led the camel back, demanding some extra money for my unauthorized gallop. When the camel kneeled for me to dismount, the driver warned me to lean back but

I was so shaken by my wild ride that my Arabic deserted me and I almost fell to the ground. Riad and Abdo laughed their heads off, but I didn't think it was very funny. Later we found my ride into the desert wasn't even recorded for posterity because Abdo hadn't understood the instructions for using the camera.

We hired a guide to take us through one of the pyramids and we hunched through the low, claustrophobic passageways with bent backs hoping for at least a mummy as a reward. Of course, we ended up in an empty room in the heart of the pyramid, but at least our curiosity was satisfied.

We spent two days exploring Cairo and the third night we boarded a train for Luxor. We shared a rickety second class compartment with two men and the trip took twelve hours. The first hour, one of the men took a whole bench for himself, stretching out with his head pillowed on his possessions, while we three, plus a jolly salesman, crowded onto the facing wooden bench. When the seat hog got off, Abdo and the salesman took one side, Riad and I the other. Our Egyptian companion threw his long cape over his shoulders, drew up his legs, closed his eyes and laid his head on his clasped knees. He appeared utterly comfortable and we looked on with envy as he quickly fell asleep. The three of us tried to sleep, but it was impossible. We were exhausted, cold and uncomfortable. It was a long night.

At first sight, Luxor, built on the ancient city of Thebes, was the filthiest, most fly-infested place imaginable. The streets were unpaved and dusty and practically everyone shouted, "Baksheesh!" at us. We found a hotel that had seen better times, washed up, breakfasted and set out. Although we had not slept all night, we could not rest because we would only have two days to see everything.

I have to say the incredible sights we saw that day and the next made us forget the train trip, the dust and the flies. We wandered around the temple of Luxor with its huge black columns and statutes in a daze, our lack of sleep making the weird ruins all the more outlandish and extraordinary. Riad, who studied history at Damascus University, could identify the different gods depicted in the bas relief drawings that covered every surface, but we were mostly happy to wander as we liked around the marvelous site and let our imaginations run free. When we were saturated with antiquities, we stumbled back to our hotel and collapsed in bed at six o'clock.

The next morning we set off early by horse and buggy, for Karnak, just outside the town, where the ruins of the temple of Amenhotep III lie. Although these ruins were around 3,000 years old, they were so well preserved that in many places the colors of the drawings were still brilliant. We were almost intimidated by the gigantic size of the columns, the statutes and the height of the walls. There were staircases, obelisks, inner sanctuaries and rooms leading into rooms until you were in total and frightening darkness.

We spent the whole day at Karnak and, after we ate, we rented bicycles and rode around town to the shock of the men leaving the village mosque after the sunset prayer. I guess women on bicycles were not an everyday sight in Luxor. At nine o'clock we boarded the train for Cairo.

After another sleepless night on the train, we spent our last day in Cairo buying presents for the family back in Damascus. Best of all, that evening I finally got to spend the night with Mohammed. There was a guard stationed at the door of the room and heaven knows who he thought I was as I brazenly sailed past him. Of course Mohammed said I was his wife, but the guard gave me a very dubious look as I entered the room. And what a room! The first time here I had hardly seen anything but the wonderful view, but this time I was comparing it to the hotel I shared with Riad and Abdo. Also, what a joy the big comfortable bed and the luxurious bathroom were after the primitive amenities of the train.

Mohammed ordered dinner to our room and we sat with the glorious view before us, watching the sun set. Our meal was a feast served by tall, Nubian waiters dressed exactly like the genie in Susu's "Aladdin" book. When they came in bearing the trays with covered dishes, they smiled conspiratorially as if they had helped us plan our stolen night. By the time we finished our meal, the sky had darkened and a new moon rose. It was a night for romance and we both sensed how lucky we were to be young and in love in such a perfect setting. We counted it as the honeymoon we'd never had and, fortunately, Mr. Kahale was never the wiser.

The next morning, Riad, Abdo and I flew back to Damascus and Mohammed followed us four days later. We found Susu well and happy and still speaking English. Tete said she would talk in English to her dolls and sing in English to herself and that she never asked for us. However, she was happy to have us back - as we were to be back.

* * *

My friend, Rita, had two children a year apart, the older was a girl, Rima, and the younger was a boy, Rami. One day, when Rami was nine months old, Rita phoned me and asked if she could spend the day with me. She sounded very distraught and, of course, I told her to come right over, wondering what in the world could upset her so. I soon found out. She said her son had not been circumcised in the hospital when he was born and now his father had decided the time had come for it to be done.

It is one thing to circumcise a newborn and quite another to perform this operation on a nine-month old baby. When the doctor came to circumcise Rami, Rita realized she could not bear to hear her little boy scream in pain and she fled to my house. I hope I was able to comfort her and distract her. She stayed all day and did not go home until after dark.

That evening, Tete, Kawsar and I sat around and talked about circumcision. Tete said that in the old days most little boys were not circumcised until they were about seven years old. They were led to believe it would be a great event in their lives, the day they when they would become "men" and they were promised lots of presents and sweets. Special white robes were sewn for them and the boys would eagerly anticipate their day in the sun and then, while their families happily celebrated, the disillusioned little boys would try to be brave.

Tete said you could easily spot these unfortunate children since they walked the streets uneasily, holding their long gowns out in front of them so as not to aggravate their sore parts. I was glad to hear that Mohammed had been circumcised the day after he was born and determined then and there that if I ever had a boy, he would be circumcised before I brought him home from the hospital.

It was Ramadan once again and Mohammed was back in Cairo, this time for a training program. He wanted me to go with him, but I didn't like leaving Susu again so soon after the last time so Susu and I stayed upstairs with Mohammed's family while he was gone. This was the second time in two years Mohammed had been in Cairo during Ramadan. Two years earlier I had been alone in New York City while Mohammed attended a pan-Arab student conference in Cairo and Susu was boarded with Connie Price. How different this Ramadan was from that earlier lonely one!

I ordinarily hated to cook when I was fasting, but it was fun to help Kawsar prepare our meals. I found it was much more enjoyable to cook with someone and every day I learned how to make some new dishes. I had a good time with Kawsar and Tete while Susu loved being upstairs in the thick of things where there were always lots of people coming and going.

There were no high buildings in the city at this time so the three minarets of the Umayyad Mosque dominated our skyline. Sunset was about 5:30 p.m. and we would stand together on the balcony waiting for the muezzins to begin the call to prayer that ends the day-long fast. "*Allahu akbar*" ("God is most great") rang out from every mosque in the city, the lights on all the minarets flashed on, and we went in to our *iftar* meal.

I am a heavy sleeper and only this year did I learn about the cannon fired around three a.m. to wake people for *suhoor*. If you missed hearing the cannon, there was always the *musaher* with his drum calling out for everyone to wake up. People worked only four hours a day, from ten to two, and the whole atmosphere of the city was different in Ramadan. Restaurants closed during the fasting hours all over the city, except in the Christian area, but at sunset were crowded with customers waiting for the call to prayer to signal the end of the fast. Special treats were sold on the street corners, especially *nayem*, a delicious, crisp, paper-thin fried bread the size of a dinner plate with carob or pomegranate molasses drizzled over it. It crumbled in your hand and melted in your mouth.

Time seemed to slow down in Ramadan. Maybe as my metabolism adjusted to fasting, it altered my perception of time. I remember sitting on the balcony one languorous spring-like day in Ramadan writing a letter to Mother. Tete and Susu were sitting on cushions on the floor, their heads bent over a tray piled with lettuce and a dish of molasses. I watched amused as they tore off leaf after leaf and dipped them into the molasses. Early spring is lettuce season and it is considered a great treat, particularly when eaten with molasses.

Tete had been fasting for several days this Ramadan since she was feeling quite well and her blood pressure and asthma were pretty much under control. However, we were all against her fasting especially because it disrupted the timing of her medicine; you cannot take medicine during the fasting hours. The day before she had not been able to keep her food down after *iftar* so this day, at least, we had convinced her to break her fast.

It was so peaceful that morning. Tete and Susu spoke quietly and the city sounds seemed muffled. While writing my letter, I had seen two planes land at the airport in the distance. I wished one was Mohammed's plane – I missed him!

Maybe it was the next day – in any case it was while Mohammed was in Cairo - Nasser came to Damascus and reviewed a big parade to celebrate three years of unity between Egypt and Syria. We saw the parade, but not Nasser. However, Susu saw both. Mohammed's brother-in-law, Wahid Beyk, was still director of the airport and he took Susu along with his children to see Nasser when he arrived. The children had a close view from the balcony of Wahid's office and Susu was very enthusiastic for she was a loyal little Arab by now.

Nasser had done a great deal for the self-respect of the Arabs and I was quite impressed with him. Two days after he arrived in Damascus, we saw him on television handing out farm deeds to a large number of previously landless peasants. The land was formerly either government land or the confiscated property of big landowners. Of course the farmers loved him, but I doubt if the landowners did. I had no premonition then that this would be the last year of unity.

When March 1st arrived, I did not fail to note that a year had passed of Mohammed's obligatory years of service to the government. I was ticking the years off, one down, seven to go.

In April, Jill came back to Damascus with Adel and their boys. She had written the previous fall that she was going to join Adel in Washington D.C. when he arrived there for his training course. Later, to my surprise, she wrote that when Adel's course finished, they would all come back to Damascus. We went to see them just after they arrived and since Adel still hadn't found an apartment, Jill was right back in the same apartment she fled from three years earlier with the same old "tribe" she couldn't stand, Adel's aunts and brothers. Not too promising a situation. I was delighted she had come and hoped against hope that this time she would settle down in Damascus.

The next day, I took Jill and her boys to meet the foreign wives I knew, hoping we all could help her adjust. The last time she was in Damascus, she had hardly met a soul. I had expected to find Jill changed, but she was as critical of Damascus as ever. To my surprise, it seemed Jill's mother was the one who had changed. Jill said her mother was talking of visiting Damascus and that would be a real turn-around since she had been very hostile to the idea of Jill's marriage.

Jill had arrived, but three of my friends were leaving. Rita was off to America where her husband had a scholarship and Pat was going back to Florida with her husband and son and both friends would never return. Also, my dear friend Rose was going to the States to see her dying father. Although Rose did come back from this trip, she also eventually ended up back in the States. Over the years, so many good friends have left Syria forever that I have lost track of their number.

As my friend, Anna Maria, is fond of saying, we foreign wives are an unstable lot. There was always at least one unhappy wife leaving forever, with or without her children, while another more persuasive wife would be convincing her Syrian husband to try life in *her* country. Then there were the trips home to visit a sick parent, to have a baby or just to see the family. So it went.

Jill and I saw a lot of each other and one day she surprised me and brought over some brownies she had made. She was finally even learning to bake. I almost dreaded her visits, though. Her children were such rambunctious daredevils that I would hold my breath and bite my tongue when they came. They sat on the arms of chairs and kicked, climbed in and out of windows, dangled precariously from the balcony wall and in general were noisy and wild.

Jill would make no attempt to restrain them, but just said things like, "Boy, are my kids afraid of Mohammed – they don't dare to breathe while he is here. They hate to come here."

Same old Jill – my blunt, but faithful friend.

10.

She'll be Coming 'Round the Mountain

Ever since Mother wrote that she planned to visit us in August, we had been looking forward to her arrival. Susu said she wanted to save her birthday party for "when Mommy comes" and every day she would ask me to sing, *She'll be Coming 'Round the Mountain*. Of course, "she" was Mother and the mountain was our Qassioun.

It wasn't only Mother we were anticipating. To our surprise, the baby we had been hoping for was also on its way. At the beginning of July my doctor confirmed that I was one month pregnant. The bad news was that, just as with Susu, I was promptly afflicted with severe nausea. This was not the typical "morning sickness" of pregnancy; it was constant and debilitating. I collapsed in bed, unable to eat a thing and looking and feeling like death warmed over.

Kawsar came to our rescue, as usual. She cooked for us (not that I could eat), looked after Susu, washed our clothes and ironed Mohammed's shirts. With all her responsibilities, I don't know how she found the time. Penny, a new English neighbor, was also a great help. She brought me books to read, made me tea and gelatin desserts and several times she and her little servant girl cleaned my apartment. With only a little over a month until Mother would arrive I hoped to feel better soon.

Susu's new bed finally arrived and the first night she slept in it, she looked lost. It was far too big a bed for such a little girl. However, now we had ensured there would be a bed for Mother. We talked of nothing else but Mother's coming.

A year and five months after I arrived in Damascus, Mother made the first of her ten trips to Syria. She once wrote: "Syria! Probably the last place on earth I would have visited but for a chain of circumstances."

Syria was a faraway country, strange and alien to her, and yet she felt obliged to visit and understand this exotic place and its people for my sake and her granddaughter's sake. She did this and more; she embraced Syria and came to love it and its people.

On August 20, 1961 Mother's plane landed at Damascus. The airport back then was very small and informal and the fact that Wahid Beyk, was in charge, made it even cozier for us. We all walked the short distance out to the plane and Susu, clutching a huge bouquet of flowers, actually ran up the stairs of the plane when she spotted her grandmother. Mother staggered down the steps with Susu and the flowers in her arms.

We stepped out of the large group of people waiting for her near the plane and hugged and kissed her. Then strange people, people *I* didn't even know, came forward and were introduced by Wahid Beyk. Each one beamed at her, shook her hand and welcomed her saying, "*Ahlan wa sahlan*." Mother's reception in Damascus, what Abdo always called "The Great Greet", more than made up for her weariness – or so she said.

As for me, now that my mother was becoming part of my Arab adventure and would meet all my new family and friends, I felt restored. Leaving behind your family, your country, your culture, your language, your religion, even your familiar food can not only cause culture shock, but also can make you feel inadequate, crippled. Many of the skills you spent a lifetime acquiring are useless or even impediments in your new world. My mother's arrival in Damascus made me somehow whole again.

I no longer felt I had severed myself from my family and my roots. I felt that the two different sides of our family, Arab and American, were now linked with bonds of friendship and understanding. Mother had already taken Mohammed into her heart; now she opened her heart to his family and his country, as they did to her.

The next morning Susu and I took her up to the roof to see the city and the mountain. I had found this mountain barren and plain, but Mother admired it and for the first time, looking with my mother's eyes, I saw what she saw: the austere beauty of our chameleon of a mountain. It rose implausibly from the flat plain, a bare, rocky outcropping which the weather and the time of day, tinted at will. Qassioun's limestone rocks ranged in colour from a rosy pink with the first rays of the sun, to amber as dawn progressed, and then to the cooler or the warmer shades of beige, grey and brown as the day wore on. At sunset the slopes could take on a golden hue. Winter storms occasionally dusted the mountain with snow and sometimes the upper reaches vanished into the clouds. However, as we three stood on the roof that August day, it was hard to believe a cloud ever marred the perfection of that intensely blue sky.

Most evenings, just as when we first arrived, visitors came to welcome Mother to Damascus. She rose nobly to the occasion and shook hands and kissed one and all as though she had been doing it all her life. My in-laws and were charmed by my mother's elegance, so unlike her casual daughter. Every morning, before Mother left her bedroom, she would get completely dressed; seams straight on her stockings, high heels showing off her trim ankles, matching necklace and earrings, her lipstick carefully applied and every hair in place. This was no act for the benefit of the Imadys. Mother was always perfectly turned out.

While Syrians are always well dressed in public, nightgowns and pajamas are the rule at home and I had quickly adopted this habit so Mother made a very favourable impression on my in-laws. Tete and Kawsar began describing her as a *sitt salon*. I think they secretly wished I were more like her.

How wonderful it was to have my mother in Damascus! I was so proud of her and pleased that all the members of Mohammed's family liked her. Mother had a gift for friendship and she won over every one of my in-laws with her gracious manner and radiant smile before she had been in Damascus two days. I am sure their opinion of me and my family rose when they met my mother.

* * *

It was Mohammed's good friend, Ahmad, the proud possessor of a car, who kindly offered to drive us to Maloula, a Christian village not far from Damascus. Maloula was built on a mountainside and there is a famous cleft – called the *sik* - in its limestone mountain which leads from a monastery at the top to a convent at the bottom. Maloula is renowned as one of only two or three villages in the world where Aramaic, the language used by Jesus, is still spoken.

Mohammed, Susu, Mother and I piled into Ahmad's car and, after a drive of a little over half an hour, we turned off the main road and had our first spectacular glimpse of Maloula. The village clings to the mountain with rows of houses rising one above the other up the steep slope like the layers of some fantastic wedding cake. The facades of the houses are painted a sky blue and the interiors of many homes are virtual caves hacked out of the cliff.

Another escarpment faced the village, this one dotted with seemingly inaccessible openings high up the sheer face of the bluff where, incredibly, tombs have been hewed out of the solid rock.

We parked at the foot of the village and walked up the winding road that ascended between the two cliffs. Halfway up, we came upon a large group of jolly women who were cooking something over charcoal in great metal pans by the side of the road. Mohammed said they were roasting *burghol* - a kind of cracked wheat that is the main staple of rural diet in Syria. The women raised their heads for a moment from their smoky, communal fire and stopped stirring the wheat to smile and welcome us to their village. Mohammed responded with the customary greeting to anyone hard at work, "May God give you health."

We soon were surrounded by children and two little barefoot boys offered to be our guides. They sprinted ahead of us and led us up to the Greek Catholic monastery. There we were received by a friendly old monk who offered us wine which he proudly said was made by the monks from their own vineyard. We Muslims politely declined, but Mother drank hers down.

The monk talked about his monastery and chapel, the scarcity of tourists coming to Maloula and how it was difficult to keep the upcoming generation of village children fluent in Aramaic – and I suddenly realized our little guides spoke Arabic to us. Finally we made our farewells and followed our guides down a flight of steps and through a low door into a small, dimly lit chapel. The monk had said this was one of the oldest Christian chapels in the world, dating from around 300 A.D. Certainly it looked very old and its plain whitewashed walls appeared to be carved from solid rock, like the village houses. The air was cool and damp and there were no windows.

A row of icons hung high above eye level in the front of the chapel. The stiffly painted holy figures all had golden halos circling their heads and their large staring brown eyes seemed to follow us wherever we walked.

The boys pointed to a painting that depicted two men on horseback and told us the chapel was dedicated to them: Saint Sarkis and St. Bacchus.

"Saint Bacchus?" My irrepressible mother wondered out loud. "When did the god of wine become a saint?"

Mohammed didn't translate her question and I hope I smothered my laugh.

I led Mother to the strange, half-oval altar in an alcove to the left of the central altar and told her the stories I had heard about it; that this altar dated back to the earliest days of Christianity before animal sacrifice was prohibited by the Council of Nicea and that it may originally have been a pagan altar taken over by the early Christians. I pointed out the groove around the altar where perhaps the blood of sacrifice collected, but if there was originally an outlet for the blood to drain down, it had been filled in. We both stared bemused at this odd relic from an earlier age. There was definitely an aura of another time in this cave-like place.

We left the chapel and found that the sun had set while we were inside. Led by our two small guides, we set off for the *sik* in the rocky cliff and descended it as night was coming on. Looking up on either side, the cliff towered high above us. At one point we heard the jingle of bells approaching us. It was a young shepherd boy with his flock of fat-tailed sheep and we crowded against the wall to let them pass, the sound of their little hooves and their bells pattering and echoing through the canyon.

It took us about fifteen minutes to walk this winding passage through the rock that narrowed in places and widened in others and all the while Mohammed was translating the legend of the *sik* as our child guides told it:

"Back in olden times, there was a young girl named Tekla, the daughter of a Roman general. Some people say she was a disciple of St. Paul. However it happened, she lost her faith in the gods of Rome and converted to Christianity. When her father learned this, he was very angry and stopped her from praying with the Christians. But Tekla was determined to keep her new religion. The first chance she had, she ran away from home. When her father found she was gone, he rode after her with a troop of his soldiers. They caught up to her just as she reached this very cliff. She prayed to God to save her and suddenly God caused the rock to crack open and she passed through it to safety."

The children didn't explain what happened to her father and his soldiers, who, I should have thought, could also have ridden through the cleft. Perhaps they were so overwhelmed by this miracle that they turned around and left, or maybe they became Christians themselves after this great sign. In any case, the little boys said that Tekla lived to become a very holy woman and after her death she was declared a saint.

At dark we came out of the *sik*, a few steps from the Orthodox convent of Saint Tekla. Tekla is buried in a cave above her convent and the water that drips from the roof of the cave is said to have miraculous curative powers. Both Christians and Muslims come here in hope of a cure. Ahmad, a Muslim, said that he had been brought to this convent by his mother when he was a little boy and that here he had been healed of some illness.

Nuns in black robes greeted us warmly and asked us to stay the night. One old nun had been to America on a fund raising drive and when she heard Mother and I were Americans, she smiled broadly and recited the names of the cities she had visited like a litany - "New York, Chicago, Detroit, Los Angeles, Houston..."

We sat for a time on the tiled courtyard of the convent with the nuns and, while Susu and I talked to them in Arabic, Mother looked at the brilliant stars above in a deep black sky. We hated to go and promised the nuns and ourselves that we would come back. And we did come back ten years later, in very different circumstances...

And so we left Maloula, taking with us some of the peace and the other-worldliness of that beautiful spot perched like an eagle's nest on its rock.

* * *

Mohammed and my mother were very close. She referred to him as her "Number One Son" and he called her "Mommy" or my dear "Mother-in-LOW" - as he invariably pronounced it since there is no "aw" sound in Arabic. Mohammed was sure that nothing would mean more to Mother than a visit to Jerusalem and he determined to bring this about. As it turned out, this trip to Jerusalem was the high point of Mother's first visit to the Middle East.

Like all true pilgrimages, it would demand a lot from the pilgrims. For one thing, it was the hottest season of the year and it would be a long tiring drive in cars without air-conditioning. Also, my mother was a nervous car passenger with the best of drivers and on the best of roads and we would be driving on a pitted two-lane highway with an Arab taxi driver, all of whom seemed to be training for the Grand Prix. Finally, I was three months pregnant and feeling dreadful. Nevertheless, we bravely set off.

At noon we reached Amman, the capital of Jordan, a dirty, dusty city back then, compared to Damascus. We changed cars and drivers and picked up a young couple and their baby who sat in front with the driver.

From now on we climbed through ever more desolate wastelands. The strident music from the car radio never stopped, but we all were subdued, even the baby was quiet. Mother was thinking biblical thoughts; I was trying to get comfortable while Mohammed and Susu were sound asleep.

At last we began to descend at breakneck speed and we went as far down as we had gone up. To our left, looking near enough to touch, was the bluest water we had ever seen. This was the Dead Sea, shimmering like a mirage. We were now below sea level on a completely flat highway. The heat was searing and oppressive and we were panting for breath. The Dead Sea stretches for miles and in the terrible heat I had the eerie feeling we were suspended in time and would spend the rest of our lives passing it and gasping for breath.

Finally, when we felt we couldn't bear it any longer, imperceptibly at first, we began to climb and breathing became easier. Soon our ears were snapping and popping and the rocky land we were passing took on a golden hue from the sinking sun. At last, the driver navigated a final curve with screeching brakes and there, to our surprise and relief, lay the city of Jerusalem before our eyes.

The next morning we set out down the cobblestone streets of the Old City, Mother, Susu and I hand in hand with Mohammed leading the way. Our first stop was the Church of the Holy Sepulchre. Inside, we were simply overwhelmed with the glitter of gold trappings and the smell of incense.

To be honest, it was not what Mother expected; she found it bewildering and disappointing. She said, "When I think of the simplicity of Jesus, all this seems out of place. And yet, I am sure these Roman Catholic, Greek Orthodox, Armenian and Coptic Christians feel they have done their best to make everything beautiful to honor Him."

Mother said it would be more satisfying to go outside where she could better imagine the wonderful events that had happened here long ago under this timeless sky so we left the church and walked along the Via Dolorosa.

Then we headed for the steps that lead up to the high platform of the Haram al-Sharif. Here is the Dome of the Rock where Muslims believe Mohammed rose to

Heaven on a white charger, which Jews revere as the site of Solomon's Temple and which many Christians, Jews and Muslims believe marks the site where Abraham almost slew his son. This tiny piece of real estate, fiercely claimed as their very own by all three religions, lay baking that day under a relentless sun. The marble paving tiles were hot and the sun glinted off the gilded dome that dominates the platform. It was hard, in the hot, bright sunshine, to imagine the gory battles that had been fought in this very place.

Near the Dome is the third most holy mosque in Islam, the al-Aqsa Mosque, or the Distant (from Mecca) Mosque. Mohammed and Susu washed their faces, hands and feet at the fountain of ablutions and prayed in this mosque. Mother and I went in and waited for them in this peaceful place. Mother, too, said a silent prayer and said later that prayer came to her more easily here in this simple mosque than in the ornate church.

Next, we set off to climb the Palm Sunday Walk to the Mount of Olives. It was one of the hottest days we had experienced, but no humidity. We thought we would never reach the top of this dusty hill and, when we did, we found ourselves at the Church of the Loaves and Fishes which, for some reason or other, was locked up. However, the caretaker, a pleasant woman, saw how hot and thirsty we were and invited us to sit down on the shady terrace of her stone cottage and, with gracious Arab hospitality, said she would get us something to drink. Soon we were sipping delicious cold lemonade as we enjoyed the sweeping view of the city.

We took a taxi down the hill and stopped at the Garden of Gethsemane with its ancient olive trees and small formal garden. Mother said it wasn't hard to imagine Jesus praying there.

Early the next morning, we sped off through the hills again in another taxi, this time to Bethlehem, about six miles to the south. Bethlehem did not disappoint Mother. It looked just like the small biblical village she expected. The Church of the Nativity is large, but more open and simpler than the Church of the Holy Sepulchre with its confusing maze of rooms. We entered the cave where Jesus' manger had been and were given lighted candles to hold. Mother shut her eyes and said a prayer.

We then went outside and climbed one of the bell towers in the wind that is constantly blowing from the desert. The surrounding hills were dotted with flocks of sheep tended by small shepherd boys and Mother said they made the nativity story come alive for her.

The next day was Sunday, but a severe attack of nausea kept me in bed and Mohammed decided to stay with me. Mother set off with Susu to hunt for a Protestant English-speaking church and found one with four-year-old Susu using her Arabic.

We left Jerusalem a little after twelve noon and as we drove away, Mother filled her eyes once more with the wonderful view of the city, now receding behind us. Its golden buildings, the spires, minarets and domes of its churches and mosques were gleaming in the sun.

The drive back seemed shorter somehow. Down we drove, then past the Dead Sea, through the rocky wastes. As we drove on and on, we talked less and less and perhaps some of us slept, but not Mother who was worrying about the two crashed cars we had passed.

Amman - the Syrian border - we were now on the last stretch. Suddenly, there were rockets and fireworks rising into the night sky and we knew we were approaching Damascus where the opening of the International Fair was being celebrated. There before us were the twinkling lights on the hillsides blending into the black velvet sky with its myriad of twinkling stars.

We all came to life and Mohammed, the two Arab gentlemen in the front seat and the driver exclaimed fondly at practically the same moment *'Esh-Sham!'*

Mother squeezed my hand and said, "I love Damascus, too."

"Home" again in Mohajareen, Mother was congratulated on her pilgrimage by Mohammed's family with excited exclamations of "*Mabruk, mabruk*!" As she was kissed, embraced and showered with presents she shed a few tears publicly, like a true Arab.

Susu had been counting the days until "Mommy" would leave on her fingers. The days flew by until the day came when, as Susu said, "only the thumb is left." The next day dawned sad and silent. We all stood in the airport and looked at each other hard and long. At the very last, Mother hurried out to board her plane only to be followed by a small person saying, "One more kiss, Mommy."

Back in Palisades, Mother wrote these words about her trip: "This visit of mine was wonderful and illuminating. I learned a great deal about life in the Middle East and about its people. Most of it made me happy and took a weight off my mind and heart.

"Before my trip, I had been a frantic mother and grandmother. Aside from Bible stories, I had known little or nothing about this part of the world. However, once in Damascus, I lived among these warm, caring folk and never felt uncomfortable or ill at ease with them. I learned to love Mohammed's mother, this little lady with blue twinkling eyes and a smiling wrinkled face. We couldn't speak each other's language but we would sit and hold hands and, as she said, we spoke the language of the heart together.

"Once, I asked her if she had grown to love my daughter, as my daughter loved her. Her answer was, "I couldn't love her more if she were my own.

"I never knew her name, nor she mine. She was always 'Tete' to me, while I was 'Mommy' to her."

* * *

One week after Mother left Syria, the union between Syria and Egypt was severed. My first thought was relief that Mother had gone before the airports and harbors were closed. For a while there was no mail service and I hoped she wasn't too worried.

The end of unity came as a huge surprise to me and even to Mohammed. I knew there was grumbling that Egypt was not treating Syria like an equal partner, However, I could not imagine that Syrians would actually dissolve the unity they had dreamed of for so long.

No one had wanted the union more than the Syrians. I heard later that Nasser was actually reluctant, but that Syria had insisted on unity. Then, when all the embassies in Damascus were downgraded to consular offices and the ambassadors moved to Cairo; when the Syrian ministries were left in charge of secretary-generals while the ministers went to Cairo, unity began to lose its appeal. The diminished importance of Damascus was felt keenly by the proud Syrians. Furthermore, Nasser made enemies of the rich Syrian landowners and industrialists who lost their property and their factories.

What is more to the point, Syrian military officers also were unhappy and, in the early hours of September 28, 1961, the army made its move. One army unit surrounded the television station, another encircled the Ministry of Defence and a third closed in on the residence of the Egyptian Vice-President, Field-Marshall Abdul Hakim Amir.[4]

The revolutionaries demanded a meeting with Amir, which was granted, but no agreement could be reached and the rebels announced the end of the union. General Amir was flown back to Cairo and that was that.

The very same day, like magic, the old Syrian flags were up all over the place and all of Nasser's pictures were down. We had a seven o'clock curfew for two nights and a twelve o'clock one the third night. Schools closed for a week, but the university delayed opening its fall semester for months, probably because of concern about militant pro-Nasserite students. Military music blared from the radio until our heads ached and the "New Revolutionary Council" kept issuing "communiqués." The city was filled with soldiers the first few days and even tanks, but we were never in the slightest danger.

Mohammed returned to work the second day after the break-up as if nothing had happened. However, he was heartsick that the unity had been so badly managed it couldn't survive. As for the staunch supporters of the union, they were furious and organized pro-Nasser demonstrations in all the provinces. Nasser's popularity in Syria with the peasants, the poor and certain intellectuals remained long after the

4 The UAR had seven Vice Presidents: five Egyptians, including General Amir and two Syrians, including Noureddine Kahale.

end of the union and for some he continued to be a heroic leader, the symbol of Arab unity, even after his death.

* * *

While Mother was visiting us, we learned that Inayat, my youngest sister-in-law, had fallen in love with a colleague in the Ministry of Finance. She kept this a secret from the family for quite a while because Hassan was a Shia while the Imadys were Sunnis. Hassan and Inayat hoped to get married but knew there would be difficulties. In fact, when Inayat broke the news to the family, Abdo and her sisters forbade her to see Hassan or even speak to him, let alone marry him. Their opposition to Hassan was rather like the objections some Americans might have raised back in the thirties if their Catholic sister wanted to marry a Protestant. Hassan's family made little or no objection because the children of interfaith marriages in Syria take the religion of their father.

The family didn't discuss the issue in front of Mother and me, but after we overheard one of the angry arguments, Mohammed told us what was going on. Our hearts ached for Inayat, but we never said anything to her; we didn't know what to say. We whispered about it when alone together and were afraid there was no hope of a happy ending.

However, Inayat and Hassan were not easily thwarted and defiantly continued to see each other. One night, after Mother had left, all hell broke loose. Inayat got dressed and said she was going to drop in on her sister, Lamat. Abdo suspected she was going to meet Hassan and followed her. Sure enough, he found them walking together and there was a terrible scene. Abdo dragged Inayat home in tears.

Up to then, Mohammed had stayed out of the picture, but several days after this incident, Hassan appealed to Mohammed for his help. Hassan said that Mohammed, of all people, should understand their predicament and take their side. After all, Mohammed had married an American from a Christian family and the world had not come to an end.

Mohammed was impressed by Hassan's character and his sincerity and promised to do what he could. He told Abdo and his sisters that Inayat would probably defy them and marry Hassan in any case, so it would be much better for them to agree to the marriage and put a good face on it rather than lose their sister, perhaps forever. It wasn't easy, but he finally managed to get their very unwilling agreement.

The minute they agreed, things rushed forward. Hassan probably feared the Imadys might change their minds so, using the pretext of a brother being on twenty-four hour leave from the army for the first time in four years – a likely tale! - he announced at two in the afternoon one Thursday that the wedding had to be *that night* for the sake of his brother.

We all went crazy trying to get everything ready and it reminded me of my slapdash wedding. Some rushed out to buy refreshments and others to invite friends and relatives. It would have been such a help if people only had phones. Some relatives were insulted by the late invitation and didn't come. In fact, very few came. Dear Kawsar, once it was clear the wedding was going ahead no matter what, had begun sewing Inayat's dress and the satin wedding gown was finished in time and was lovely.

Weddings here come in two stages, the *kitab* when the contract which legalizes the marriage is signed and the *irs* which is an optional party to celebrate the actual wedding night. Unlike a Christian wedding, there are no vows and a wedding is not a religious ceremony. The fathers of the bride and groom hold hands while a prayer is said to solemnize the joining of the two families in marriage and then the bride and groom sign the contract. However, in this case, neither the bride's nor the groom's father was alive, so Mohammed and Hassan's brother – of the "twenty-four-hour leave" - did the honors. Finally, Inayat in her bridal gown and Hassan in his best suit, sat quietly elated in the salon while the guests offered them their congratulations. The happy bride and groom had overcome everyone's objections and were now legally married.

In the usual fashion, they did not set up house together at this time, but every day an eager Hassan came to visit his "wife". As it turned out, they never did have an *irs*, to celebrate their wedding night. They simply moved into Inayat's apartment when their furniture was ready and the tenants left.

A few days after the *kitab*, the women of the family held an *imbarakay*, a sort of "bridal shower" for Inayat. She sat radiantly happy in her wedding gown and seventy women came bearing gifts, including many who missed the wedding.

Hassan was tall, wore glasses and had an earnest, dependable look. He was dark, Inayat was fair and both were slim. They made a handsome couple He was very intelligent and well-read, a self-educated man. Unfortunately, the fact he didn't have a university degree was one more thing some Imady family members initially held against him.

Inayat's marriage turned out to be the happiest of her sisters. Even though she had two boys and a girl, she kept her slim figure and for forty-four years, until Hassan died, she would celebrate her wedding anniversary dressed in her bridal gown. Eventually, Hassan won over every member of the family with his quiet, self-effacing charm and we all mourned when he died a brave, uncomplaining death of cancer.

* * *

One evening in October, shortly after we had arrived at a party, I got a blinding headache and felt hot and faint. Mohammed rushed me home, put me to bed and took my temperature. It was 104. To make a long story short, after running a high temperature for five days, I finally was diagnosed with typhoid fever.

My doctor prescribed chloromycetin, the drug of choice for typhoid, and said to take it round the clock. The next day I got another severe headache, one of the symptoms of typhoid, and took some aspirin for the pain. In a very short time, my temperature plummeted from 104.5 to 94. I had a dreamlike feeling I was slipping away and I thought, quite calmly, this is how you die. My friend, Dolores, was visiting me and I could see her mouth moving, but couldn't hear a word she said. It was as if I had floated away from my body and could see us both down below. I was sure I was dying, but I remember feeling peaceful and unworried. I knew Susu and Mohammed would be fine. They would miss me for a little while, but Kawsar and Tete would take care of them.

Then something intruded – did Kawsar come in the room? the phone ring? – and I could feel myself being pulled back. Strangely enough, there was a sense of reluctance, even sadness at this return.

"Well," said Dolores, "I guess I'm boring you – you went to sleep there for a while."

Over the years, this strange episode has comforted me. If this was truly a preview of the moment of dying, then there is nothing to fear.

However, everyone around me was very alarmed and another doctor was brought in. This doctor decided it was the combination of aspirin and chloromycetin that caused my temperature to plunge. They took the aspirin away from me after that.

As soon as I felt a bit better, I wrote Mother about my typhoid since I had promised to write her all our news, good or bad. I wrote: "I have typhoid fever! Everyone here is terribly impressed. Even the doctor who gave me the blood test told Mohammed not to tell me, but with the new medicine it is no worse than a mild case of measles."

I made light of my illness to Mother, but, in fact, it was no joke to be pregnant with typhoid fever. After three weeks in bed I felt better and got up, but after a week I had a relapse. The burning fever came back, I felt worse than before and I ended up spending another two weeks in bed.

I was so tired of being ill. I had not felt well almost the entire five and a half months of my pregnancy. Finally, more than six weeks after I came down with typhoid fever, my doctors pronounced me well enough to get up.

I got out of bed and found it was winter. The temperature hovered around the freezing point and there was lots of rain and cold wind. However, with our heaters on, our apartment was warm and cozy. I began to look forward to my expected baby, who I was sure, was a girl.

More good news was that the university wanted Mohammed back and this time not as a substitute professor. He would be teaching a sophomore course in English called "An Introduction to Economic Planning" whenever the university decided to re-open. Classes hadn't resumed since we broke off the union with Egypt and it would be the middle of December before they would start again.

Meanwhile, Mohammed began compiling his own textbook in English on economic planning and I helped out by typing and editing it for him. Later on, I also helped Mohammed correct his exam papers.

This month we finally got a phone, but so few people had them I wasn't sure how useful it would be. Of the relatives, only Lamat had one. The waiting list for a telephone was ten years and we only got one because Mohammed's ministry speeded things up. I supposed they wanted to be able to reach him at any time.

11.

Muna

My friend, Holly and I had the same obstetrician and both of us were due to deliver in February. We hoped to be in the hospital at the same time and share a room, but Holly had her baby girl, Sara, early, near the end of January.

Our second daughter arrived February 18th on a Sunday afternoon in Ramadan. Her birth was much easier than Susu's and I was quite alert. Mohammed was with me in the delivery room and the doctor handed her – wet, bloody and slippery - to him the moment she was born. I marveled at my first glimpse of her in her father's arms, at her compact little body, snub nose, and her pink and white complexion. All our worries about the Rh negative problem were for nothing. To our great relief, we had a beautiful, healthy baby girl, *al hamdu lillah* (thank God).

Not long after my baby was born, a nurse brought her to me all cleaned up and placed her in my arms. I was surprised when, instead of a soft, wriggly little baby, I was handed a stiff little bundle, swaddled tightly from neck to toe. Like Indian papooses, Syrian babies are packaged. Their arms are placed straight down at their sides and their feet are straightened and then they are wrapped snugly several times in a blanket the end of which is secured by tucking it in. They are completely immobilized except for their little heads. Syrians feel this "is good for their postures" and that the firm pressure on their little stomachs is "good for their digestion." Of course, since it was winter, they also added that it "keeps the babies warm." However, I found out when summer came that babies are wrapped just as tightly in the blazing heat of summer.

My daughter was very fair with blond fuzz on her round head and her eyes were firmly shut as if she were reluctant to face her new surroundings. It was not until the next day she finally opened her sky blue eyes and when I looked up from her little pink face I was surprised to see snowflakes swirling past the hospital window, the first snow I had seen in Damascus.

My first visitor was a young Saudi friend who had been with us in New York. He came into my hospital room bearing a huge bouquet of flowers and made more of a fuss than the Imadys who had been hoping for a boy. Only Mohammed, Tete, Susu and I were not disappointed.

Susu had wanted this baby sister more than anything in the world. From the time Susu arrived in Syria at the age of two and a half, she had pestered us for a sister.

"All my cousins have brothers and sisters," she would say. "Everybody has brothers and sisters. Please get me a baby sister." In the end, it was Susu who chose the name "Muna" for her little sister.

My friends Holly and Jill also welcomed Muna's arrival with enthusiasm. Jill, who had only boys, was delighted I'd had a girl and declared herself Muna's "godmother". She came visiting a few days after Muna's birth with a present she had made herself: a lovely small crib on rockers, just the right size for a newborn.

When it came time to take Muna home from the hospital, the nurses were horrified when I unwrapped Muna and dressed her American fashion.

"She will catch her death of cold," said the nurses.

I just laughed as I put her into her quilted, hooded baby suit. At home with my new baby, I ran into more cultural differences. The day after we left the hospital, I decided to give Muna her first bath. I got out the plastic baby tub, put it on the floor in front of the heater and filled it with warm water. Kawsar and Tete watched anxiously and Susu excitedly as I kneeled on the floor, tested the water with my elbow and lowered Muna into the warm water. Syrian babies are only sponged off for the first weeks, especially if they are born in the winter because it is feared they will catch cold. Even though Tete disagreed with some of my American ideas about infant-care, she never interfered or criticized. Sometimes she even became convinced that one or another of my methods had some merit and would tell me so and, conversely, from time to time I would adopt one of her suggestions.

On my first check-up visit after Muna's birth, my doctor casually told me, "If you had to have typhoid while pregnant, the fifth month when you had it was the best possible time."

"What do you mean?" I asked.

"If you'd had typhoid in your first trimester, the chloromycetin could have caused birth defects in your baby. On the other hand, coming down with typhoid after the fifth month, might have caused you to deliver prematurely."

Good grief, I thought. Thank God none of us knew of these frightening possibilities before Muna was born!

On March 1st, Mohammed was sent to Washington D.C. on an official trip with the Governor of the Central Bank of Syria. Their mission was to negotiate loans from the International Monetary Fund for several economic projects and a loan to stabilize the Syrian currency. As usual, Mohammed was given only twenty-four hours notice of this trip, but even with the frantic preparations, I didn't fail to remember that two years had elapsed since we came to Syria and six years remained of his government service.

I was disappointed to miss this chance to see Mother, but Muna was only eleven days old, too young to be left and too tiny to travel. Mohammed promised to take a side trip to New York – and he did. The best part of this trip for Mohammed was his two-day visit in Palisades with Mother, Jo and Dave. He showed pictures of our new baby and Susu and assured them that all their dear ones in Damascus were well and happy.

No sooner did Mohammed get back, than he was sent on yet another official trip, this time to West Germany. He was away two weeks and came back with a severe case of hepatitis. He turned as yellow as a lemon and was in bed three weeks. The Syrian custom is to visit people when they are sick and visit they did! They came in droves, starting in the early morning. The doorbell would ring and Susu would run to answer it and then whisper to me, "It's more of Baba's frogs." Poor Mohammed really had a miserable time and only by the last week of April did he begin to get his strength back

Muna was an easy baby. From the age of one month, she began sleeping eight hours every night and during the day was on a four-hour feeding schedule. She first smiled at four weeks and soon would smile and gurgle very obligingly at any friendly face. Susu was gentle with Muna and there was never a hint of jealousy.

In April we got the sad news that our good friends Adel and Jill were leaving once again, after just one year in Syria. Adel had been hired as a UN expert and was assigned to Niger. He flew off to Africa and Jill took the boys back to her mother in the States a few days later. I wondered if we would ever see them again.

* * *

Not long after Jill and Adel left, Mohammed and his friend Ahmad decided we should take advantage of the four-day holiday of the Eid al-Kabeer and go on a family trip. The plan was for Ahmad to drive us to the north of Syria where we would visit different towns in the mountains and on the Mediterranean Sea. When I say "us" I mean Mohammed, Susu, Muna, Fowzieh (our newly arrived ten-year-old servant) and me. This brave bachelor undertook an eight-hour car trip with Mohammed in the front seat and two children, a baby and me in the back! I hope he never regretted it.

On our way north, we spent a day on a beautiful beach in Latakia. The Mediterranean was just the color of Muna's eyes and Susu and Fowzieh collected sea shells on the beach. The sand was the cleanest and whitest I had ever seen.

I was very surprised to see how green the northwest of Syria is. Thick virgin forests cover the mountains and, after we left Latakia, we drove up a winding road through pine forests where trees met over the road and not a house was in sight. Ahmad parked the car at a lookout place and we all got out to watch the sun set into the Mediterranean Sea far below. The sun was such a red, fiery ball, I almost expected the water to sizzle when it touched the sea.

Finally we reached our goal, a hotel in Kessab, a mountain town near the Turkish border. Kessab is a small, charming village mostly populated by Armenians whose families fled Turkey during World War One. It is also a popular refuge for Syrians escaping the hot summer weather and although it was May and the season had barely started, we appreciated the cool weather after the heat and humidity of Latakia.

I am not sure what kind of holiday it was for Ahmad, but I know the rest of us had a wonderful time. Susu and Fowzieh played together and picked wildflowers in the fields near the hotel and Mohammed and I enjoyed the delicious Armenian meals served in our hotel, the spectacular views of forests and green valleys and the fresh pine-scented mountain air. Even baby Muna seemed to enjoy herself and was no trouble at all. Since I was nursing her, the only extra work was keeping her supplied with clean diapers for this was long before disposable diapers appeared in Syria. Fowzieh was a big help in washing and changing the diapers.

Ah, Fowzieh. Although I had sworn to never have one of these child servants, two years in Damascus had changed my perspective. When Muna was born, my in-laws decided that I must have help in the house and brought me Fowzieh, a little girl from Houran, a southern district of Syria where many of the peasants were impoverished. I caved in, feeling very guilty and determined to make her time with us as pleasant as possible.

Muna seemed well and happy during our vacation although, before we left Damascus, I had worried about taking such a young baby with us. When Muna became ill not long after we returned, I began to think we definitely made a mistake to take her along.

The family had their own idea about what caused Muna's crisis and were sure the evil eye was to blame. My nice Italian neighbor visited me often and her daughter was about the same age as Muna. Bianca had a beautiful face, like a Raphael Madonna, and her little girl looked very much like her mother. However, their looks were not to the Syrian taste. Bianca was slim and her baby girl had her mother's olive skin, brown eyes and hair and was not a chubby baby. When Bianca visited, she would often hold Muna and I would hold her baby. Several times Kawsar walked in on us and saw this and reached her own conclusions. She was convinced that Bianca was comparing her baby with Muna and was jealous of Muna's blonde hair and plump, rosy cheeks. Bianca never suspected that after Muna almost died, my sister-in-law would invoke God to protect Muna from Bianca's evil eye every time she visited our house.

Muna's ordeal began one night when she ran a high temperature and cried for hours. We took her to two different doctors on two different days but when she didn't get any better my friend Holly suggested her baby's doctor, Dr. Oum al-Khair, a well-known woman pediatrician.

Dr. Oum Al Khair took one look at Muna's bloated stomach and told us to get X-rays of her intestines. I had been reading Spock and found the only condition which matched Muna's symptoms was a blocked intestine. The X-rays were taken and, sure enough, they showed an obstruction. Emergency surgery was scheduled.

As she was carried off for her operation, she looked back at us trustingly over the orderly's shoulder, a blue pacifier in her mouth. Mohammed, Kawsar and I sat outside the operating room and were soon joined by Riad, Abdo and Wahid Beyk. Not a one of us was dry-eyed. Finally, the pediatrician came out smiling and handed me Muna's pacifier. The operation, she said, was a success and they were stitching her up.

That night, the surgeon dropped in our room to check on Muna. She seemed much better to me, but the surgeon only said, "So far, so good." As it turned out, his words were ominously to the point.

Next morning, while Holly was visiting us at the hospital, Muna went into convulsions. Holly ran for the head nurse and dragged her into the room. The nurse took one look at Muna and told me to call my pediatrician. While I rushed to phone, Holly, who was much more assertive than I, got hold of a doctor and convinced him that Muna needed oxygen.

Before Dr. Oum Al Khair arrived with her quiet competence and confident air of hope, the senior hospital doctor entered our room and, lifting Muna's eyelids, he directed his flashlight into one eye after the other. Then he turned to us saying dismissively, "Tsk" while he jerked his chin up – the Syrian gesture for "No" – in this case meaning "No hope." "Take her home," he said.

Holly had to leave at this point to nurse her own baby and promised to call Mohammed. When he arrived I was holding the oxygen tube while tears streamed down my face. Muna's temperature was a dangerously high 107 F. and the pediatrician had packed ice around her in an attempt to lower her temperature. Muna was gasping and gurgling with every breath and there was fluid in her lungs. She had almost no pulse and her arteries and veins had collapsed. Her condition was critical.

Meanwhile, Holly came back to stay with me. She brought tissues, (which I cried into) a cotton housecoat (mine was too heavy for the hot day), cake, black coffee in a thermos and best of all, sympathy. I'll never forget how she helped me get through that day.

I also will never forget that Dr. Oum Al Khair saved Muna's life. She never stirred from Muna's side for four and a half hours on this hot day in a room without air conditioning, trying one thing after another, including the *kasat al howa*. This frightening and ancient procedure involved making little cuts in Muna's back and then placing small glass cups over the cuts and throwing lit matches into them to create a vacuum. The idea was to suck the fluid from her lungs. Amazingly, it worked. Finally, Muna's temperature began to drop and the crisis ended. All this time Mohammed had been standing by Muna's cot and the doctor said later that he had nerves of iron.

I learned later that what happened to Muna is called "intussusception" and is caused when the intestine collapses into itself, precisely like a telescope being closed, causing a blockage. This obstruction usually occurs in small babies and I don't think anyone knows why it happens.

When I became pregnant, everyone, except Susu, had hoped for a boy. When Muna was born, most of the family members could not hide their disappointment, but Mohammed, Tete, Susu and I welcomed her with all our hearts. Dear Tete said to me, "I had six girls in a row, God bless them, and I welcome whatever God sends, boy or girl." As for Mohammed, I think he secretly prefers girls. But the rest of the family definitely wanted badly for our second child to be a boy.

However, when Muna nearly died, everything changed. By the time we brought her home from the hospital, she was everyone's favorite baby. Her uncle carried her everywhere, her aunts vied with one another to feed her and to make her smile and she wrapped us all around her little dimpled fingers. She must have been too young to have her head turned because all this attention did not spoil her.

In a few weeks, Muna was completely over her ordeal. She was a happy baby and smiled all the time. She could turn over and tried to crawl a bit. She also learned to take her pacifier out of her mouth and plop it back in with her own little fat hand. She had so little hair that I began taping a ribbon on her blond fuzz so people wouldn't take her for a boy. If I were a Syrian mother, I'd have had her ears pierced for earrings like all the little girl babies wore here, but I couldn't bring myself to do this. They said it didn't hurt, but that was hard to believe.

* * *

The brief, mostly disappointing, spring of Damascus had gone. We had one or two picnics in the Ghouta under the blossoming fruit trees while the weather was still pleasant and suddenly it was hot again. I spent long days sitting with Tete and Kawsar nursing Muna and listening to them reminisce about times gone by as Tete did some mending and the wheel of Kawsar's antique Singer whirred. Their talk often turned to my departed father-in-law, who, Tete would never fail to tell me, was "difficult."

"Amik (your father-in-law) was difficult," she would say with a smile. Those were her words, but like a mother describing a loved, but problem child, I could sense sympathy and understanding behind her words.

The more I heard about Jowdat Imady, the more I was intrigued and I was glad when Mohammed, to while away hot summer nights, began telling me more of the old stories, especially those about his father.

"We don't know much about Abi's childhood," said Mohammed, "for, while he might tell a family story or two, he was not given to talking about himself. However, there was one event he witnessed when he was a young boy that made such a huge impression on him that he actually told me about it several times.

"When Abi was around fourteen years old, the family moved from Qaymaria to Khudariya, near the spice and seed market, and it was this same year that fire destroyed the Umayyad Mosque and Abi and my grandfather saw it burn."

II. Tales of a City and a Family, 1893-1923

As the first rays of the sun gilded Jebel Qassioun on October 14, 1893, it promised to be a beautiful autumn day. As always, the three minarets and the dome of the Umayyad Mosque nestled on its octagonal base rose serenely above the tightly packed buildings of the city. This particular morning, a workman could be seen standing on the western side of the narrow platform topping the base of the dome. He was enjoying the crisp morning air as he performed one of the routine yearly tasks necessary for maintaining the mosque: repairing cracks in the leaden dome to ensure there would be no leaks when the winter rains came.

From his lofty perch, the man had a truly magnificent view. To the north rose Qassioun and all around him lay the city, its flat rooftops, rounded domes and pointed minarets gleaming in the early morning sun while down in the warren of narrow alleys and lanes the sun still cast long slanting shadows. Where fingers of sunlight reached the paving stones in front of the stalls crowded up against the mosque, he saw the merchants begin to push up the metal shutters that secured their shops at night. The loud clanking of the shutters as they were rolled up signaled that the shops were open for business and drew out some early customers.

Time passed. The sun climbed higher, but the brisk west wind kept it from being unpleasantly hot. Finally, the workman finished his job, paused to look out over the city and may have thought that the only thing lacking to truly enjoy the view would be his *argheelay*. He shouted down to a fellow worker to bring it to him. It was handed up and he settled down for a rest. As he puffed away, the man never noticed when several large chunks of burning charcoal fell from his pipe to the sun-baked wood of the platform around the dome. Fanned by the stiff breeze, little curls of smoke began to rise. The man finished smoking and descended the ladder, unaware that he left behind him a small patch of smoldering wood. By the time he and the other workmen realized what had happened, it was too late. Flames already encircled the platform and smoke was billowing into the air. Loud shouts rang out from one alley to another: "Fire! Fire! The Umayyad Mosque is burning!"

Like all those who witnessed this awesome and frightening sight, Jowdat never forgot it. Years later when his son, Mohammed, would ask him to tell the story "just one more time", Jowdat would begin like this:

"*Ya* ibni [Oh, my son], I'll never forget the day the Umayyad Mosque burned down. It was a Saturday morning - the fourth day of Rabie' al-Thani,[5] 1311.

"When the news reached our alley, my father – your grandfather - took my hand and we ran like crazy people. As we got nearer, we smelled smoke and, *ya Allah*, there it was! Flames on the roof of the mosque and a black cloud in the sky!

"Some brave men raced into the prayer hall and carried out carpets and copies of the Qur'an. Others poured pails of water on the fire. I saw men chopping down the wooden walls, to prevent the fire from spreading, but the flames were faster. Soon it was too dangerous to enter the mosque.

"*Ya Allah*! The heat and smoke were terrible! We stood and watched. What else could we do?

"Fire department, *ya* ibni? Back then we had neither fire fighters nor a fire brigade.

"The heat became fiercer and the smoke made me cough and stung my eyes. Everyone moved back, but nobody left. I thought of *jahennam* [Hell] and wondered if this is what hellfire is like.

"Whispers went around that the fire was started by a careless workman and his *argheelay.*

"One man said, '*Haik maktoub*' [This is what is written] and someone answered, '*Allah yajeerna min shee a'tham*' [God save us from what is worse].

"My father said, '*La howla wa la kowata ila billah*' [There is no power or strength except God's].

"*Ya* ibni, the fire left nothing standing except the stone walls of the mosque. When it was time for the noon prayer, the fire was still smoldering. It was hard to breathe because of the smoke, but the muezzin gave the call to prayer and we prayed in the courtyard on the ashes and soot fell down on our heads like black rain.

"The imam reminded us that the first mosque in Islam had been very simple and had neither minaret nor dome. He told us that only our mosque was destroyed, not our faith – and a mosque could be rebuilt.

"And, thanks be to God, it was. Hundreds of men and boys offered to clean up and carry away the fire rubble from the mosque and I am proud that I was one of them. Although the work was hard and dirty, we did it from our hearts. When we finished clearing the mosque, it was we Damascenes who rebuilt the mosque with-

5 Rabie al-Thani is the fourth month in the Islamic lunar calendar.

out waiting for the Ottoman government to help. It took nine long years, but finally the Umayyad Mosque again took its place as the most beloved and most beautiful mosque in the city.

"*Ya* ibni", Jowdat concluded, "don't forget this is the only building remaining from the glorious time of the Umayyad Caliphate when Damascus ruled from China to Spain. This mosque reminds us of our history and makes us proud. God keep it safe."

"So ended my father's story", said Mohammed, and added that one positive result of this disaster was the long-overdue establishment of a fire department in Damascus.

* * *

Like most old Damascene families, the Imady family lived for centuries within the walled city; first in the quarter called Qaymaria and then briefly in Khudaria. Sometime in the early twentieth century, Saeed Imady, my husband's grandfather, moved his family out of the old city to a large walled-in compound in Salihiya, on the lower slopes of Jebel Qassioun. In addition to Saeed, there was his wife Kulthum, their oldest son, Jowdat, a much younger brother and six daughters.

After Jowdat married, he moved into one of the two houses in the compound and several of his children were born there. Of them, only my sister-in-law, Lamat, remembers living in Salihiya. I asked her why her grandfather decided to move there and she said it was at the request of his sister, Hamida Imady.

Lamat said, "When Aunt Hamida's husband Hikmat Pasha Mardam Beyk died, she inherited a lot of land, including the compound on Jebel Qassioun and she offered this place to her brother – our grandfather - for as long as he liked.

"Aunt Hamida," continued Lamat, "made a brilliant connection when she married into the Mardam Beyk family. Although the Mardam Beyks, were relative newcomers in Damascus compared to the Imadys, they were fabulously wealthy. They were also part of the elite and politically influential society of Damascus in the early twentieth century. The family owned land in Lebanon and Syria including properties in Salihiya and this is where Aunt Hamida lived, in a big stone mansion. Perhaps because she was a widow, she wanted her brother near her. However, he died in 1907, a few years after moving near his sister. After his death, Grandmother, Uncle Hamdi and our aunts stayed on in this home until the late thirties but, after Father quarrelled with his family, we moved out in 1926."

* * *

The district of Salihiya is an area outside the city walls and to the northwest of the old city. Originally, perhaps one thousand years ago, Salihiya was a separate village, a peaceful town where religious scholars congregated and opened *madrasas* for their students. It was officially declared a town in 1159.

Much later, about 200 years ago, it became a place where packs of fierce dogs roamed at night and travelers were not safe after dark from brigands. Engravings of Salihiya from the early nineteenth century picture it as a wild and desolate place. However, at the time the Imadys moved there, it had again changed character and was now considered an attractive and healthful district in which to live where one could escape the hot and crowded city. Because of its elevation, Salihiya has fresher air and cooler temperatures than the old city.

When I arrived in Damascus, the former town of Salihiya had been reduced to not much more than a main street called "Salihiya" and the area around it. It was one of the only two shopping areas in the city, the other area being "the souk" – Souk Hamadiyeh and the smaller souks surrounding it. Kawsar would say, "Today we are going to Salihiya to buy some fabric," and we would hop on the tram in Mohajareen and in minutes we would be there.

Salihiya Street runs from Afeef on the mountain slope to Bawabat al-Salihiya, the Gates of Salihiya. I suppose there must have been gates to the town in this spot at some long ago time, but today there is only a traffic circle. The trolley cars ran along Salihiya Street in my first two years in Damascus, but service was discontinued in 1962 to make way for cars and busses. Now, not even cars are allowed on this street and it has become a pedestrian walkway.

Shortly before the Imady family's move from the Old City, Salihiya had been incorporated into Damascus city proper. Even so, it was still sparsely inhabited and there were many open areas and farms with vegetable fields and fruit orchards, especially in the upper reaches of Salihiya where the Imadys settled, the area called Afeef. Yellow chamomile grew wild on Jebel Qassioun and Isabel Burton remarked that when she and her husband, the British Consul, Richard Burton lived in Salihiya in 1869 and 1870, the whole area was perfumed with its odor. Mohammed says this was still true in his childhood in the 1930s.

In 2002, Mary S. Lovell, author of the definitive biography of Richard and Isabel Burton, *A Rage to Live,* was in Damascus hoping to locate where the Burton's house had been. To help in her search, she had a photocopy of a painting by Frederic Leighton of the Burton's house with Jebel Qassioun in the background.

Mary and I had become friends a few years earlier when she gave a talk in Damascus on Jane Digby, the heroine of *A Scandalous Life*[6], another of her excellent biographies. After reading Mary's description of the Burton's home in Salihiya, I was sure I could help in finding its location. The house, wrote Mary in *A Rage to Live,* "was flanked on one side by an old mosque and on the other by the local *hammam* (baths). Behind it was a garden through which wended a river." Also, Mary told me

6 published in the USA as *Rebel Heart.*

that Isabel Burton wrote she could hear the sound of the water-wheel in the neighboring orchard while sitting on the roof of her house in Salihiya and that behind her home rose "a saffron-hued mountain."

"The mosque near the *hammam*", "the river with its water wheel" and "the mountain rising behind the house" – all this sounded very familiar because Tete and my sisters-in-law had described just such a place to me many times. I took Mary to Afeef, and we stood facing the mountain below where the Imady home had been. We had the copy of Leighton's painting in hand and the outline of the mountain in front of us was exactly the same as in the painting. The Burton's house apparently stood just below the Imady family compound. Today, both compound, and Burton home have vanished.

Lamat remembers the family compound vividly. Several years before Mary and I went hunting for the Burton house, Lamat said she would show us where the home had been. Mohammed and I drove her to Salihiya and just above the tiny park in Afeef, she told us to park the car.

"It was here where the al-Sikkar building is now," said Lamat, pointing to a large building on the road leading up the mountain. "They have widened the road; the western wall of our land was where the middle of the road is now. Our compound took in all the land of the Sikkar building as well as the land of the Armanazi family villa behind it to the east.

"I remember a mosque and a public bath stood side-by-side near our home. You see," she pointed, "that mosque over there – it's a new one built where the old one was - but the *hammam* is gone.

"The main gate to our home was on the western wall and opened out on this street which runs up the slope of Jebel Qassioun to the cemetery above - and the cemetery is still there.

"To a little girl," continued Lamat, "our home was a green and pleasant paradise. As you entered the compound, on your right was the Yezid River that ran through our land. On the river, a large wooden water wheel groaned night and day as it watered our trees and gardens. The comforting noise it made is one of my earliest memories. It put me to sleep at night and woke me in the morning. I could not imagine life without it.

"In the middle of the compound were two large stone houses built years earlier by an important Turkish official of the Ottoman government. There was also a large stable for my father's horses and a chicken house built on the bridge over the river. We had more than twenty-five bitter orange trees on our land and I remember how the scent of their blossoms filled the air in the spring.

"The entrance to the larger building was up a flight of stairs and this grand house had many rooms including two very large reception rooms, one upstairs and one downstairs. The latter was more impressive and was on two levels. It had a fountain on the lower level, the marble walls were decorated with geometric designs and water ran down a grooved section of the wall for cooling the room. The windows had colored glass and pleated curtains framed them.

"One of my favorite rooms in our compound was the *tayara* on the roof of the larger building. This room had windows on all four sides and when I climbed there, I felt like a bird flying above the city.

"Potted plants were everywhere since Amti [paternal aunt] Shahwar, the second of our six aunts, had a green thumb and took a great interest in gardening. She supervised the gardener who looked after our trees, flowers, vegetables and herbs. Amti Shahwar was also the one responsible for the all-important coffee-making. The servant girl would grind the beans, roast them on the *men'al* [a portable brass charcoal stove] and then Amti would prepare the coffee. She always had a pot of coffee on the *men'al* ready to serve any family member or any guest who might come calling. Amti Shahwar suffered from heart trouble and died in her forties, the first of her sisters to die.

"My aunts," continued Lamat, "led a busy life in these delightful surroundings. The Imady family was a sociable family, known for its hospitality, and there were always many visitors. My grandmother and aunts loved to have parties for their friends and they would bring *'oud* [Arabian lute] players and singers to entertain the guests. Of course, all the guests and musicians at these parties were women.

"Like most women of their generation, our aunts never learned to read, except for Amti Bahjay, the youngest, but they were very modern for their time. There was a tennis court near their compound and they learned to play tennis. They could ride horseback, swim – they learned in the river that ran through our fields - and one of them, Amti Zekieh, was taught to shoot by Abi. Our aunts not only rode, but also took an interest in the care of Father's beautiful horses and often would help curry and comb them. Amti Zekieh, in particular, had a way with horses. At a word from her, any one of Abi's horses would stand still."

...So ended Lamat's pleasant memories of her family in Afeef. However, on other occasions, she would tell of the darker side of life there.

"Our grandfather," said Mohammed as he took up the story, "owned large tracts of rich agricultural land in the Ghouta. In addition, along with all heads of the Imady households, he had a share in the large al-Imadia Bistan [field] near the village of Jobar to the east of Damascus. Strangely enough, with all the property he owned, Grandfather never thought it important to buy a home for his family, but was content to live and die in the compound provided by his sister, Hamida.

"His oldest son, our father, expected to be a rich man on the death of his father and, meanwhile, he indulged his passion for horses. Abi raised pure bred Arabian horses and was very good at it. Two of his horses achieved fame when one, sold to a Frenchman, won the Derby race at Epsom in the twenties and another was bought by Emir Faisal when he was King of Syria.

"Abi always had a favorite Arabian and one of his greatest joys in life was to ride his horse to northern Palestine to visit his uncle, Abu Ismaeel. This uncle lived in Qadas, a village north of Safad, around 110 kilometers from Damascus. Abi was very fond of Uncle Abu Ismaeel, probably because he shared Abi's love for horses. They would ride their horses to the desert where they would camp out for days under the heavens. Nights they would sit around their campfire, smoking their water pipes under the star-studded sky and talk until their fire burned low."

I thought their talk might run to politics, but no. Mohammed tells me that most of their talk was of horses - comparing horses they had raised, discussing the qualities of horses they owned, sharing remedies for curing ill or injured horses and tracing the lineage of different horses.

Mohammed said that their only other favorite topic was the old traditional story of fair Abla and her dark cousin, Antar. This epic is older than Islam and is a kind of Arabic "Romeo and Juliet" story (but with a happy ending) as well as an adventure story. Antar fell in love with his cousin, Abla, and wanted to marry her, but her father refused his suit because, although Antar was the son of his brother, his mother was a slave. Most of the story revolves around the heroic deeds Antar undertook to prove his bravery to his uncle in order to win the hand of Abla. Finally, Antar's father frees him from slavery and Abla's father consents to their marriage. The story has been told and retold in prose and poetry for centuries and, like many others of his generation, Jowdat never tired of it. Mohammed said that in his old age, his father would often ask his mother to come sit beside him as he read passages aloud to her from the stories of Abla and Antar. She would laughingly indulge Jowdat, but probably understood little of the classical Arabic in which the story is written.

* * *

When Mohammed's grandfather, Saeed Imady died in 1907 he left behind his widow and eight children from the ages of twenty-five to four. Jowdat, the oldest, became the head of the family, but he was not the rich man he always assumed he would be. The family story – told to me by many family members - is that Jowdat prevented his sisters from marrying which so angered them that they retaliated by cheating him out of his share of the Imady wealth. I started out investigating this story with a skeptical attitude. How likely is it, I thought, that women could get away with disinheriting their older brother in Damascus in 1907?

The story of Jowdat's lost inheritance is a strange story and, after all these years and with all the people involved in the event long dead, we cannot be absolutely sure how it actually came to pass. However, if we know what kind of man Jowdat was, it becomes more believable.

Jowdat never held a job in his life. Men of his generation and his class, those whom the old English books on Damascus always call "the notables" (*al a'yan*), came from the scholarly, wealthy, landowning and governing families of Damascus and they did not have "jobs". They might hold a sinecure from the Ottoman Government, or they might oversee their land; nothing more. Jowdat, as I have said, kept himself busy raising horses.

Jowdat, all his children maintain, was also a religious man. He was observant in his religious duties, never missed a prayer and was completely honest in his dealings. He would not lie, not even a white lie to save someone's feelings, and he hated liars.

Everyone agrees he was an aristocratic, upright, pious man, but was also opinionated, stern and worst of all, had a terrible temper and was totally lacking in tact or diplomacy. Jowdat, say his children, ruled his six sisters with an iron hand, and in this respect, he was typical of many men of his society and generation.

According to Tete and my sisters-in-law, Jowdat's sisters all hoped to get married, but not a one of them did. In a way, this was the fault of their Aunt Hamida who, by marrying into the immensely wealthy and influential Mardam Beyk family, made all her nieces' suitors suffer by comparison. Their families were compared to the Mardam Beyk family and none measured up. First the girls' father, and then, after his early death, Jowdat turned away all suitors because, "none of them were good enough for the Imady girls".

However, there was undoubtedly another reason for rejecting the suitors. If the girls did not marry, the family money would stay in the family. Perhaps it was in Jowdat's interest for his sisters to remain spinsters. Although their father was also partly responsible for this, it was Jowdat they blamed and they never forgave him. Even their mother sided with her daughters against her oldest son and together, the mother and daughters planned a spectacular revenge. They must have been very determined, self-confident women.

From all I have been told by my sisters-in-law and Mohammed, what follows is a possible scenario. No one will ever know exactly how Jowdat lost his inheritance; we only know it did happen.

In those long ago times, no one kept their money in banks. Money, usually in the form of Ottoman gold coins, was kept at home. It seems Saeed Imady had entrusted his money to his wife and, when he died unexpectedly at fifty-two, his wife immediately turned over all the family money to her daughters and they hid it away.

When Jowdat went to his mother and asked for his share of his father's money, she looked him in the eye, shrugged her shoulders and said, "There is nothing. He left nothing but the land." Jowdat was astounded. He did not believe this was true, but, strangely enough, he never accused his mother or sisters of robbing him – not then or later. The story of how Jowdat was disinherited was always told by his wife and his children – but Jowdat also never contradicted them.

It amazes me how these women, with the help of their mother, cheated their older brother out of his inheritance back in 1907 in a patriarchal Muslim country where females allegedly had little control over their lives, but it actually happened. The proof is the lavish life style these women led over the years which was in great contrast to the modest circumstances of Jowdat and his family.

Lamat remembers hiding as a young child behind a cupboard in her paternal grandmother's bedroom and catching her oldest aunt unlocking the large chest at the foot of the bed. Lamat was astonished to see it stuffed with gold Ottoman coins, each one nestling in its own small bag. The coins were sewn into cloth bags so they would not make a tell-tale chinking sound when the maid moved the chest to clean under it.

The Imady property – all farm land in the Ghouta - was divided among Saeed's heirs strictly according to Islamic inheritance law: Jowdat's share was 17.5%, Hamdi got the same and the remaining 65% went to his six sisters and his mother. Of course, Jowdat became the manager of the land for his siblings and his mother, but his heart was not in it. This was not something he did well nor was it something he enjoyed. His bad temper and intolerance of crooked dealing were serious handicaps in overseeing the people who farmed the family land. Also, supervising the land was too much like work and Jowdat far preferred to spend his time with his horses, reading his books or playing backgammon.

Hamdi was only around seven years old when his father died. As he grew up, he turned out to be very unlike Jowdat, his much older brother. He was sociable, easygoing, fun-loving and likeable with a *laissez faire* attitude towards his religion. The enormous difference in temperament plus the eighteen-year age gap between the brothers meant they would never be close. However, the sisters adored their little brother and made a pet of him. My sisters-in-law say this was partly to spite Jowdat, partly out of frustrated maternal longings, and partly simply because their little brother was irresistible. He became the spoiled favorite of his sisters and they indulged all his weaknesses.

Eleven years after their father died, when Hamdi reached the age of eighteen, Jowdat was relieved to turn over the management of the family land to him. In fact, Hamdi turned out to be far better at the job than his older brother had been. Unlike Jowdat, Hamdi was a "hands on" manager and got the land to turn a good profit. Also, as soon as Hamdi became of age, the sisters continued their vendetta against Jowdat by signing over their shares of the land legally to Hamdi. In this way, if they should die before Jowdat, he would not inherit anything from them. So it was that Jowdat completely lost his rightful share of the money and was left with the smallest share of the land.

Even this small share, Jowdat did not bother to manage himself, but turned its stewardship over to Hamdi. Although Jowdat badly needed an income for his growing family and although Hamdi did not always give his older brother a fair share of the profits, Jowdat knew his own shortcomings. He was aware that with his hot temper it was better if he did not have too many dealings with people outside the family. Since Jowdat had no job and got very little income from his land, as time passed, he began to sell off parcels of his land to his brother. Hamdi grew richer and Jowdat, poorer.

The collapse of Jowdat's financial expectations marked him forever and was the defining factor in his life, but he did not for a moment consider taking his sisters and mother to court and suing them for his rights. To publicly brand his mother a liar was something he would never do. His mother and his sisters must have known him well enough to be sure they could get away with their scheme.

* * *

It was five years after he was disinherited that Jowdat sent his aunts – instead of his mother and sisters - to find him a bride. When Jowdat and Yisra were married, they moved into the smaller house in the family compound. Jowdat was angry at his family, but they were seven illiterate females and a little boy and he was their sole guardian. He could hardly turn his back on them. In fact, he never cut off relations with his mother and sisters. He continued to see them, to be part of their lives and to help them when necessary to the end of his days.

Tete told me she was fourteen and my father-in-law was thirty when they were married and she would add "girls were married off early when I was young" and that the difference in their ages was not considered unusual then. She didn't mention the year she was married – she probably didn't know it - but it was 1912. She did tell me with a frown that her in-laws changed her name to "Yisra" as soon as she was married. but would add with a smile that the next year her first child was born, a beautiful little boy they named Sadaddeen.

Yisra and Jowdat were happy with the arrival of their first child in 1913, but unfortunately Sadaddeen's birth, infancy and childhood took place in very inauspicious times. War, economic problems and crop failures all combined to make these years difficult. The year Sadaddeen was born, the Balkans successfully revolted against Ottoman rule and, shortly after that, the First World War began and Turkey came into the war on the side of Germany.

Back in the sixties, when I heard the older generation talk about the past, they always lumped the Balkan War and the First World War together and referred to them as the *Safar Barlik*, the Long March. They never failed to pronounce *Safar Barlik* with a shudder as they recalled those dark war years. They were a time of suffering and privation, not only for the young soldiers who were forced to fight in distant lands, but also for the Damascenes left behind. The headquarters of the combined German and Turkish forces of Greater Syria was garrisoned in Damascus and the priority of the Ottoman Governor was feeding his soldiers, not the population. Although the harvests were bad because of drought, food was requisitioned for the troops and, as a result, there were severe food shortages all over Syria.

Jowdat was conscripted as an officer into the Ottoman Army and spent his entire military service in Damascus because he was registered as the sole guardian of a family of ten. It was his great good fortune to have so many legal dependents because large numbers of young Syrian soldiers were sent off to war, never to return.

Lutfiya Khanum, the Turkish aunt of Wahid Beyk, Mohammed's brother-in-law, was the widow of one of these soldiers who marched off to war a few months after their marriage and never came back. I was very fond of this old lady who would sit and roll her cigarettes with a secret smile on her lips and a faraway look in her eye. She waited years and years for her handsome young husband to come home, or for just a word as to his fate, in vain. The lute she used to play for him gathered dust on top of her wardrobe and the photographs she sometimes showed us of a dashing, mustachioed young man in military uniform had the much-handled patina of age. Only these few mementos and her memories of their brief six months together remained.

In her very old age, Lutfiya Khanum lost touch with reality and the present. Once again she was young and would whisper proudly that her parents had arranged an engagement for her to a young, good-looking soldier. She started sneaking out of the house and wandering the streets, "looking for her fiancé". After the neighbors found her and brought her home several times, Lamat and Wahid Beyk began locking her in the apartment. Not long afterwards, she died.

* * *

The First World War meant different things to different people and this was particularly true where the Middle East was concerned. For many Arabs, the *Safar Barlik* was a bloody war between far-away countries and they wanted no part of it. The British and French governments, however, saw it as an opportunity to enlarge their colonial empires and their influence and power in the world. The European Zionists saw it as a chance to fulfill their dream of establishing a Jewish State in Palestine. In Istanbul, the idea of Turkish nationalism was emerging as the Ottoman Empire weakened. Finally, Arab nationalists saw it as an opportune time to throw off Ottoman rule and achieve independence. These conflicting motives and goals were a certain recipe for disaster and disappointment for the Arabs.

On May 6, 1916, Jamal Pasha, the Ottoman Governor of Damascus, hung twenty-one Syrians and Lebanese in Marjay Square. Their crime was belonging to a clandestine nationalist movement. It was to be the last gasp of Ottoman oppression in

Damascus. One month later, the Arab Revolt began when the Shereef Hussein, Emir of Mecca, and his Bedouin troops, attacked the Ottoman forces in the Hejaz. The British government had encouraged this uprising by fueling Arab hopes of independence in the McMahon-Hussein correspondence of 1915-1916 and by sending T. E. Lawrence, a British officer, to Shereef Hussein to ensure the success of the campaign. Hussein's army grew as deserters from the Ottoman army joined it and, led and advised by the military expertise of Lawrence, it successfully pushed north. Together, the Arab and the British forces drove the Turks and the Germans out of the Arabian Peninsula, Jordan, Palestine and headed for Damascus.

News of this revolt was met with enthusiasm by most Damascenes. Some, it is true, felt that to turn against the Ottoman Empire was to betray Islam. However, with the emergence of the secular Young Turks as the real power in Istanbul, fewer Damascenes still saw the Ottoman Empire as a defender of Islam. In the waning days of the Empire, many Damascenes had chafed under heavy-handed Turkish rule, and hoped for the dawn of a new Arab era and they cheered Emir Faisal, son of the Emir of Mecca, when he entered their city in triumph on October 1, 1918. Among those cheering, was Jowdat Imady, who had been a reluctant conscript in the Ottoman Army. The only lasting souvenirs of Jowdat's service as an officer in the Ottoman Army, were his military sword and the title, "Effendi".

While the Damascenes were still rejoicing in the Arab victory, the betrayals had already begun. The British had encouraged the Arabs to side with them against the Turks by promising Arab independence, a promise which the secret Sykes-Picot agreement of 1916 made clear they had no intention of keeping. This French/British agreement spelled out how the Arab territories of the Ottoman Empire would be divided between them after the war was won. England was to get Egypt and Mesopotamia; France would get Lebanon and Syria.

Next, came the Balfour Declaration in 1917, which promised the establishment of a Jewish National Home in Palestine. The indigenous inhabitants, the Palestinians, were not consulted about this plan to bring in European Jews to settle in their land although they constituted the overwhelming majority of the population of Palestine throughout the entire Christian era. The Balfour Declaration was one of the first steps on a path which would lead to the creation of the State of Israel and the *Nakba*, the Catastrophe, which uprooted and dispossessed – without compensation - around 780,000 Palestinians and ultimately led to the violence and suffering which continues unabated today.

Of course, back in 1918, all these behind-the-scene machinations were unknown to the Damascenes who rejoiced in the Arab victory. The defeated Turkish soldiers and officials fled the city and only deliriously happy Damascenes were left to welcome Faisal's Arab army.

From October 1918 to July 1920 Syria had a ruler who was not only an Arab, but also a Hashemite, a descendent of the Prophet. Faisal's brief rule as King of Syria, if it accomplished nothing else, gave the Syrians a taste for independence which would only grow as their hopes were frustrated time and again.

The twenty-two months Faisal reigned were memorable to the Imady family for a personal reason: he endeared himself to them when he had the discernment to buy a pure bred Arabian steed called al-Hamdaneeya, from Jowdat Effendi.

In January 1918, President Wilson announced his Fourteen Points with the famous principle of self-determination. The twelfth point specifically called for the unhindered development for the nationalities previously under Ottoman rule. Later, at the Paris Peace Conference in 1920, President Wilson sent the King-Crane Commission to the former Ottoman provinces to discover what kind of postwar government the Arabs envisioned for themselves. The Syrians told the Commission they opposed the idea of a French Mandate, they rejected the Balfour Declaration and they wanted an independent, sovereign state.

Syria's wishes were totally ignored. The French sent an army headed by General Gouraud to enforce the Mandate on the unwilling Syrians. A small ill-equipped Syrian army made a quixotic stand at Maysaloun, thirty kilometers outside Damascus. After the defeat of these brave men led by Yousef al-Azma, who fell in battle, the French Army marched into Damascus on July 25, 1920. The first demand General Gouraud made was to be taken to the tomb of Salah al-Din. There, it is reported, he insolently said: "We are back, Oh Saladin. My presence here consecrates the victory of the Cross over the Crescent."

To me, this gratuitous announcement seems like an echo of the Western hate that helped fuel the Crusades and it also reflects a remarkable ignorance of the Arab World. Did Gouraud not know that there were Christian Arabs who were as nationalistic, if not more, than their Muslim brothers? The French Mandate, which was to last for twenty-six years, had begun with the usual posturing arrogance of an occupying force.

* * *

The years of the First World War had been bad for Syria, but the terrible year of 1920 was even worse. The country was not only occupied by a foreign army, but also endured a very severe winter which ruined all the crops that year and actual starvation and epidemics resulted, not only in Damascus, but all over Syria. One of these epidemics, scarlet fever, ended the life of Sadaddeen.

This blond, blue-eyed little boy was greatly loved and greatly mourned when he died at the age of seven. My mother-in-law was just twenty-two when she lost her only child and it was a terrible blow to her. Years after Sadaddeen's death, she would tell me about him with tears in her eyes; how he promised he would build her a castle when he grew up, get her servants to do the housework and buy her whatever she wanted. She always said he was the kindest, the best-looking, and the cleverest of all her children.

He must have been very intelligent because he managed to complete reading the entire Qur'an by the age of seven. The family held a big celebration – called the *kutme* (the "Completion") - for Sadaddeen to commemorate this achievement and his mother sewed him a white gown with gold embroidery and a white cap with gold thread for the festivities. The sheikh from his *madrasa* and his classmates were invited to the party along with many family members and all feasted on the lamb slaughtered for the occasion.

Years later, Mohammed, who was born ten years after Sadaddeen's death, would be told every time they passed a certain school in Mohajareen: "This is the school where your brother learned to read the Qur'an." Mohammed told me once that part of his burning ambition to succeed was fired by his desire to fulfill his brother's promises to their mother.

Not only was Mohammed constantly reminded of Sadaddeen. Yisra and Jowdat never failed to point out to all their children where the brother they had never known had gone to school. Riad says they would all get sick of hearing about their wonderful dead brother, especially since their mother would always cry when she talked about him. Riad would tell her, "Sadaddeen is gone and after him you had us five girls and two boys. Isn't it enough for you? Forget Sadaddeen!" Her mother would answer that no child could take his place and that she would never forget him.

Sadaddeen died of scarlet fever in 1920. My sister almost died of it in 1940. Sulfa, the new wonder drug, saved Janet's life, but there was no modern medicine to save Sadaddeen. Sadaddeen caught scarlet fever from his cousin Essmat, Bahira's daughter. Essmat lived; Sadaddeen died. However, Essmat was also fated to have a relatively short life.

What has always seemed strange to me is the fact that Sadaddeen, throughout the seven years he lived, was an only child. When talking about these years my mother-in-law would always say to me, "Times were very hard. I didn't let myself get pregnant." She said she remembered seeing people so hungry they were happy to eat the orange peels, potato peels and watermelon rinds people discarded.

Still, I always wondered... how, in those long-ago days, long before the Pill was even dreamed of, how did Yisra control her fertility so successfully? According to her, she avoided pregnancy at will and became pregnant whenever she wanted. Amazing. Of course, I never had the nerve to ask her what the secret was.

In fact, when Sadaddeen died, Yisra immediately became pregnant and had another boy called Khaled. This child died of measles at the age of four months. When her second little boy died, Yisra was twenty-three, childless again after nine years of marriage.

However, in the next seven years she delivered six girls, one every year or so in her pursuit of a son to please her husband. Kawsar, born in 1922, was the first girl and had green eyes and chestnut hair. She would become her mother's great helper and a second mother to her youngest siblings. One year later, Lamat, blond and fair, came along. Some of the relatives nicknamed Lamat, "The French Doll" and all were charmed with her although they had hoped for a boy.

12.

To Palisades and Back

One summer night in 1962, we went to the airport to welcome Haidar, his Danish wife, Anna Maria, and their little boy to Damascus. We knew them from the days when we had all been together in New York and used to run into each other at the Arab Students' office. Haidar rented an apartment in Mohajareen near us and I soon learned Anna Maria and I shared a love of books, art, cooking, the BBC and much more. Before long she was part of my circle of good friends.

Except for Anna Maria, by the fall of 1962, it seemed as if all my friends had left Syria for one reason or another. Bianca was visiting her family in Rome, Rose was in the States, and Jill had also gone to the States last spring when Adel got a UN job in Africa. Now, her most recent letter said she and the boys had joined Adel in Niger. In addition to these three, there were at least half a dozen other friends who had gone home to visit their parents in the last few months.

After two and a half years in Syria, I felt it was *my* turn for a visit to the States. I was homesick and wanted to show off Muna to my family. As a first step, I took Muna to the American Embassy and registered her birth as an American citizen, born abroad, and had her put on my passport. Susu had a passport and now Muna was all set.

Getting us to Palisades wasn't going to be easy, however. As usual, the problem was money. I wrote letters to Mother going into detail about the exchange rate and Mohammed's salary. I wrote, "Although Mohammed's salary is 'chicken feed' in dollars, the ironic thing is we're well-off here with this salary. It is just when you have to convert to dollars that we seem so poor."

And, of course, we would have to pay for the airline tickets in dollars. Mohammed could only come up with half the cost of the tickets and said the sensible thing to do would be to wait a year until he could save up the whole amount, but I was in no mood to be reasonable.

I wrote Mother suggesting all kinds of wild schemes to finance the trip and finally asked her point blank to send me four hundred dollars. Worse, I gave her an ultimatum; I wanted her answer by return mail. It seems incredibly selfish of me now. Of course she sent the money, money she could ill afford to part with.

By the time it arrived, I had been hired as the music teacher at the Damascus Community School (DCS) and committed myself to teach until the Christmas break. If I had just waited a week or so, this solution would have turned up before I importuned my mother for money. With remorse, I asked Mother to cancel the remittance and get her money back - which she did.

The DCS was informally called the "American school" and was a private elementary school with an American curriculum. Most of the students were the children of embassy and United Nations personnel. In fact, this was the very same school we had hoped to send Susu to until the American vice-consul told us that as a child of "mixed parentage" she was not eligible. Actually, this turned out to be not only insulting, but also untrue; there *were* children with Syrian fathers in the school. However, in the end we preferred to have Susu attend a Syrian school where she would learn Arabic and English and not feel like a stranger in her own country.

I had no training as a music teacher, or any kind of teacher for that matter, but I did play the piano and loved music. The job sort of fell in my lap and it came to pass because at one point Jill had been the neighbor of Mary Bitar, the Palestinian principal of DCS. This very capable woman was the founder of the school and, when I first met her, she was not only handling all the administrative tasks of the school, but was also teaching math to the upper grades and music to all the students. She told Jill that she desperately needed to hire a music teacher and Jill suggested me. I jumped at the chance. Tete and Kawsar immediately offered to look after Susu and Muna while I taught, although I sometimes took Susu along with me to my classes.

There were about sixty children of many nationalities in the school and their ages ran from six to thirteen years old. I gave lessons to the first and second graders four days a week and the older ones twice a week. Music had always been an important part of my life and I was happy to share my love of music with these children. Also, it was wonderful to be able to play the piano again. However, much as I enjoyed my new job, I was not deterred from my plan to visit my family in December.

In November we began rehearsing for the school Christmas celebration. I was in charge of the music program and. in keeping with the international makeup of the school, I included Christmas carols from many different countries. Some of the children had lovely voices and I gave them solos. I taught the older children a descant for one of the songs and many of the songs were in two-part harmony.

While I was happily rehearsing my students for their Christmas program, back home my family was living through a tense and traumatic time. This was the autumn of the Cuban missile crisis, but truth to tell, to me in Syria, it all seemed very remote and far away. I found it hard to believe, as Mother later told me, that at the very height of the scare, many people in America felt it was the end of the world. Jo and Dave told Mother that they wished they could have lived long enough to have children and see them grow up! Mohammed and I were impressed at the way Kennedy handled the confrontation and were very relieved when it was defused.

Meanwhile, Mohammed and I continued to argue about my plan to visit Mother in December. He had a fund of objections: the time was not right; I should wait until we could save up more money; and since my sister, Jo, and brother-in-law, Dave, were living with Mother while their new house was being built, we would be three more "burdens" on my mother.

He probably had another unspoken objection. I think he privately worried that I might take the children to the States and never come back. A lot of stories circulated in Damascus about foreign wives who had done just that. Mohammed never actually forbid me to go, but made it perfectly clear that he was against it.

I brushed aside his opposition and Mother encouraged me when she wrote that Jo and Dave wanted us to come and there was plenty of room for us all.

Holly was also going back to Oklahoma for Christmas with her little daughter and we hoped to fly together as far as New York. However, she left early in December, while I couldn't go before the Christmas program on the 21st of December.

Finally, a very unwilling Mohammed put our airline tickets in my hand. We would be traveling by Pakistani Airlines to London where we would change to BOAC for the New York leg.

The Christmas program went well. My children sang sweetly and I was very proud of them. The next day Susu and I climbed aboard a Pakistani flight with Muna in my arms. A very grim Mohammed saw us off, but I soon forgot his chilly farewell in the excitement of our departure. Susu's earlier fear of airplanes was forgotten and she was thrilled at everything she saw. Over and over she urged me to look out at the clouds, the Mediterranean Sea, the mountains, the sunset and I would close my eyes and pretend to look. My fear of flying, which I thought had ended with my trip to Egypt, returned redoubled now that my children were with me. I kept thinking, if anything should happen to them, it would be my fault.

The only time I conquered my fear enough to really look out the window, was when we circled New York City. I decided to get at least one last glimpse of my beloved city before we crashed.

After a perfectly dreadful trip, we finally arrived. Everything that could go wrong, went wrong. Worst of all, we were so late into London that we missed our BOAC flight to New York, so PIA kept us on. The flight was terribly crowded with

American college students going home for the Christmas break. Their skis and luggage were all over the place. I even think several students ended up sitting on the stewardesses' jump seats to make room for us.

Jo, Dave and Mother were waiting for us in Idlewild Airport and when the BOAC plane arrived without us, Mother was frantic and called Mohammed – who, of course had no idea what had happened. Not knowing what else to do, Dave drove them back home.

Our PIA flight landed an hour after they had left the airport and I was devastated to find no one to meet us. Choking back tears, I called my family to come get us – and learned it would be their second trip to the airport that night. Muna went to sleep in my arms while we waited, but Susu happily went up and down the escalators while humming along with the Christmas songs that came over the loudspeakers. She also marveled at the big Christmas trees scattered around the airport – the biggest ones she'd ever seen, with ornaments the size of her head.

My family finally arrived and when we got home at four in the morning, I called Mohammed, who had spent a worried few hours, to tell him we were safe in Palisades. Poor Jo, Dave and Mother immediately fell into bed for three hours sleep because they all had to go to work in the morning.

It seemed so strange to be in Palisades without Mohammed. Susu talked about him all the time and when I said, "Baba," Muna, looked all around the room for him. Much as the children missed their father, I missed him even more.

Before we had been in Palisades very long, David and Jo fell in love with our girls. Jo befriended Susu while Dave's favorite was Muna. Every night when we ate supper, Dave put Muna over his knees and whispered little nothings in her ear. She would laugh and we said they had their own secret language. Then, he rubbed her back until she fell asleep. Jo, like Kawsar back in Damascus, took Susu along on all her shopping trips.

It was nineteen days before I got a letter from Mohammed and this was back when it took only four or five days for a letter to arrive from Damascus. The day I got Mohammed's first letter, I had given Mother a terribly angry letter to mail him. When she saw there was one from Damascus, she didn't mail it. All my family members found it very strange that he waited so long to write and so did I.

Then, when I read it, it was a chilly, formal letter and I began to imagine all kinds of things; that he no longer loved me and was planning to get a divorce or at the least that he didn't miss me at all.

Susu looked every day for a letter from her father. She would ask, "Why doesn't Baba write us? After a while she didn't ask anymore, but she constantly worried that her Tete might be sick.

I was sad and depressed. Every other time there was trouble between us I could at least telephone. I felt now as if there was an enormous barrier between us, more than just space in miles. When I went to get the mail, the postmistress, the old busybody, would ask if I wasn't worried since I so seldom heard from my husband.

Mohammed's next letter was worse, full of accusations: this was a selfish, unnecessary trip; I had insisted on going when he said not to; didn't I realize we could ill afford this expensive trip; hadn't my mother visited Damascus recently - and more in the same vein. I wrote him, "Don't write anymore negative things. They are so permanent on paper. It's one thing to think, another to say and still another to write."

Mother and Jo would innocently ask me to read Mohammed's letters and I recall making up nice things to tell them that were *not* in the letters. Finally I got some news I could truthfully read – Inayat had given birth to a baby boy, but no details were included – not even the baby's name.

It was a bittersweet three-month visit with my family. There were so many good times, but all of them were clouded by Mohammed's stiff and infrequent letters.

Muna took her first steps in Mother's old house and Susu learned to read in Mother's old school. Shortly after we arrived, we enrolled Susu in kindergarten and by the time our visit ended, she could read her primer all the way through and was trying to read other simple books.

We celebrated Jo's birthday in January and Jan came in the middle of February, in time for Muna's and Mother's birthdays. Jan stayed about five days and Mother's old house rang with the laughter and talk of two children and five adults. It was the first time we three sisters had been together in three years and we treasured every moment of it.

Finally I got a really hostile letter from Mohammed and I wrote him, "Like you, I am writing and tearing up letters. You should have torn up the last one..." I went on to say that if he was not ready to start over again and welcome us back with open arms, for him to let me know at once so I could change my plans about coming back.

In the midst of all this, not even sure whether I was going back, I still remembered that March 1st marked the third year for Mohammed's government service, with five years to go.

While our little drama was playing out by correspondence, another drama was unfolding on a much larger stage. Back in Syria, the country was divided between the separatists in power and those who opposed the break-up of the unity. The latter group included the Nasserites and members of the largest opposition party, the socialist Baath Party. A group of officers who had been dismissed and briefly imprisoned for belonging to the Baath party, began plotting with the Nasserites to overthrow the government. Among these officers was Hafiz al-Assad, who at this time lived with his family in Mohajareen two doors from us in a simple apartment. None of suspected then that he would be President of the country for almost thirty years.

The Baathist and Nasserite officers took over the government without firing a shot on March 8, 1963. For a short time, these two parties worked together, but relations between them deteriorated when it became clear the Baathists had no intention of restoring the unity. In May, the Nasserites staged huge riots and the Baathists ruthlessly put down the demonstrations. The Nasserites were thrown out and General Amin al-Hafiz (no relation to Hafiz al-Assad), who as Minister of Interior, had crushed the pro-Nasser rioters, became President.

The socialist Baath Party was now firmly in control of Syria and brought about swift and overwhelming change. Private enterprise, except for small shops, was eliminated with the nationalization of all industry, banks, and insurance companies. Import was put under government control as well as the export of all basic commodities and rent control went into effect.

Many wealthy Syrians who had money outside the country fled, but most middle class citizens were unable to leave and were badly hurt by the nationalization decrees, including our Abdo. He had put all his modest inheritance from his father into stocks in different factories and he lost everything.

Down in Oklahoma, my friend Holly was horrified by the news of the March 8th Revolution even before all these drastic changes were enacted and decided a socialist Syria was no place to raise her little girl. She phoned me and said she hoped her husband would join her in Oklahoma, but in any case, she was not returning to Damascus. Then she asked me about my plans. I didn't tell her about our differences or that Mohammed had finally written a letter saying he couldn't live without me and begging me to come back. I simply told her I would be going back. The truth is, the revolution did not affect me as it did Holly. Whether I returned to Syria or not only depended upon Mohammed; nothing else mattered.

So we came back to Syria, Mohammed was his dear, loving self once again and all was well. I think the anger in his letters was simply a reflection of his fear that he had lost us forever when we went back to Palisades. He thought we would be seduced into this easier world and not want to return, but he was wrong.

We came back from the cold and snow of early spring in Palisades to the blossoming fruit trees of early spring in Damascus; from cozy rooms with wooden floors and central heating to high-ceilinged rooms with tiled floors and *sobas* (heaters). How loud voices seemed to me as they they ricocheted from the lofty ceilings to the tiled floors. It sounded like everyone was shouting. After so many years I still find this small but striking change an unnerving difference between here and there. You only notice it for a day or two when you return from a trip, then you get used to it and no longer hear it.

The day after I arrived back in Damascus was a Sunday. Mohammed got the day off from work and we took the children to a park where Muna had great fun looking at the ducks and showing her Baba how well she could walk. When we got home, Lamat and Wahid Beyk came and took Susu on a picnic to the Ghouta with her cousins.

That afternoon, in our sunny living room, I wrote a letter to Mother while Mohammed worked on a report. Muna and Fowzieh, our child servant, sat together on a black lambskin quietly playing games with things from the toy drawer. It was a typical afternoon in Damascus and I could hardly believe that forty-eight hours earlier we had been in Palisades.

On our arrival, everyone was amazed, including me, to discover that Susu couldn't speak a word of Arabic. She understood what people said, but answered everyone, even Tete, in English. Her little cousins were mystified. Fowzieh, however, had not forgotten her English and she became Susu's official translator. Fowzieh's English was inside-out, but fluent.

In the first few days after we returned, Susu cried hard three times for "Mommy" and one morning, before going to school, she sang *My Country 'Tis of Thee* and said the Pledge of Allegiance to the Flag and, after that, she settled down to being a loyal little Syrian again. Muna latched onto her Baba as if she wanted to make up for the three lost months. She wouldn't look at anyone else if he was in the room.

By the time we had been back three weeks, it was just as if we had never left. Susu began speaking Arabic again before a week was up and Muna began drinking boiled milk with as much enthusiasm as she'd had for American pasteurized, homogenized milk. The flocks of people who came to pay their respects for our safe return tapered off, and Inayat had the whole family over to see her new baby boy, Ammar.

After all Susu's fears, we were happy to see that Tete's health was no worse than usual. Kawsar and Riad caught me up on all the family news of the last three months and Abdo was glad to be able to practice his English again. The old family building in Mohajareen once more was full of the voices of children and the endless tramp of feet going up and down stairs. We sent Susu to a nearby nursery school with some of her cousins and I returned to the American school. In short, life was back to normal.

I realized after this first trip back that from now on, wherever I was, I would feel torn. If I were in Palisades, I would miss Damascus. If I were in Damascus I would want to be in Palisades. For the rest of my life I would exist between two worlds, never completely at home in either.

In April, Holly wrote me and said she was definitely not coming back. Fuad was broken-hearted and haunted our house asking advice as to what might get Holly back and begging me to write her. How history repeats itself! Two and a half years earlier, it was Adel sitting in our living room asking advice and begging me to write Jill.

Holly said she wanted "Fred" to come to America and I think he would have if it had been possible. However, he hadn't served in the army and therefore couldn't get a passport. He promised Holly a new apartment (their old one was nice) with central heating if she came back, but she wasn't tempted. The next letter I got from Holly said she had gone back to her old teaching job in a local school and shortly afterwards, Mohammed went into Fuad's office and found him crying.

The weather that April was in tune with Fuad's bleak mood. It was not only unseasonably cold, but wet. It rained as often as any April in Palisades. It was good for the farmers, but some illegal mud brick homes built by the very poor on the upper slopes of Qassioun were actually washed away. All the streets that ran down the mountain turned into streams and stones, even some large boulders, loosened by the heavy rain, rolled dangerously down these steeply inclined streets. We stood in the rain on our balcony and watched this unusual sight. At least the underground water level, which they always fret about here, rose. After days of rain, I began to long for some typical, sunny Damascus weather.

When my school closed the end of June, I started my belated spring cleaning. In Damascus this is a very serious business that takes several days and entails washing all the rugs, sprinkling them with soap flakes to discourage moths, rolling them up and storing them up on the lofts; taking down and cleaning the soot from the stove pipes and putting them and the *sobas* away; washing the walls, ceilings and windows and taking down the curtains to wash and iron them. My in-laws even took their doors off the hinges to scrub them!

My ceilings were fourteen and a half feet high and to clean my walls and ceilings I was given a ladder like no ladder I'd ever seen. It looked as if it had been hacked out by hand with primitive tools since there wasn't a single smooth, straight piece of wood used in its construction. Also, it wasn't a folding ladder; it just had the one piece with the steps. Obviously, this kind of ladder should never be used without having someone hold it.

Fowzieh was helping me clean and offered to hold the ladder for me, but I waved her away and asked her to hand me a cloth. As I stood at the top of the ladder, almost fifteen feet up, the ladder suddenly slid down the soapy floor and me with it. It happened so fast I didn't cry out or even feel myself fall. It was my good fortune the ladder slipped down the wall and didn't flip over backwards.

I was knocked unconscious, giving poor Susu and Fowzieh a terrible scare. They ran screaming for Kawsar and even Tete climbed down the stairs to see how I was. I came to quickly and the worst that happened was a cut on my chin. Also, my left arm and foot were a bit stiff for a few days, but I was very lucky. The same day, Mohammed bought us a proper folding ladder.

The American Embassy usually had a cocktail party on the Fourth of July, but this year they had a picnic near the village of Ijdaydeh "for all Americans in Damascus, including their foreign spouses and children" as the invitation read. In the early sixties, there were only narrow gauge trains in Syria with Swiss steam engines made in the 1890s and it was one of these quaint, old trains that was chartered to take us to Ijdaydeh. Susu and I were excited because it would be our first train ride in Syria. What a pleasant surprise it was to see the sides of the steam engine hung with bunting and the Syrian and American flags crisscrossed on the front of the engine!

The picnic was held on an island and to reach it we had to ford a little stream. It was only knee deep, but there was a strong current, the water was icy cold and the bed of the stream was full of pebbles which made it rather an adventure. Once across the stream, there were donkeys for the children to ride and hot dogs, hamburgers and coke for all. The Girl Scout troop from the DCS had a flag ceremony and for entertainment someone played the guitar and a men's quartette sang gay-ninety and patriotic songs. Fireworks finished off a lovely day. On the train ride back, someone played Arabic songs on an accordion and a young girl and Susu danced all the way home.

I realize now that observing these American holidays - the Fourth of July, Christmas, New Year's and Thanksgiving - helped me feel there was some continuity between my old life and my new. It not only was a link to my past, it also enriched my children's lives as they grew up with not one culture and its traditions, but with two.

* * *

Shortly after Susu's sixth birthday, Fuad invited us for dinner to the Sahara, an outdoor restaurant in the "desert" on the road to Zebadani. Damascus was at its hottest, but at night outside the city and under the stars it was many degrees cooler. We had a light supper while Fuad monopolized the conversation hashing over and over Holly's refusal to return, trying to come up with ways he could get her back to Damascus and telling us with tears in his eyes how much he missed her and his daughter. If only we could have steered the conversation in any other direction, it would have been a pleasant evening. Finally, drained and talked out, Fuad drove us home.

Since the next day was a Friday, our "Sunday", we did not wake as early as usual. When I finally opened my eyes, I turned to Mohammed and was jolted awake. What was wrong with his face? He was asleep, but his left eye was strangely half open. On the same side, his face sagged and his mouth drooped. He had gone to bed whole and well and in the night something had happened to his face. Crazy thoughts of curses, spells and the evil eye tumbled in my mind.

We soon found out how bad this affliction was when Mohammed awoke. He was in no pain, but on the left side of his face, he simply could not smile, frown, chew or close his eye. It was a terrible blow for him and for us all. For Mohammed's heart-sick mother, sisters and brother it was particularly hard since they had been through this three years earlier when Bara'at had come down with the very same thing.

I didn't let Mother know right away, because at first we all hoped this strange facial paralysis would vanish overnight, the way it had appeared. When it didn't, we began to think Mohammed should go abroad and see a specialist.

Meanwhile, Mohammed's aunt, Amti Bahajay, took matters into her own hands. She was now in her sixties, and like many Damascenes of her generation, she was very superstitious. She believed that this strange malady was clearly the result of the evil eye. Some jealous colleague who wished Mohammed ill had brought this upon him. She was also certain that to cure this paralysis, you only needed someone who could counteract curses, the evil eye and suchlike. She had heard that in the Haret al-Yahood, the Jewish Quarter, there was such a man and she persuaded a very skeptical Riad to go with her to consult him. As Amti described her nephew's paralysis to the healer, he stared at Riad. He hardly listened he was so taken with her slim elegance. Finally, he took his eyes off Riad long enough to say this was a simple matter which would cost them twenty-five Syrian pounds. Although this was five times more than the fee of a medical doctor, Amti agreed and the man began an incantation in an unknown tongue. Then he handed them a folded paper on which he had written some sentences and told them that they should soak the paper in a glass of water and, when the patient drank the water, the cure would take effect. Mohammed doesn't remember whether he drank the water or not. Probably he was just handed a glass of water without being told it was supposed to cure him. Of course, it didn't.

Amti Bahajay was not one to give up easily. Next, she decided to take Mohammed to the tomb of Sheikh Raslan, a 12th century poet and "saint". There, she said, they would recite the *fatihah* (the seven verses which make up the first chapter of the Qur'an) over his grave and the blessing this would confer would open the gates of Heaven for a cure. Mohammed humored his old aunt, but again there was no improvement.

I only learned about these well-intentioned attempts of Amti Bahajay to cure Mohammed years and years later. Perhaps they didn't tell me at the time because they thought I would object and say things like "superstition" and "witch doctor".

While Amti put her faith in healers and prayers, in my American fashion, I turned to the best medical expert I knew. I wired Mother to contact Dr. Haagensen and ask his advice. In the meantime, the Syrian government sent Mohammed to London to consult a Harley Street specialist. Mohammed was already in England when I finally heard from Dr. Haagensen who said Mohammed's paralysis was called Bell's palsy and was caused by a virus that attacks the facial nerves. He recommended a short course of cortisone to kill the virus and said time would bring about a cure.

The specialist in London agreed with Dr. Haagensen and told Mohammed to go home. Mohammed's family was disappointed he didn't come back cured, but I was confident that with time he would recover and did my best to make him think positively.

It wasn't easy. For someone like Mohammed who had been good-looking all his life, the psychological effects of Bell's palsy were the most difficult to deal with. As he said, one's face is all-important; with it we face the world. For about two months, he was depressed, didn't want to see anyone and stayed home from work.

Eventually, Mohammed took a philosophical view of the episode and decided it had been good for him to experience what it was like to lose his good looks. He said before he got Bell's palsy, he had put too much stock in his appearance and had even been a bit dismissive of those who were not attractive. His paralysis brought home to him in a very personal way how desperately everyone wishes to be attractive and that beauty is a gift which is randomly bestowed upon some and not upon others. He told me he came away from this experience with a better appreciation of the fact that no one can take credit or blame for his or her looks and that everyone deserves to be met with kindness and courtesy irrespective of their appearance.

I have to add that whatever Mohammed privately thought, he had always treated all people graciously, no matter what they looked like.

Mohammed ended up with close to a one hundred percent recovery. Anyone who meets him for the first time would not think anything was amiss, but if you had known him before the Bell's palsy, you would notice a slight difference in his smile.

* * *

While Mohammed was in London for treatment of his Bell's palsy, he bought me a platinum wedding ring for our seventh anniversary. We celebrated by going out for dinner and reminisced about our wedding day; about our long bus drive from New York to Palisades in a big traffic jam and how Mohammed had teased that he was going to get off the bus. As he gave me the ring he said, "I'm glad I stayed on that bus." We remembered Jo driving us to the George Washington Bridge and the friendly attention we attracted as we rode the subway to our apartment, our radiant faces and the sprinkles of confetti on our clothes clearly proclaiming we were newlyweds.

Now that Susu was six years old, we decided to enroll her in an excellent English/Arabic private school called Rowdat al-Ahdass. However, when we went to register her, they told us she would have to begin in kindergarten with the five-year-olds unless she passed a reading test in Arabic and English. The children Susu's age had already finished a British primer as well as the first Arabic primer. I took the books home and Riad tutored her in Arabic and I took care of the English. Susu passed with no trouble and was near the top of the class when her first report card came out. She was happy at school and before long was reading on her own for fun in Arabic and English.

One day Fowzieh's father came to take her home because her mother was sick and, as with Najah, we never saw her again. I began looking around for an older helper, a responsible woman I could depend on if I worked full-time since I had heard about the possibility of a secretarial job with the UN. However, I ended up with another child, Wazira.

This pretty little girl had never worked before and was trouble from the first day. She was homesick, hated our food and cried all the time. We sent her home to visit her family and she came back with her long, thick hair infested with lice. Of course Muna and Susu caught them and it took Kawsar and me a week of cutting hair, combing out nits and soaking the children's heads with kerosene to get rid of the lice. Wazira's mother arrived in the midst of this battle and was furious we had cut her daughter's hair. She grabbed her daughter by the hand and angrily flounced out shouting that they would never return. We all breathed a sigh of relief.

Meanwhile, the chance to work for the United Nations actually materialized and it came about through my friend, Lillian, who worked for one of the UN organizations. She asked me if I could type and whether I would be interested in working for FAO, the Food and Agricultural Organization of the UN. I made 140 Syrian pounds a month at the school working part-time, but the UN job would be full-time and would pay five times more than that. When I started to think of pianos and trips to America, I decided to take the typing test. I did fine and began the long wait, which could take months, for my appointment to go through.

When I told Mrs. Bitar, the school principal of my plans, she said she would be sorry to have me go and told me I was "irreplaceable", something no one had ever said to me before. She even raised my salary, perhaps hoping I would change my mind. I promised to continue teaching until school let out in June.

December came and with it another Christmas entertainment. This year it was held at the American USIS (U.S. Information Service) Library which, unlike the school, had a small auditorium with a stage. The children gave a wonderful performance and afterwards the chairman of the school board presented me with a bouquet of flowers.

By now, we foreign wives in Damascus had become a circle of close-knit friends who dropped in often on each other with our babies and children in tow. When friends came to visit me, the children would head for Susu's and Muna's bedroom and we mothers would gather in the living room with our babies over coffee and cake to talk, commiserate, and exchange recipes, shopping tips, books and advice on coping with life in Damascus. Because someone was always pregnant or leaving, there were always baby showers and farewell parties being planned.

That winter Adel came back from Niger alone. Jill, he said, had gone back to the States in September to put the boys in school. In December, I had a farewell party for one of my friends who was off to the States for good with her Syrian husband. As usual, their departure was sudden and unexpected. To my dismay, Penny and Farouk left the following month, supposedly for ever, but after two and a half months they returned because Farouk had difficulty in getting permission to resign from his ministry. I was so glad they came back. Also, around this time, another friend went to live in Kuwait where her husband had a new job. Then, in February, Anna Maria and Haidar went to Geneva for three months. Anna Maria was happy because she and her boys – there were now two - got to make a side visit to her folks in Denmark. A few months later, an American couple who were good friends left after a flurry of farewell parties. It seemed as if I was always saying goodbye to someone.

On March 1st, I ticked off another year for Mohammed. It was the half-way mark with four years left of his governmental service. On March 8th, a holiday was declared to mark the first anniversary of the Baath revolution and a big military parade was held. We took the children to see the parade and how Muna enjoyed herself! Airplanes flew overhead as tanks, jeeps and anti-aircraft guns rolled past, but Muna only had eyes for the helicopters and clapped for joy every time one appeared. That night we watched the fireworks from Tete's balcony.

This celebration was barely over when the Baathists faced serious unrest all over the country, particularly in the city of Hama. The economy was in bad shape and some religious leaders, unhappy with the secular Baathists, preached fiery anti-government sermons which led to riots. Finally, there was an armed uprising of the Muslim Brotherhood in Hama and President Amin al-Hafiz ordered the army to crush this clandestine opposition movement. About seventy Muslim Brothers were killed, many were arrested while others went into hiding in neighboring countries. No one imagined then that this was just a precursor of an all-out and doomed attempt to overthrow the government eighteen years later.

The articles that appeared in American newspapers describing these events were far from reassuring to Mother. She read every word printed about Syria and was disturbed and anxious about our safety. She asked cagey questions in her letters and I wrote back that we had never been in any danger. It was true and I hoped she believed me.

The only time Syrian news made the American papers was when there was a coup d'etat or political violence of some kind. Unfortunately, during the sixties, Syrians provided plenty of opportunities to journalists who specialized in this kind of news. Since this was all Westerners ever heard about Syria, they were getting a very skewed idea of the country. Imagine if the only news coming out of America in the sixties was about violent crime and racial discrimination. I felt it was very unfair.

Haidar's Garden

Below our hillside district of Mohajareen, extensive fields of cactus sloped down from Malki Circle with its statute of an assassinated officer, to the much larger Umayyad Circle, which then marked the western edge of the city. The clumsy, stumpy cactus plants, studded with prickly fruits, did not grow wild, but were cultivated for their fruit, *sabara* (sa-BA-ra), which Syrians consider a great delicacy. In addition to the cactus fields, numerous vegetable farms and orchards dotted the Malki area below us. Mud brick walls enclosed these rural enclaves within the city and, inside these walls, life was still ruled by the age-old rhythm of the seasons.

All this was about to change. Up to the time of the Baath Revolution, Syria had been ruled by *al a'yan,* the urban aristocrats or "the notables" as they are usually called in English. However, with the establishment of the socialist government, the newly empowered rural population began flocking to the capital for jobs, for education and for a better life. Damascenes looked askance at what they privately called this "march of the peasants", but the trend was irrevocable. The population of the city would soon jump from 400,000 to 2,000,000 and the fields and farms of Malki were swept away as the city grew. A large boulevard connecting the Malki Circle to the Umayyad Circle was cut through the cactus fields and, not long after that, the fields were leveled, the mudbrick walls knocked down and the farms razed to make way for a fashionable new city district called West Malki. Almost overnight, expensive apartment buildings sprung up to replace the fields and orchards.

At the same time, another huge, new district was rapidly sprouting to the west of the Umayyad Circle. It was called Mezze after the name of the small village swallowed up as development spread westwards. Where there had been mostly barren land, street after street was paved and apartment buildings were built. The metastatic growth of Mezze was only stopped on the south by the last remaining cactus fields and on the north by hills.

Before all these drastic changes came to pass, one of the walled-in orchards in Malki was owned by the family of our friend, Haidar. A rippling stream ran through it and small birds nested in the trees and feasted on the fruit. Anna Maria often invited me and other friends to bring our children to what she called "Haidar's Garden". There we would spend the day and picnic beside the stream. As we opened the gate and entered into this bit of country in the city, I always felt as if I had stepped into a secret garden, an enchanted place where nothing unpleasant could ever happen. Today, when I drive around the streets of West Malki, all lined with apartment buildings, I cannot even guess where this marvelous, secret garden was. It has vanished without a trace as though a genie, summoned by the rubbing of a magic lamp, had whisked it away overnight.

What remains are the pleasant memories my children and I have of that place and some photographs taken there. This miniature farm of perhaps three acres was filled with small fruit trees including apricot, fig, pomegranate and mulberry as well as tall walnut trees. There was a peasant who looked after the land and he planted vegetables under the trees. Large, colorful roses bloomed four or five times a year adding bright splashes of color to the garden.

Throughout the summer of 1964, we went there several afternoons a week and, amazingly, it was only a short fifteen-minute walk from our home. The children had a wonderful time exploring and getting into mischief with Anna Maria's two boys. They climbed the trees, fell into the stream, picked the flowers and ate the fruit.

We were often joined there by a new friend, Janette, from Glasgow, whose Syrian husband, Souad, was a doctor. They had two boys close in age to Susu and a girl about Muna's age.

Of all people, Michel, my hairdresser, introduced us. Janette was under the hairdryer and I was having my hair rolled up when he said, in Arabic, "You two are both English – you should get to know each other."

Janette immediately bristled and answered him in Arabic, "I am certainly *not* English! I'm Scottish."

And I said in Arabic, "Well, *I'm* not English either! I'm American."

Then we both laughed and did introduce ourselves. Janette had a very exotic – to my ears – Glaswegian accent, a wonderfully wicked tongue and could make a stone laugh. We soon were visiting back and forth and I introduced her to my friends and met all of hers.

School was out and hot weather, swimming weather, was back. One scorching Friday, Mohammed persuaded Abdo to come swimming with us. He did a complete about-face and all his objections to my swimming were forgotten. Perhaps having an American sister-in-law was making him more open-minded.

We took Abdo to the old "embassy pool" that we used to go to. It had been closed for about a year and a half and we realized why when we got there. This pool formerly was surrounded by orchards, but the land had been sold and apartment buildings were going up with cement mixers and construction debris everywhere. We could hardly recognize the place and it was the last time we went. We found another pool further out from the city in an area that was still unspoiled.

Sometimes the whole city seemed to be one big construction lot, including our block where the building next to ours, Bianca's house, had been torn down, making the street almost impassable. The site was a great gaping hole on our block, like a pulled tooth. Bianca and her husband moved into an apartment in Lamat's building while all this was going on. Of course their old Arabic house was replaced with a four-story apartment building like ours. The old homes were coming down all over the city.

As soon as school let out, I began working at the Food and Agricultural Organization of the UN (FAO) with my friend Penny, who was secretary to the Resident Representative or director of the FAO in Damascus. Like all the foreign secretaries, I was hired as a temporary employee, which meant I was paid by the hour and there were no benefits, but the pay was so good that these drawbacks didn't matter. My salary came to almost as much as Mohammed earned. By the end of my fourth month at FAO, I was thrilled to be able to buy a piano. Growing up, we had never been without a piano; to me it was an essential part of a real home. I could do without a car, but not without a piano.

Most of the FAO foreign advisors were not native English speakers although English was the official UN language, so one of our main jobs was to edit their reports, put them into proper English and type them up. A lot of the reports we edited were very informative and some were bizarrely hilarious such as one by a Russian veterinary expert on the artificial insemination of cows in southern Syria. This expert, who was thick-set, bald and had some steel teeth, spoke only Russian so he had with him a young translator. Penny and I had many funny and embarrassing sessions with this shy young boy as he struggled to translate all kinds of graphic sexual terms from Russian into English. He told us he was good at "literary translation", but had never learned the words he needed for a report on artificial insemination. He would blush and stammer as he tried to explain what word he wanted and we worldly young married women would try to help him with straight faces.

I enjoyed the work and particularly liked working with Penny. She was not only an excellent secretary; she was fun to be with. The hours at work passed very pleasantly.

Riad's ministry, the Ministry of Public Works, was in the same building as the FAO so we came back home together. In the mornings we went separately because Riad had no children to get up and get dressed and no breakfast to prepare so she was always out of the house long before I flew out the door.

Suad

Now that I was working full-time I needed help with the housework. After a succession of child maids – Najah, Fowzieh and Wazira – I promised myself that Wazira would be the last, and she was.

I am indebted forever to Penny for introducing me to Suad who ended up working for us for seventeen years. I first met Suad at Penny's home one day when we were invited for a dinner and was impressed to learn Suad had cooked the delicious meal. When, some months later, Penny mentioned Suad had three free days a week, I said send her to me! So it was that Suad came to work for us, to do the heavy housework and cook. The days she came she would cook for two days which made life a little easier for Kawsar. We had been eating upstairs since I started working for FAO, but Kawsar had her hands full without having to cook for us.

Suad was a short, stocky woman with the dark skin, broad nose and kinky hair of some distant African ancestors. She was amazingly capable and would go through the apartment thoroughly and efficiently and never needed to be told what to do. She was a wonderful cook and could prepare all the Damascene delicacies as well as some Turkish dishes she'd learned from Penny's Istanbuli mother-in-law.

She also took over the laundry and I soon found she could iron better and faster than anyone I had ever seen. I offered her the ironing board, but Suad preferred to iron on the floor and this was something to behold. She would ensconce herself on a rug on the floor with several thicknesses of folded sheets in front of her, a bottle of water and a heap of ironing beside her. She then would take a mouthful of water and spray it in a fine mist on the clothes. When they were dampened to her satisfaction, she began to iron with a flourish. She was truly a professional. When we praised her ironing she would tilt her head, give us a fiendish look and say she was going to quit working for us as soon as she earned enough money to open her own laundry!

Bit by bit, Suad began telling me her sad history. Her parents had been poor Bedouin living in the Jordanian desert. When she was only two years old, they sold her to the family of a prominent Syrian lawyer (and she named the family) who brought her to Damascus. This was probably in the late 1920's and even then such transactions were not legal, but who was to report the crime? And who was to enforce the law?

She said she remembered sweeping floors when she was hardly old enough to hold a broom and washing dishes when she had to stand on a chair to reach the sink. She was a feisty woman and must have been a feisty child. She told us about finding a huge snake in the kitchen when she was just a tiny girl. Instead of screaming for help, she chased it back into a hole in the wall with a stick.

When she was a teenager, one of the young boys of the family tricked her into thinking she was married, and she ended up pregnant. As she told us, when she delivered her baby girl, the family came to the hospital to see the baby and when they found it "more white than black" as she put it, they took the baby from her. She then developed a serious infection that kept her in the hospital for months. She finally recovered, but could no longer have children.

At this point, her life took a turn for the better. She managed to leave her "owners" and somehow ended up living with Penny's in-laws who treated her kindly. Penny's mother-in-law took Suad under her wing and taught her to cook. For the first time in her life she was a free person and was getting paid for her work

Several years passed uneventfully until she met and married a good-looking man who was as tall as she was short. Her husband was from the city of Homs, but he had found work in Damascus as a maker of ladies' leather handbags. They settled down in a small apartment in the east of Damascus that Suad kept spotlessly clean.

When she didn't show up for work, it was usually because she had rushed her husband to the hospital with a hemorrhaging ulcer. He had a chronic problem with ulcers, but could not resist hot, spicy food. Sometimes when he overindulged, he would have an ulcer attack and Suad would install him in a private room in the best hospital in the city. Over the years, I am sure a good part of her salary went to pay her husband's medical expenses. She used to say that if he had been left to the mercy of his family he would have died long ago. I believed her.

She often muttered to herself as she worked and had many colorful expressions. She would always say as she carefully set the table and arranged the serving dishes on the table, "The eye also needs to be fed." "*Ya khrafunnah*!" she would exclaim when annoyed or angry and Mohammed told me it was a made-up euphemism. She always called me "*Malemti*" and Mohammed, "*Maalm*i" – both meaning "my teacher". She loved to tell and hear risqué jokes and her eyes shone and she cackled appreciatively at a good one.

When you think of Suad's deprived childhood, how much she missed out on in the way of parental love and family life, it is amazing she turned out to be such a self-confident and capable woman. She was also fiercely independent and, understandably, could be rather prickly.

She must have had a very resilient nature to have survived her early childhood without a scarred or warped personality. It is a great tribute to her that she ended up an honest, respectable woman and certainly no credit to the heartless people who bought her and put her to work as a little child.

Suad's life actually had turned out rather well except for one huge problem: she had no identity card. In this part of the world you are a non-person if you lack an identity card. You cannot attend school, you can have a religious marriage – as Suad had - but it cannot be legally registered; you cannot leave the country or even be buried - your body will end up as a cadaver in the Medical School. I think this latter fact is what bothered her the most.

Now and then, I would confide to Tete some of Suad's stories of her early childhood. Tete would listen with sympathy and say that many child servants in Damascus had difficult lives although Suad's case was especially dreadful because she had no family to turn to. How sad, Tete would say, to know your parents abandoned you – worse, sold you to strangers!

I made no comment, but was thinking that Tete had not been much more than a child herself when her parents married her off to a man more than twice her age and into a family of six unmarried sisters-in-law and a stern mother-in-law...

III. Tales of a Family and a City, 1914-1960

Tete often told me how hard the fourteen years were when she was Yisra, the young daughter-in-law living in the Imady compound. No one could be easier to get along with than my mother-in-law, but even she got entangled in the family quarrels. Jowdat's sisters resented Yisra, his beautiful wife who was blessed with everything they lacked: marriage, children and the love of their elder brother. They envied Yisra and made life as difficult as possible for her.

In a pattern that was to be repeated over and over, the five older Imady sisters, lavished their frustrated maternal instincts first on their little brother, Hamdi and their even younger sister, Bahjay, and later on their nieces and nephews. As soon as Kawsar was out of diapers her aunts took her from her mother and made her theirs. She slept with them, ate with them and eventually seemed to prefer them to her parents. Yisra was sad, but could do nothing about it.

The sisters also excluded Yisra from the very social preparation of meals in the family compound because, as they unkindly said, her hands were "contaminated" from changing babies' diapers.

With a mixture of pride and regret, Tete would tell me of the incident that permanently spoiled her relationship with her in-laws. It happened like this: one day several *khatabeen* (women looking for a bride) arrived at the Imady home. In a family with six marriageable girls these visits were routine. The women were taken into the reception room and ushered to seats at the "head" of the room where honored guests were seated. They were served the obligatory coffee and made small talk while they eyed the many young women in the room and, to the dismay of the Imady sisters and their mother, they quickly focused their attention on Yisra. At this time, Yisra was around twenty years old and a mother, but (as Tete's daughters would interject) was far and away the most beautiful girl in the room. Before anyone could say a word, one of the *khatabeen* announced she was interested in Yisra as a bride for her son. Poor Yisra! When the insulted hostess explained their mistake the visitors left abruptly and Yisra was left to face her angry in-laws. From then on, they made sure to keep her out of sight when *khatabeen* came calling.

* * *

All the Imady family discord was overshadowed when, in 1925, the Druzes attacked the French in the south of Syria. This uprising against the French occupation, called the Great Syrian Revolt, quickly spread to towns in the Ghouta, the green belt near Damascus. Fierce battles broke out between the French army and the Syrian irregulars and the peasants rallied to the cause. The rebels came to the Imady farms in the Ghouta and asked Jowdat Effendi to join the resistance, but, once again, his large family disqualified him. The rebels then suggested he support their cause by providing them with wheat to feed their men and Jowdat willingly agreed. According to Lamat, they asked her father to leave large sacks of wheat in front of the *beladiya* at certain times and they would pick them up. To me, this seems a very strange place to leave anything meant for the rebels because the *beladiya* was the municipal headquarters of the city. However, perhaps the *beladiya* was not guarded at night.

As attacks by the rebels increased, the French counterattacked with increasing determination. Damascus was no longer a safe place to live. Fearing for the safety of his wife and young daughters, Jowdat Effendi sent them by train to Beirut to stay with Ezzat Beyk al-Idilbi, Yisra's maternal uncle, until things calmed down. Jowdat's sisters hated to part with Kawsar, but knew she would be safer in Beirut. Kawsar was three years old, Lamat was two and there was now a third little girl, Bara'at, just a few months old.

It was Yisra's first trip outside Damascus and years later, when she recalled it, her eyes would sparkle. For her, it was a great adventure. When the train pulled into the Beirut station, Yisra found her uncle's grand horse carriage waiting to take her and the girls to his home, a big villa overlooking the Mediterranean. As they drove up the carriageway, Yisra got her very first glimpse of the sea.

Uncle Ezzat Beyk was a prosperous merchant who imported wool fabric for men's suits from his brother, who lived in Manchester, England. Beirut was a beautiful, lively city and its inhabitants, including Uncle Ezzat Beyk and his family, lived a different, an easier more open life, than the conservative Damascenes. In fact, the relatives in Damascus always said that Uncle Ezzat "lived like a king". There were many servants to do all the house work and help with the children and Yisra had a wonderful time as her uncle went out of his way to make his favorite niece happy.

After some weeks in Beirut, Yisra's sister, Bahira, sent word for her to bring the girls to Palestine for a visit. Bahira had married a cousin, Mahmoud al-Idilbi, (called "Abu Mustapha" after the birth of his son) and was living in Haifa. Yisra missed her sister and was happy to accept the invitation. Her uncle was sorry to see her go, but kissed her goodbye and put her and the girls on the train to Haifa.

It was a good time to be in Haifa – in fact, to be anywhere other than Damascus where the situation was getting more dangerous by the day. On October 18, 1925, a large number of rebels attacked the Azem Palace, the home of the French High Commissioner. The Commissioner managed to escape and sent in French reinforcements to smash the rebels. However, the narrow streets of the Old City favored the rebels and the French soldiers had to retreat.

The same night, the French retaliated with an aerial bombardment of the Old City that lasted two days and two nights. It is estimated that at least 1,414 people died as a result and 150 homes were destroyed.

Even after this, Damascus was not pacified. In April of 1926, trouble broke out in the district of Midan and a French soldier was killed. Troops were sent to root out the rebels and suspected rebel homes were destroyed, just as today, eighty years later, the same thing is happening in occupied Palestine.

On May 7th, Midan was bombed and a fire started. The High Commissioner shut off water to the district and refused to allow fire engines in to fight the blaze. As a result, the fire burned out of control and ended up destroying more than 1,000 homes and killing 600 people.

With this demoralizing defeat, the Syrian Revolt ended. The rebels realized they could never defeat the French by force of arms. In 1926, the Syrian nationalist leaders announced that independence would only be achieved by diplomacy.

* * *

Yisra came back to a quiet, but devastated city. The country was in a bad state and so was the Imady family. The seeds for a serious rift in the family had already been sown and things came to a head one night when Hamdi came home drunk after carousing in some "questionable places" with some "women of ill-repute". Hamdi had done this before, but this particular time his brother's patience snapped. Jowdat was disgusted with Hamdi's behaviour and could no longer tolerate the way his sisters and mother condoned anything he did. It was time, he decided, to move out.

But first, he had to sell the last of his beloved horses. He had begun selling them off a few years earlier and it must have been a wrenching thing for him to do. He had outlived the golden age of the horse and never would learn to drive a car, the newfangled contraption that replaced the horse.

Finding a home to buy would take time and Jowdat was in a hurry to move. To his relief, Adeeb Agha came to the rescue and offered his son-in-law and daughter one of his houses in Bahsa, near Marjay Square, until they bought a home. Jowdat thanked him and started packing.

As Jowdat and Yisra were leaving the Afeef compound with Lamat, Bara'at and all their worldly goods, a frantic little voice was heard shouting, "Baba, Mama, wait for me! Wait for me!"

Down the stairs pell-mell, her hair flying behind her, came running a little barefooted girl with her shoes in her hand. Four-year-old Kawsar threw herself at her mother as her shocked and disbelieving aunts stood at the door and watched her go. Undiscouraged, these women would try again, with better luck, to separate Hamdi's future children from their mother.

If Yisra expected life to improve after leaving Afeef, she was disappointed since the years the family spent in Bahsa were not happy ones for her as new problems replaced the old. Now that there was a border between Palestine and Syria, Jowdat's Uncle Abu Ismaeel had moved from Qadas to Damascus. The camping trips in Palestine the two men had enjoyed so much were over and Uncle Abu Ismaeel now spent most of his time visiting Jowdat in Bahsa. He would usually arrive with a group of men and Jowdat would invite them all for dinner. Yisra was kept busy planning and cooking meals for Uncle Abu Ismaeel and the other guests. Yisra's father did provide her with a servant, but even so, keeping up with her husband's visitors and his endless dinner invitations was not easy.

And that was not all. The family lived in Bahsa from 1926 until 1930 and, during this time, three more girls were born. First came Riad in 1927, then Fatima in 1928. While Yisra tried to cope with the constant stream of dinner guests, little Fatima, who was not a strong baby, spent a lot of time in her cradle in the kitchen. The stone floors were cold and damp and low lying Bahsa was not the healthy place to live that Afeef had been. There, the children had played in the fields in fresh air, but the house in Bahsa had no garden, only a paved courtyard. Baby Fatima became ill and didn't live long. For the third time, Jowdat and Yisra had to bury a child. Because the lives of children in those days were so precarious, there was almost a taboo against counting one's children. There is an Arab proverb that says: "Go count your father's camels, not your children."

Lamat remembers how she and her sisters cried inconsolably when their baby sister died until their mother, who was pregnant at the time, said, "That's enough my children. Stop crying. Did I die? *In sha' Allah* (God willing) we will have another baby soon."

Sure enough, a few weeks later, Yisra gave birth to her sixth daughter. She was a pretty baby with very fair skin, blue eyes and auburn hair and they named her, "Inayat" which means "protected (by God)" in hopes she would have a long life.

Yisra was pregnant every year they lived in Bahsa as she tried to give Jowdat a son and I am sure her health and strength were strained to the utmost by her many pregnancies and the responsibility of caring for her small children. At the end of 1929, Yisra had five little stair-step girls - from seven-year-old Kawsar to five-month-old Inayat - and she was pregnant yet again. Finally, on a hot day in August in 1930, Mohammed, the long-awaited son was born. How happy everyone was! He was blond and green-eyed, like his brother Sadaddeen had been, and his mother and sisters insist he was not only a wanted baby, but also a happy, easy baby.

Meanwhile, Jowdat Effendi was collecting money to buy a house in Mohajareen near his in-laws. To do this, he had to sell all his remaining land except for a piece in Kabun and Yisra had to sell most of her land, as well. She had inherited some shares in several shops on Marjay Square from her father as well as land from her oldest sister, Aisha.

This was the unlucky Aisha who was briefly married to a rich, old man who soon left her a wealthy widow with a small son. However, first her son died and a few years later, Aisha herself died, leaving her siblings, Ghaleb, Yisra, Bahira, and Yezda, large tracts of property in four different villages.

Now, Ghaleb was a rogue and a ladies' man, but a charmer. He was fond of his sister, Yisra, but was not above taking advantage of her if he needed money and he was always short of money what with his wives, ex-wives and ten children. He would drop in on Yisra and cajole her into letting him sell some of her land. Invariably she agreed and put her thumbprint on the bill of sale. Of course she could not read the selling price of the land so, after the sale went through, she happily took whatever amount her brother gave her. Ghaleb could not pull the wool over the eyes of his other two sisters, because they could read. Needless to say, all this transpired behind Jowdat Effendi's back. Most of the money Ghaleb gave Yisra after these transactions went to help buy the house in Mohajareen.

Eventually, after briefly renting a house near his in-laws, Jowdat found a house in Mohajareen to his liking and bought it when Mohammed was one year old. In the margin of one of his books Jowdat wrote: "Today, Sunday, the 9th of August, 1931, marks the day we moved into our Mohajareen house, the house God gave us."

The building is on Jareer Street which runs horizontally along the slope of Jebel Qassioun and crosses Shutta, one of the streets that run up the mountain. When Jowdat bought the building, Yisra's parents lived in the next block and Jowdat's family was also not far away. This building, rebuilt, would also be the home Mohammed brought me to in 1960.

In 1935, in this building, Yisra gave birth to Abdulgane, the tenth and last Imady child. Now they were a family of nine with seven children. I have often mused on my in-laws' unusual family – actually you could say their *three* different families. For seven years they were a family of three with Sadaddeen, as their only child. After his death and Khaled's birth, for a few months they were again a family of three with an only child. After little Fatima died, they ended up with seven surviving children. Their first two sons never knew each other or their younger brothers and sisters and the surviving seven never knew their two older brothers. How sad. How strange.

Abdo was as dark as his brother was fair and, as a child, people would tease him by saying he had been delivered to the family by the charcoal seller in a bag of charcoal whereas his blond brother had been brought by the milkman in a yogurt pail. But Mohammed's schoolmates also teased him because of his blond hair and fair skin and called him "The Albino".

Sometime after the move to Mohajareen, Yisra used Imady family connections to get Jowdat Effendi a job as a government official. He was appointed to collect taxes from peasants bringing their agricultural produce into the city for sale. He went off unwillingly the first morning and was back in a dudgeon after only a few hours. When asked what had happened, he said someone had dared to order him around! He quit on the spot and that was the end of his working career. Mohammed defends him saying the job was really unsuitable for a man of his father's standing. But since Jowdat Effendi considered working for a living beneath his dignity, he had to pay his bills by selling plot after plot of land.

* * *

Around 1938, Yisra's sister, Bahira, and her husband Abu Mustapha fled their home in Haifa, Palestine, leaving behind all their worldly goods, and came to live near the Imadys in Mohajareen. As a young man, Abu Mustapha had been an officer in the Ottoman Army and then, after he married Bahira and moved to Haifa, he went into the textile business with his relatives in Beirut and Manchester and prospered. However, as Jewish immigrants poured into Palestine unchecked by the British Mandate authorities, Abu Mustapha became increasingly concerned about the future of Palestine – as did all Arabs. In vain, they demanded the democratic institutions the British had promised them and the right to set limits on Jewish immigration. Finally, the Arabs called a general strike and, when it achieved nothing, the Arab Revolt of 1936-39 broke out in Palestine.

Abu Mustapha was very involved in the resistance and, when a price was put on his head by the British, he escaped with his family to Damascus. He was sentenced to death in absentia by the British, which made him a hero in Damascus, but a penniless hero. He had left everything he owned in Palestine and he was never to regain the comfortable life he had led in Haifa. Bahira spent years nagging him to find a job that would make their fortune again, but it was never to happen. He managed a small shop owned by his son-in-law for a time, but it was not successful and after this, he never worked again. He and Jowdat Effendi became fast friends and spent hours together every day playing *tawlay* (backgammon).

The Idilbi and Imady cousins also visited back and forth. Bahira and Abu Mustapha's daughters, Essmat, Najah and Hedayat were around the same ages as Lamat and Riad and the five cousins became close. Lamat remembers how, when her Aunt Bahira was busy, she would send her youngest child to the Imadys and she would say innocently to her Aunt Yisra: "My mother says to tie the goat to the post," which was

Damascene women-speak for, "Please keep my child with you for a while so I can have a break."

* * *

Yisra's second trip outside Damascus took place around 1938 and again it was to Lebanon, this time for the wedding of her cousin Ali, the son of Uncle Ezzat Beyk Idilbi. The wedding party from Damascus, in addition to Yisra, included Jowdat Effendi, fifteen-year old Lamat, Bahira and her husband, Abu Mustapha. Lamat remembers that Kawsar sewed her a very special wine-colored silk dress with a lace collar for the occasion. Kawsar, herself, was left behind to take care of her younger brothers and sisters.

Uncle Ezzat Beyk was a gracious host and the relatives from Damascus were welcomed as honored guests. Jowdat Effendi was very impressed with the beautiful home of Ezzat Beyk and, long after this visit, would describe to his sons the imposing villa that looked out over the Mediterranean and the huge dog that guarded it.

All went well until the day of the wedding which was held in Souk El Gharb, a Lebanese summer resort in the mountains. There, as the wedding guests began arriving, Jowdat Effendi was stunned to see couples walking in arm in arm. This was unheard of in Damascus where separate wedding parties were held for men and for women. When the band struck up and the guests began to dance, Jowdat Effendi could hardly contain himself. He was ready to jump out of his seat and denounce the whole occasion and everyone present. He got up and began to circulate among the guests and Yisra and Lamat, who well knew what was on his mind, walked anxiously beside him. He stalked among the dancers with his hands behind his back and the tassel of his tarboosh swung back and forth as he looked disapprovingly right and left.

"Tell me, Yisra," he said, "shall I ruin the whole party?"

Lamat felt faint when she heard this and she wished fiercely her father had stayed in Damascus, but her mother gently took his arm and pulled him closer as she whispered, "*Ya* Abu Mohammed (Oh, Father of Mohammed), please. We are the guests of my relatives and it will be scandalous if you do this. Please, Abu Mohammed, for my sake, restrain yourself."

This is all Lamat heard because she stood transfixed with apprehension while her parents walked ahead, her mother talking quietly and earnestly for several minutes until, to Lamat's great relief, her father nodded his head in assent. Once again, her mother's gentle, loving touch had managed to calm him down. The festivities ended uneventfully and the Idilbi family never knew how narrowly their wedding escaped disaster.

It is Mohammed's thought that once his father was persuaded to come round, he might have enjoyed himself. An extravagant wedding such as this with its lavish food and beautifully dressed guests, was not a spectacle he would be likely to ever see again and he was not immune to its appeal.

Whereas, Lamat's comment about this incident was, "Immi was the only one who could swallow the volcanoes of anger that Abi periodically spewed out and convince him to behave."

* * *

You may wonder what Jowdat Effendi found to keep himself busy after he no longer had his stable of horses. Unfortunately for his family, he had too much time on his hands and began to take far too great an interest in the minutia of household affairs; in what his children were up to and what his wife and daughters might be cooking. He would go into the kitchen and criticize what had been planned for the day's meal and even the way some dishes were prepared, as in Lamat's story of the day her mother made *kibbeh b'labaneeya* (*kibbeh* in yogurt).

The preparation of this dish has been aptly described as "an exercise in patience and stamina". The first step is pounding raw lamb and *burghol* (wheat grains) together in a mortar until it forms a smooth paste, an exhausting time-consuming process. Then the paste is formed into round hollow shells which are stuffed with a fried mixture of ground meat, onions and pinenuts. The stuffed *kibbeh*, which are about the size of golf balls, are cooked in yogurt, after stabilizing it with a raw egg and cornstarch so it doesn't curdle.

On this particular occasion, Jowdat Effendi looked into the bubbling pot in the kitchen and saw the *kibbeh* balls were different sizes and said, "You call this *kibbeh b'labaneeya*? Not one is like the other!"

Yisra, who had been in the kitchen all morning, was quiet, but Lamat spoke up bravely in defense of her mother. "Do you think Immi is a machine to turn out forty identical balls of *kibbeh*? If I were her," said Lamat daringly, "I would throw the whole pot off the roof!"

Her father frowned at Lamat and said, "Are you giving your mother lessons?"

Another story Lamat told involved a huge *tanjera* of rice with lamb and fava beans – *riz-ef-fool*. On this particular day, Jowdat Effendi made his usual trip to the kitchen to see what was being cooked and found Kawsar, hot and sweaty, just putting the finishing touches on the *riz-ef-fool*. He stalked over to the pot, lifted the lid and tasted it.

"Can't be eaten!" he said spitting it out. "Too salty!"

That isn't all he said and his voice boomed to every room in the house. Perhaps it was Kawsar who had learned Lamat's "lessons" because, giving her father a look of despair, she turned the pot upside down on her own head! She probably would have loved to empty it on her father's head, but didn't dare.

"Come see, come see," shouted Jowdat Effendi. "Come see what this crazy girl has done!"

Before Lamat finished telling these two stories, she was in tears over these upsetting events that had happened more than sixty years ago. Then Riad took up the story.

"Mother, my sisters and I," said Riad, "liked to listen to music on the radio and keep up with the new popular songs, but this kind of music sung by 'women of doubtful morals' was frowned upon by Father so the radio was only tuned to the news when he was home. It was not really music he objected to because he sometimes liked to have me or one of the neighbor's daughters sing for him.

"One of Father's rules," continued Riad, "was that we children had to be in the house by sunset and, to this day, although I am now almost eighty, I feel apprehensive if the sun goes down and I am still out."

Riad never told me the worst thing that happened to her as a child, but I heard the story many times from other family members. To excuse and explain what their father had done, they would preface the story by saying that their father was always anxious about the safety of his beloved son, Mohammed, because he was born after the death of two sons and the birth of six girls.

Then, they would go on: "One day when Mohammed was perhaps two years old, Riad dropped him and his leg was broken. Our father was beside himself. He said he didn't want to see Riad's face for a long time and banished her to her maternal grandparents for several years."

At the time, Riad was only five years old.

* * *

Abdo was the youngest child in the family and his father was old enough to be his grandfather. Besides the big difference in age between them, there was also a great difference in personality. It is my guess that Abdo reminded Jowdat Effendi of his brother, Hamdi. Like Hamdi, Abdo was easygoing and fun-loving and like Hamdi, Abdo was never able to please Jowdat Effendi.

Abdo only once managed to put something over on his father and he smiled with satisfaction as he told me the story:

"Father used to raise pigeons and chickens on the roof of our building," said Abdo. "From time to time, Mother would cook us *riz kurdi* (chicken on cinnamon rice with toasted almonds) and we always had fresh eggs.

"When I was young, everyone believed that eating raw eggs would make you strong so one day I decided to become the strongest one among my friends. I watched Abi's chickens for several mornings until I knew the sound they made when they laid an egg. The next morning I got up very early and waited on the stairs until I heard the special clucks and then I ran to take the eggs.

"Every morning I would hurry to the roof at the first cluck of the chickens and grab two or three eggs, whatever they had laid that day. I cracked them, swallowed them raw, threw the shells over the roof and then sneaked down the stairs. Abi would come up shortly after and get angry to find that day after day there were no eggs.

"Abi said, 'I can't understand what is wrong with these chickens. They cluck and cluck and don't lay an egg.'

"Then it occurred to him that unearthly beings might be stealing the eggs and, just to be on the safe side, he invoked God to protect him and his chickens from the *jinn*.

"This went on for about a week until early one morning Abi happened to be sitting on the balcony when an eggshell fell on his head. He guessed immediately where the missing eggs had gone and rushed up to the roof where he caught me with an egg in my hand. I got such a tongue lashing from him that day that I never again dared to take another egg."

Mohammed remembers opposing his father just once and it happened like this: "When I was about nine years old," said Mohammed, "Abi came home with a young lamb to add to his menagerie. I adopted it as my own and named it 'Jobie'. Every day I fed the lamb by hand and it would come when I called it. Perhaps I should have realized what the fate of my pet would be, but I was young and did not. The day came when Abi decided the lamb – now a sheep – was ready to be slaughtered. I could not believe my father would really bring the butcher to kill my Jobie. I cried, I begged and finally with the tears streaming down my face, I pounded my father's chest with my small fists crying, 'Baba, Baba, Baba - please - no, no, no.'

"But Abi gently removed my hands and said, 'Sheep were created to be slaughtered,' and the deed was done.

"I was broken-hearted and had no dinner that day and for a long time afterward I ate no meat. This was the last time my father brought home a lamb to fatten it up."

The Imady children obeyed their mother out of love; her wish was their command. However, Jowdat Effendi had the last word on everything. Yisra was the loving spirit that tried to soften and, whenever possible, circumvent Jowdat's strict rules.

Mohammed said, "When we were little, my mother made rag dolls for us to cuddle and play with. If Abi found them he tore them up in the belief they violated Islam's ban against idols. Immi would turn around, comfort the child and, when no one was looking, sew up another doll.

"I am sure that Abi loved us all in his own way. I remember the nights when Riad and I used to stay up late going over our school lessons. Abi would come around and take the school books from our hands and turn out the light saying, 'Enough, enough, my children, time to sleep.' Then he would look in on the rest of his sleeping children to be sure they were covered."

To be fair, some of Jowdat's behavior as a father was typical for fathers of his generation. For example, Jowdat Effendi never sat any of his children on his lap and rarely kissed or embraced them. Fathers were expected to handle the discipline of children and mothers to ladle out the affection. Also, some of the awe and respect Jowdat Effendi inspired in his wife and children was characteristic for that society and that time. Even a grown man in those days would not dream of smoking in front of his father or lolling in his chair in his father's presence. What made the usual, domineering, patriarchal role worse in Jowdat Effendi's case, were his fits of temper.

Finally, everyone made it clear that in all Jowdat Effendi's angry explosions, he never struck a child or his wife. His ferocious anger and his loud voice were intimidation enough.

Fortunately, Jowdat Effendi eventually found a project that kept him busy - and out of the kitchen - up until the last years of his life. He decided to tear down his one-family traditional home and have it rebuilt into a modern four-story apartment building, one apartment of which could be rented for income. This was done gradually, beginning in the nineteen forties. Jowdat Effendi did some of the work himself; most of it he closely supervised.

* * *

There are at least two positive legacies Jowdat Effendi passed down to his children. One was a strong Islamic faith and the second was a love of learning. Jowdat had a library of well-read books which was unusual for his day and age and, by example, he instilled in his children a desire for education.

Kawsar, who was as intelligent as any of her siblings and who probably wanted to go to school as much as they did, was not to have their opportunities. She had just finished her first year of school when Mohammed was born and was then kept at home to help care for her little brother. With her selfless, accepting personality, she never gave any sign that she resented this. When she was around ten years old, she was sent to a nearby seamstress to learn to sew and became an accomplished dressmaker. However, each of her four younger sisters, partly as a surprising and unexpected result of the family's lost inheritance, got an exceptionally good education for girls of their generation.

In Syria in the forties and early fifties, practically no rural girls were sent to school, very few Damascene girls finished high school and just a handful of these went on to attend Damascus University. Most families were too conservative to permit their daughters to get more than an elementary education and practically all families were opposed to having their girls attend the university with its coeducational classes. Jowdat Effendi was conservative himself, but with the reduced circumstances of the family, he could see the advantage of educated, salaried daughters.

Lamat attended a prestigious private girls' school on a scholarship arranged by her father's Mardam Beyk cousins and was the first Imady to attend Damascus University. Her three younger sisters, on the other hand, attended government elementary and secondary schools. Bara'at dropped out before graduation when she was offered a post teaching in an elementary school. She was the first of Jowdat's children to get a job and more than fifty years later her grateful siblings still remember how her salary "helped put the bread on the table."

Riad and Inayat soon followed Bara'at's example and all three became teachers while they were still in their teens. Lamat, however, did not start teaching until she married, and then only at her husband's insistence. He made Lamat drop out of the university in her third year and got her a teaching post in a girls' school. Eventually, the three younger sisters went on to careers with the government while Lamat continued to teach in a girls' secondary school until she was promoted to a position in the administration.

Riad was the most determined of her sisters to get an education. After secondary school, she enrolled in the Institute for Teachers and upon graduating, was hired by a girls' boarding school in Hasake, the remote northeastern part of the country. Riad told me that when she returned to Damascus after three years in Hasake, her father praised her warmly and kissed her for the very first time. In fact, as one daughter after another pursued her education, Jowdat Effendi became proud of his girls and was pleased with their success.

Riad taught by day and studied by night for the baccalaureate exam which would enable her to enroll in Damascus University. She eventually passed the exam and entered the university while continuing to hold down a full-time teaching job. When she finally got her university degree at the age of thirty-two, she was burned out from years of teaching and got a job with the Ministry of Public Works. The high point of her career came when she was appointed director of the personnel department in this ministry.

Lamat, who cannot forgive her father's laziness, insists on adding that while the four young Imady girls were working as teachers, their father was spending hours every day playing *tawlay* with Abu Mustapha. Mohammed never criticizes his father like Lamat does, but it is telling that he chose to follow a path as different from his father's as possible.

13.

Turbulent Times

Christmas 1964 was the second year we put up a gaily trimmed Christmas tree. At first the family was unsure how to take this – was I reverting to Christianity? Trying to change my children's religion? When they saw that none of this was true, they accepted the tree for what I intended it to be: a delightful American custom which made me less homesick. Our American family never forgot to send Susu and Muna Christmas presents so now we even had Santa Claus and the children would hang up their stockings. They always knew Santa and his visits were "just pretend", but they enjoyed this game of make believe.

Scarcely had 1965 begun, than it was Ramadan again. In the peculiar way of the lunar calendar, Ramadan was moving steadily back through the solar calendar at a rate of around eleven days every year. My first Ramadan in Syria had begun the day I arrived – March 1st. Since then, the first of Ramadan had moved back to the 18th of February in 1961, then the 7th of February in 1962 and now Ramadan began in January. Mohammed told me it took thirty-three years for any day in the lunar calendar to make a complete circuit back through the solar calendar.

This was our first Ramadan with Suad and during this month, she came an extra day every week. As a treat, she sometimes surprised us by preparing stuffed carrots, a delicious speciality of her husband's city. She would bring an armful of fat, red carrots from Homs which were hard as rocks and were sold already cored out by an electric appliance. Suad would stuff them with rice and meat and cook them until tender in an appetizing tomato broth flavoured with garlic and cumin. No matter how hard I tried, my stuffed carrots never tasted as good as hers.

* * *

The previous September Fuad had been sent to the States by the Ministry of Planning to attend a conference in New York. Naturally he went to see Holly and Sara and somehow he convinced Holly to give Syria another chance. They arrived in November and we went to welcome them back. Although Holly's appearance had changed a bit - she had gained weight and "frosted" her hair - like Jill, she hadn't really changed her opinion about life in Damascus. I wondered if she would be any happier here this time than she had been before. Why did she come back? I think the main reason is she really loved Fuad; it was life in Syria she hated. Perhaps she even nursed the hope Fuad would come to agree with her that Syria was no place for their daughter and would decide on his own to return with them to Oklahoma. Of course nothing of the kind happened.

Another reason Holly agreed to come back was this: Fuad gave Holly his solemn promise that if she was not happy after three months, she and Sara could go back to Oklahoma. Holly even had this promise put in writing and signed and notarized, not realizing it would have no legal weight in Syria. They no sooner got to Damascus, than Fuad broke his promise and tore up her American passport. It was a fatal mistake. As Holly later told me, this was the moment she made up her mind to leave Fuad and Syria.

She said she had not minded living in Syria as long as she had no children, but once Sara was born, everything changed. Holly did not want to raise her daughter anywhere but in the States. With each passing month, she became more desperate and finally she began planning her escape. The only two friends she let in on her plans were Rose and I.

Her first step was to go to the American Embassy one day when Fuad was at work. She told the consular officials her husband had destroyed her passport and the consul agreed to issue her a new passport good only for her and Sara to travel back to the States. That was fine with Holly.

Next, she had to find a way out of the country. To this day, I am not sure how she and Sara got across the border to Lebanon. She must have crossed in a diplomatic car because, as the wife of a Syrian, she needed written permission from her husband for her daughter to leave the country. However, passengers in diplomatic cars are not questioned.

Finally, everything was ready. She decided to leave the house one day about fifteen minutes after Fuad went to work. By the time he got home, she would be beyond his reach, in Beirut Airport or maybe even flying on the first leg of her long trip home.

The night before Holly's planned departure, we went to the movies with Holly, Fuad, Rose and her husband. We three women sat in that movie theatre unable to think of anything but what was going to happen the next morning. I have no recollection of the film we saw that night, but I do remember sitting there staring unseeing at the movie screen while questions raced through my head. Would Holly really get out or would Fuad stop her at the last moment? Were Rose and I doing the right thing by keeping Holly's plans a secret? Should we try to talk Holly out of it? In the end we were silent and said nothing.

I never saw Holly again. The next day arrived and she and her daughter slipped out of Syria. I remember it was in February, not long after Muna's third birthday party. Holly promised to call my mother from JFK Airport and assure her we were all fine and she did. Before the year was up, Holly was back at her old job teaching high school home economics and Fuad was married to a young Syrian woman.

After Holly went, there was the usual letdown I experienced every time a good friend left Syria forever. I always felt - temporarily - abandoned and left behind as everyone flees the sinking ship. Then I realize how silly this is and snap out of it. I tell myself Syria is no sinking ship and I belong in Damascus with my husband and children. Not long after Holly left, I belatedly noticed another March 1st had come and gone leaving three more years of service Mohammed owed the government. It hardly seemed possible I had been five years in Damascus.

* * *

As if Holly's escape from Syria had not been upsetting enough that spring, our lives were touched by several other disturbing and troubling events. Sometime in the previous fall, Rose and her husband, Riyad, told us about a friend of theirs, Walid, who had come down with Bell's palsy. As it turned out, I knew the man's American wife. Riyad told us how depressed his friend was and suggested that Mohammed visit Walid and assure him that he would recover.

"Fine," said Mohammed, so one evening Rose and Riyad took us to visit Walid and his wife. Helen was an attractive girl from Brooklyn whose Arabic was the envy of all foreign wives. Both her parents were Syrian-Americans, but Helen insisted she had never spoken Arabic before coming to Damascus. However, once here, she learned it effortlessly. Helen brought out their two cute children before putting them to bed and afterwards we had a pleasant visit. Walid's case of Bell's palsy was not as severe as Mohammed's had been and Mohammed did his best to cheer him up. After a few weeks, Riyad told us that Walid was getting better.

Several months later, terrible rumors began to circulate about Walid. People whispered that he had sold information to America about Syria's Russian missile technology. Then we heard he had been arrested and charged with treason.

Before long, things got even worse. Walid was put on trial and the court sessions were televised nightly. Rose and Riyad often came over to our house to watch with us and we sat, horrified, as the trial proceeded and Walid got thinner and less recognizable. When the prosecutor asked Walid where he had been on a certain date, we would hold our breath. Would he be asked about the night we visited him? Would we hear him say that the four of us were at his home that night? Rose and Riyad worried more than we did because these people had been their friends and they had often socialized together whereas we had only met Walid that one time.

The trial seemed to go on forever and we watched mesmerized with our feelings in turmoil. We were concerned for Helen and their children, who, people said, were in Latakia with her in-laws, and were filled with shock, disbelief and pity for Walid. It was clear he was being mistreated and we could not decide if we thought he was really guilty or not. It seemed incredible to us that a happily married man with two children would take the extraordinarily dangerous risk of selling military secrets. Whatever the truth of the matter, he was finally found guilty and condemned to death by public hanging in Marjay Square.

That appointed morning, Penny and I watched as most of our fellow FAO employees set off for Marjay Square to see Walid hanging by the neck. Penny and I did not share their morbid curiosity and we stayed behind. My heart ached for Helen and her children.

Months later, we heard the American Embassy had helped Helen and her children leave the country and return to her family in Brooklyn. Of course American newspapers covered this story and Mother read about it and was distressed.

Another troubling event which occurred that spring, involved a pleasant young man in the FAO office with the double name of "Ibrahim Ibrahim". In addition to his job, he was studying English Literature in Damascus University and I often loaned him books from my student days at NYU. When his wife had a baby, I chipped in with the other office colleagues for a baby present. I considered him a friend.

One day, Mohammed got a phone call from an old classmate of his who asked him to drop by his office. The man was working for the *mukhabarat* (secret police) and he said he had something Mohammed should see. Mohammed went immediately and the man came right to the point. He told Mohammed there was a dossier on his wife, but that he, as an old friend, was going to destroy it. He also said Mohammed should advise his wife to be careful with whom she discussed politics.

He showed the file to Mohammed and all it contained were several anti-Syrian statements I had supposedly made. One in particular Mohammed quoted to me later, word for word and I remembered saying something of the kind to Ibrahim Ibrahim, but with the exact opposite meaning. I had been defending Syria, not attacking it. This was no misunderstanding. Ibrahim's English was excellent; he had deliberately twisted my words. I felt so betrayed that it was hard to go to the office the next day. You can be sure I never spoke freely about anything political with that young man again – or indeed with anyone but my closest friends.

Amazing news came in January from Jill. She wrote she was coming to Syria by sea in the spring and was bringing not only her children and a lot of household goods, but also a dog. This would be her third try at life in Syria. Adel took us to see the apartment he'd rented for her and the boys. It was huge and lovely with seven big rooms, central heating, a good-sized courtyard with a fountain and a modern kitchen. If this didn't please her, I thought, nothing would.

In April, Adel went to Beirut to meet Jill's ship and she finally arrived here, children, dog and all. I found her older, a bit thinner, and somewhat more easygoing. It was good to have her back and, before long, I talked her into coming to work with Penny and me at the FAO Office.

We saw a lot of Jill and Adel in the next few months. The weather was lovely that spring and we went on a lot of outings to the Ghouta in their big car. One fine day, they drove us to Houran in the south of Syria where there is a very well preserved Roman amphitheater in Bosra.

It was the first time I had been in this part of the country and I was surprised at the black volcanic rocks which dominate the landscape. Low stone walls of basalt rock divided the farms and the bright green of the fields was in sharp contrast to the black stone. The farm houses were also built of the black rock and the scenery was very different from the areas around Damascus. The amphitheater was incredible and of course we had to test the acoustics. We were told a whisper from center stage could be heard in the farthest reaches of the amphitheater and this turned out to be true.

Some time after Jill's arrival, Dr. Haagensen and his wife came to Beirut, and although her schedule was very tight, Mrs. Haagensen took the trouble of getting her friend's chauffeur to drive her to Damascus for a flying visit to us. The round trip took twice as long as her three hours in Damascus, but she wanted to be able to assure Mother that she'd seen us and found us well and happy.

When it came time for her to leave, Mrs. Haagensen insisted that I go back to Beirut with her to see Dr. Haagensen and meet some of their friends there, particularly Dr. MacDonald, Dean of the Medical School of the AUB. Dr. Haagensen put me up in their hotel, the Phoenicia, which Mrs. Haagensen dismissively described as an "aggressively luxurious American hotel", but which I thoroughly enjoyed.

That night they took me to a party given by Dr. Haagensen's favourite Lebanese protégé and his charming wife and I finally met the gracious Dr. MacDonald and his wife. Like them, most of the other guests were medical doctors and their wives and all seemed to speak English or French – or both – fluently. The Lebanese women were slim, petite, and elegantly dressed and coifed; their flawless complexions carefully made up. I began to think my rose linen suit, sewn by Kawsar, was perhaps not the thing, not the latest fashion. Also, Mrs. Haagensen and I seemed conspicuous and ungainly – too tall, too pale, our hands and feet too large - next to these sleek, small women.

One of the Lebanese guests said to me, "I know an American in Damascus, Patricia H. – she's married to a Syrian doctor – lovely girl, do you know her?"

I said, yes, I'd met her.

The woman then said, "Patricia has adjusted very well and her in-laws are very fond of her. She's very happy in Damascus, but of course the fact that she's married into a Christian family has made all the difference."

I was really taken aback. I never heard this kind of sectarian remark in Syria. After a pause I said, "Well, *my* husband's name is Mohammed Imady and *his* family made me welcome from the very first day and I'm sure I am just as happy and adjusted as Patricia is."

Now it was her turn to be rattled. She fumbled in her small handbag for a cigarette, lit it with a gold lighter and smilingly asked me how I knew the Haagensens. Some others then came up to us and joined our conversation and the awkward moment passed.

Meanwhile, the apartment was filling with the appetizing smells of dinner, but it grew later and later with no sign of food being served. Mrs. Haagensen whispered to me that the hostess was waiting for the guest of honor, Charles Malik, the prominent Lebanese politician and former head of the UN Assembly, to arrive. When he finally came, well after midnight, the food had been re-heated too many times and most of the guests had lost their appetites and were ready to go home.

Back in my hotel room, I had trouble falling asleep as I thought about the people I had met that night. I truly liked the hostess, but found I had little in common with most of the other women with their talk of European vacations, spas, jewellery and Paris fashions. I also found it odd that they seemed more at home speaking French than Arabic.

The next morning, I went with Mrs. Haagensen and Mrs. Malik to a very exclusive flower show where I was introduced to all the elite women of Beirut – whose names I promptly forgot. Around noon time the MacDonalds and I saw the Haagensens off at the airport.

When they returned to Palisades from their trip, the Haagensens asked Mother for dinner. Dr. Haagensen met Mother at the door, kissed her and said (according to Mother), "You don't have to worry about that daughter of yours – she is a great success."

As they had their dinner on the terrace overlooking the Hudson, Mrs. Haagensen gave Mother a glowing account of all our news. Best of all, she encouraged Mother to seriously think about visiting us again the next year.

We had a terrible heat wave in June. It was up around 100 degrees Fahrenheit day after day. Even the evenings were hot. Thank heavens there was little or nothing to do at the office because it was just too hot to work. I was so glad that Suad was doing most of the cooking although no one was very hungry in this heat. Fortunately, the apartment below us was no longer rented so Tete and the others moved downstairs for the summer. It was much cooler than their apartment upstairs, maybe as much as fifteen degrees cooler – and cooler than ours, as well. When we got too hot, we also went downstairs.

The weather improved as the time for Susu's eighth birthday approached. I got permission to hold her birthday party at the DCS School playground because this year we had invited twenty-seven children and fourteen adults, far too many for our apartment or even for the roof. Susu came to the party wearing a dress made from Tete's wedding dress and looked like a little princess. Tete once impulsively promised to cut down her wedding dress to fit Susu and Susu nagged her about it for a year. Finally, Tete found the strength to do it. She managed to cut out two dresses from the one; one for Susu and one for her cousin, May. She worked on this project whenever she felt well enough and after the dresses were finished, she spent three weeks lovingly sewing on all the missing decorative pearls. As she sewed, she must have thought about her wedding day so many years ago when she had been only a girl of fourteen.

Not long after Susu's party, I got some expected bad news. Penny and Farouk had been talking about leaving Syria for some time. I knew that Farouk was not happy working for the government so I was sad, but not surprised when Penny told me they would probably be leaving permanently in December. Farouk was in Switzerland on a training course and she planned to join him before Christmas and from there they would go to England. Another good friend had already gone. Janette and her children were now in Scotland with her mother and her husband soon followed. My Swiss friend, Jocelyne, was the next to go when her husband decided to move to Saudi Arabia. I hated to see them leave. All three of these women, Penny, Janette and Jocelyne, were among my closest friends, along with Jill, Anna Maria and Dolores.

We foreign wives clung together. Our common circumstances bound us together like castaways on a desert island. We became surrogate sisters for each other and helped each other cope. "Old timers" showed the newcomers the ropes; where to buy books or imported food or where to find a school or a doctor for their children. Your friends would tell you how to navigate a funeral visit or how much to pay a taxi. When they went "home" for a visit, they would mail packages for you and call your family to reassure them you were fine. We helped each other with all these situations and more. We even taught each other some useful Arabic words and expressions. Some of us were American, but since Syrians acquire wives from all over, we were an international lot. Through the years, I've had close friends from England, Scotland,

Ireland, the Dominican Republic, Columbia, Switzerland, Italy, France, Germany, Belguim, Denmark, Sweden, Poland, Finland, Russia and Czechoslovakia. Most of them spoke English, but some did not and then we spoke Arabic together. Several of the friends I made in the early sixties are still my friends today.

September came and we sent my "baby" to nursery school and Tete's "baby" to England for graduate studies. Muna was thrilled to ride the school bus with Susu and Abdo was happy with his university in Leeds. Abdo would be away for about a year and before the first week was up, Tete missed him. In fact, we all did. His enthusiasm and jokes always kept us stirred up. Life was much quieter without him.

In October, I got a long letter from Holly and she said that Fuad may have received his divorce papers on his wedding day. Of course, he didn't need a divorce to remarry here. Holly said she was not only teaching home economics in a nearby high school, but also taking courses towards a Masters degree.

When Fuad got back from his honeymoon, he installed his new bride in the same apartment where Holly had lived, across the road from Jill. I hoped this new marriage would bring him happiness. I met his wife and liked her. She was a pleasant, placid young woman, very different from Holly with her drive and ambition and probably a better choice of wife for Fuad.

Penny left Syria one day in November and I quit my FAO job the next day. Penny had been training me to take over her job, but a woman who was the laziest person in the office was appointed instead "because she knows steno". Even worse, since her English was not very good, she expected me to edit her correspondence. That was more than I was willing to do, so I resigned, naively thinking they wouldn't be able to manage without me and would beg me to come back. In fact, since the director was Swiss, he probably didn't even notice his new secretary's grammatical and spelling errors. Jill couldn't stand working under this woman, either, and quit shortly after I left. I was going to miss my salary, but even more, I would miss Penny. Working with her was the best part of my year and a half with FAO.

Although I didn't know it, I was about two weeks pregnant when I left FAO. People later thought I gave up my job because of this, but actually another baby was the last thing I expected – and still another surprise lay ahead. Mohammed came home with the good news that he was nominated for a four and a half month course at the World Bank in Washington D.C., to begin in March. At first, I hesitated to tell Mother because things were always so iffy here and I didn't want to raise false hopes. However, when Mother said she planned to make a second trip to Damascus in June, which meant we would see each other one way or the other, I decided to tell her.

Christmas, the first day of Ramadan, and New Year's Day arrived in that order – all within a week or so. Next came the Eid and this year we sent Muna down with her big sister into the swirling noise and confusion of what the children simply called "the Eid" – the children's fair in front of our building. Susu had their Eid money in one hand and clutched her sister's hand with the other while I kept an eye on them from the balcony until the older cousins showed up to shepherd them around the booths and the rides. They stuffed themselves with garishly colored candy, rode the rickety, makeshift rides, dodged the popping firecrackers and were ecstatically happy. Somehow they managed to survive it all with no ill effects.

Well, maybe that isn't completely true. After the Eid, Susu came down with scarlet fever. She didn't seem very ill and I guess, what with antibiotics, scarlet fever is no longer the dread disease it was in 1920, when it ended Sadaddeen's life, or in 1940 when it almost killed my little sister.

* * *

You never knew what would happen here next. On a February night not long after Muna's fourth birthday, a series of explosions jolted us awake. It was pitch dark outside, still well before dawn. Shivering with cold and fear, I followed Mohammed into the girls' room and we got them up.

"Heavy artillery," said Mohammed. "Let's go upstairs." We hurried upstairs to Tete's apartment dragging our half-awake girls behind us. Tete, Kawsar and Riad were all up and, it seemed to me, rather blasé about the whole thing. Of course they had been through this and worse many times before. Mohammed and I followed Riad to the balcony where she pointed out flashes of shell fire against the dark sky off to the southeast. Now we heard for the first time the chatter of machine guns as well as the boom of big guns.

"How close it is!" I thought and stared hypnotized at the traces of light. They slightly anticipated the noise of the shells exploding and were answered by staccato gun fire. Obviously, some group was trying to overthrow the government. I recalled that when Syria split from Egypt four years earlier, not a shot had been fired.

This is the first time I've heard a gun fired in anger, I thought. My hand instinctively went to my belly as I wondered what kind of world my baby was coming into.

Not knowing what was happening or whether the shooting would come closer was the worst of it for me. Even Mohammed had no inkling this coup was in the wind or who was behind it. All we could do was speculate about what was going on and what might happen next. Tete got back in bed and we put the girls into bed with her and they soon fell asleep again.

But for the rest of us there was no thought of sleep and, before long, the uncertainty seemed to spur our hunger. Kawsar, with Riad and me helping, prepared a huge breakfast. We nervously wolfed down bread, yogurt, cheese, jam and eggs and washed it all down with scalding glasses of strong, sweet tea. As we ate, Mohammed tried in vain to get some news about the coup on the radio, but even the BBC didn't have any information yet, and the Syrian radio station didn't begin its morning broadcast until 7:15 am. When the Syrian station finally came on, all we got was military music. It was a Wednesday morning, but of course no one would be going to work or school – or even leaving the house.

The battle continued and eventually neighbors, who had gotten the news by telephone from relatives living near the shooting, passed the word from balcony to balcony that President Amin Hafiz was under attack. That wasn't very encouraging news since he lived just a short walk away from us. What we were hearing, the neighbors said, was a battle between rebel tanks firing at close range on the presidential villa and a valiant, but foolhardy, defense thrown up by the President himself and his guards who were armed with nothing more than machine guns. The President and his men fought on until almost noon when they ran out of ammunition and finally surrendered. By that time, most of the guards were dead or dying, one of Hafiz's children was wounded and later lost her eye, and his home was in ruins. He was unceremoniously carted off to prison while his traumatized family was allowed to return to their home city of Aleppo.

In the afternoon, the blaring military music on the radio was interrupted long enough for the first of the usual "communiqués" that follow every Syrian coup. "Communiqué Number One" was broadcast by the rebels who styled themselves, "The 23rd of February Movement" and it confirmed that Amin Hafiz had indeed been overthrown. Schools and governmental offices were closed until further notice and a city-wide curfew was imposed.

Two days later, when the curfew was lifted, everyone in the city was seized by the same impulse and single-mindedly headed on foot for the presidential villa. We were no exception; we joined the throngs who wanted to see with their own eyes the scene of the recent battle. It was a beautiful day with a cloudless sky and unseasonably mild weather for February. Entire families with children in tow, like us, walked through streets empty of traffic towards the presidential villa. As I looked around me at the crowds of well-dressed people walking in an atmosphere that was almost festive, I had the bizarre thought that it was like the Easter Day parade on Fifth Avenue in New York.

This fleeting comparison evaporated as the ruined villa came into view, and everyone's mood turned somber. The gutted building was a sobering sight and a reminder that people, we would never know how many, had died in this place. Whole walls had been knocked down, exposing battered rooms with damaged furniture and broken chandeliers hanging askew. Looking at the house you wondered how anyone in it had survived. Some parts of the building showed extensive fire damage and water leaked from broken pipes.

Surrounding buildings in the area bore scars from the battle, as well. The homes in this area are not far apart and many of them were pockmarked by shellfire. Looking at the damage, I wondered how many ordinary citizens had been caught in the crossfire and were wounded or killed.

Later, we learned this was an intra-party feud between the "progressives" and the "old guard", the followers of Michel Aflaq and Salah Bitar, the founders of the Baath Party. There were minor outbreaks of trouble in different cities around the country, but the rebels prevailed. The victorious faction, the "progressives", threw the supporters of the former regime out of their jobs and many were imprisoned with Amin Hafiz, the former president. How glad I was that Mohammed did not belong to any party!

Hafiz Assad, who did not personally participate in the coup, was appointed Minister of Defense. Since this was a power struggle within the Baath Party, not all ministers in the cabinet were changed. However, Mohammed got a new Minister of Planning.

I was getting used to these "governmental changes". There was nothing any of us could do about them except hope for the best. A few days after this one, we went on a picnic with Jill and Adel. Mohammed and the girls were home for four days and it was like a holiday. Our February weather continued to be unseasonably warm, like late April in Palisades. For days we had no heat on and were perfectly comfortable – and imagine, picnics in February.

In fact, we had a rash of picnics that February as people rapidly resumed their customary lives after the coup. One memorable picnic was held on a balmy winter day in the Ghouta near a little stream. We were sixteen: Lamat, Wahid Beyk, and their three children plus Wahid's old auntie, Lutfiya Khanum, the four of us, Kawsar, Riad, Tete, two of Bara'at's boys and Sheeha, Tete's little maid.

Wahid Beyk made the charcoal fire, while Lamat and I helped Kawsar put the chunks of tender lamb on skewers and the boys helped fan the fire as the meat cooked. Is there any better smell than the aroma of broiling meat outdoors over a smoldering charcoal fire? By the time the meat was cooked, Mahair, the oldest cousin at eleven, had caught several fresh water crabs in the little stream with which he terrorized the girls, Muna had managed to fall into the water, and we all were dizzy with hunger.

This happy day, which gathered together so many members of our large family, sticks in our collective memory, in part because it was the last family picnic before our circle began breaking up and also because someone took a lot of photographs. Years later, we sometimes reminisced about our "winter picnic" as we looked at these photographs and pointed out the family members who were no longer with us.

In December, I had told Mother there was a possibility Mohammed would be sent to the World Bank course in Washington D.C., which would run from the middle of March to the end of July. By the end of February, the latest word was that Mohammed had permission to attend the course and I wrote Mother the good news.

I was marking the days off on the calendar and, of course, I did not fail to note March 1st which meant only two years of Mohammed's service remained. Our trip to Washington was originally planned for March 11th, with a two-day stopover in London. However, on the 7th, Tete became ill; her blood pressure shot up and she had a small stroke which briefly affected her speech. We postponed leaving and when Tete seemed a bit better we decided to leave on the 17th. Tete was told the trip was off and Kawsar planned to break the news that we had gone, gently and gradually.

Our bags were packed, presents had been bought for all the American relatives and we were set to leave at six the next morning. In fact, up until 9:30 the evening before, I thought we were going, but it was a doomed trip. All that day, Tete had been getting worse. We took her to the doctor and the results of her cardiogram were very ominous. The doctor said hardening of the arteries was affecting both her heart and brain and there was the possibility of a serious stroke. Finally, he said, if it were his mother, he would not consider traveling.

That clinched it. We unpacked our bags and called off the trip. I hope I was more worried about Tete than I was disappointed. After this illness, Tete was very weak and frail and we were afraid she would never be the same. She either wandered mentally, or, when she was lucid, cried because she couldn't express herself. She didn't eat enough to keep a bird alive and much of what she ate didn't stay down. Even Tete's doctors were discouraged.

The weather turned icy cold again after one month of false spring. Appropriate, I thought; false hopes and a false spring. After temperatures as high as 70 degrees Fahrenheit at noon, it now went down to the thirties. Everyone either had flu or was just getting over it.

By April, Tete was finally a little better although every so often she would have another bad day with her blood pressure rising alarmingly. Now the government was insisting that Mohammed go to Moscow as part of an official delegation. The mission was supposed to last only five days, but with the government you never could be sure. Mohammed said his mother was ill and did everything he could to get out of going, but without any luck. He decided to tell Tete that he was going to Aleppo and hoped that the trip really would last only five days - and it did.

Tete had become very sensitive. One day she got upset because Kawsar invited us to eat with them and we refused so as not to make extra work. Tete even began saying that we should write Abdo and tell him to come back from England, that he'd been away long enough. That was very unlike her. The doctor said it was "irreversible arterioscleroses". Time proved the doctor wrong. As the weeks passed, she slowly became her old self again, although she never got her strength back. Eventually, she was as alert and as interested in everyone and everything around her as ever.

With all our fears for Tete, death struck from a totally unexpected direction carrying off a young family who lived down the street from us. Hilda, a pretty, blonde German girl, her Syrian husband and their little boy were all killed in a dreadful car accident on the way back from a vacation on the Mediterranean Sea. I stood on the balcony as the funeral vans bearing their bodies passed our house and burst into tears as their names were broadcast. It seemed unbelievable that an entire family could be gone in a moment.

I wondered if the van was heading for the Qassioun cemetery and a picture of this grim place where the Imady family plot lay flashed through my mind. This old cemetery was on the slope of our mountain, up the road from where the Imady compound had been. It was surrounded by a wall and reached by climbing a flight of stone steps. Inside the stark enclosure there was not a tree, a bush, a flower or a blade of grass. There was nothing but packed hard dirt with tombstones placed so close to each other that it was difficult to make your way around them to reach the Imady plot.

The first time I saw this place, I compared it with dismay to the Palisades cemetery with its tall shade trees and graveled paths winding past grassy plots where five generations of my family are buried. I warned Mohammed that if I were buried in the Qassioun cemetery, my bones would never lie at rest. I begged him to find a better place for us to be buried. He just laughed and said I would outlive him and in any case I could always be shipped back to Palisades. I thought of the line from Ruth which says, "Where you die, I will die, and there will I be buried". This was the one sticking point in this verse for me. My friends also laughed when I told them of my objections and wondered why I would care where I was buried. But I did care.

This year had certainly begun inauspiciously what with Susu's scarlet fever in January, the coup d'etat in February and Tete's illness and our cancelled trip in March. Also, while Tete was ill, Muna came down with chicken pox and in April, both girls caught the mumps. Then, there was our friends' fatal car accident and now there was sad news about Jill and Adel. Just when I had begun to think they were settled in Damascus, Jill told me they had decided to try life in America. She would be going ahead to see if Adel could get a job with the United Nations in New York. I worried what might be next, but actually there were good times ahead.

Now that Tete was getting better, all our thoughts turned to Mother's planned visit and my expected baby. Since the baby was due the first week of July, I wrote Mother that it would be better if she arrived earlier so she would miss the worst of the heat and I would not be tied down with a newborn. And that is what Mother did. She arrived on June 18th which gave us almost three full weeks before the baby's birth. Everyone was happy to see Mother again and even Tete seemed to rally with her arrival.

Five years had passed since Mother's last visit and, as she discovered, things were not exactly the way she fondly remembered them. The sheep in the neighbor's house across the street were gone, as was the house itself. Construction was underway to replace their old family house with a four-story apartment building as had already been done with Bianca's house next-door. All over the city, the traditional Arab houses were making way for modern apartment buildings.

Mother was sorry to learn the quaint little trolley rattling and clanking along the street was also gone. Up on the roof, she found the skyline of the city marred by television antennas and several high buildings partially cut off our view of the Umayyad Mosque. When Mother asked about the little goats that used to scamper down our street every day at sunset, we told her they no longer passed through the city. She had returned to a changed city.

Initially, she was a bit sad that the city was not quite as she recalled, but she soon found that many things hadn't changed. The buses were still decorated, as the trolleys had been, with feather plumes, plastic flowers, worry beads, photographs, pictures from magazines, hanging mottoes and amulets against the evil eye.

The country milkman with his black and white Arab headdress and baggy pants, still came pounding on the door in the early morning and turned his back when Kawsar or I (or any woman) answered his knock. The first time Mother saw this happen, she thought he was being rude, but I explained that by averting his eyes from women who were not kinfolk, he was actually being respectful and polite from his point of view. I would talk to his back and tell him how many kilos of milk we wanted and hand him my *tanjera*. He measured out the milk from his metal milk can into my pot and passed it back to me without ever turning around. Mother watched bemused as I then boiled the fresh milk, still warm from the cow, and afterwards strained out the hairs. "Cow hairs?" asked Mother.

The smoke stacks still belched forth black smoke on Fridays when everyone lit their *mazote* stoves to heat water for the weekly bath. Soldiers were still pinching the pretty girls and little boys in the souk were still shouting, "Madame, well-come, *tafuddily* (come in)!" to every foreign woman and pushing their wares right up under your nose. There was still plenty for Mother to see and exclaim over.

On this visit Suad and my mother became friends. From this time on, whenever Mother was in Damascus we would all take Suad to the fair and have a great time together. When Mother left Damascus she always asked Suad half-jokingly to look after her family. Invariably, Suad put her hands on top of her kinky head and said, "*Ala rasi*!" which means "Your wish is my command!"

About a week before my baby was due, we took a long trip by taxi to the port city of Tartous on the Mediterranean. Mother worried that the five-hour car ride might cause me to begin labor far from my doctor, or indeed any doctor and had visions of me delivering my baby on the sea shore. However, we arrived at the Island Beach

Motel without incident and the fun the children had on the clean beach and in the warm, sparkling water of the Mediterranean made us forget the tiring drive.

We were assigned a little wooden bungalow right at the edge of the beach and, as long as you stayed in your cabin during the very hot middle of the day, the heat was bearable. Mohammed stayed out of the sun as much as possible because his fair skin burns easily, but Mother and I parked ourselves on beach chairs under a big umbrella and kept our eyes on Susu and Muna as they splashed about, played in the sand and collected shells and small, colorful stones. Mother told me as she gazed out at the sea that now and then her thoughts wandered back to her vacations as a young girl on the beach in Ocean Grove, New Jersey - how far away in time and space!

"What", Mother wondered out loud, "would my Papa and Mama have made of this faraway land and their little great-grandchildren babbling away in Arabic?"

The fresh sea air was invigorating and there was always a sea breeze in the afternoon that cooled the air and banished the noontime flies. This is when Mohammed would join us and we would walk along the beach and look out over the water to the small island of Arwad, directly in front of us, and enjoy the glorious sunsets. Mohammed offered to take us across to the island, but when Mother saw the little motorboat packed with people, precariously bobbing across the water, she declined. She said she preferred to remember it as a fairy island, shimmering on the horizon. Evenings in Tartous the moon hung over the sea and lit up the beach.

We had a peaceful time except for Mother's worries about me, but the trip back was horrendous. I must admit I was dreadfully uncomfortable as I braced myself against the bumps and turns of that interminable ride. The worst moment came when we passed a shepherd with his flock and hit and killed a large sheep. We were already going fast, but when this happened the driver gunned the car even faster to escape the furious shepherd who was shaking his staff threateningly at us. Mohammed begged the driver to stop so he could offer the man some money, but the driver refused saying that the shepherd would kill him. Besides, he said, it was God's will and the fate of that particular sheep to be hit by our car. I'm glad it was also God's will that the car didn't go out of control and kill us all!

Back in Damascus, I plunged right into the preparations for Susu's ninth birthday, planned for the day after our return. We decided to hold it on the roof after sunset since the daytime temperature hung around a very dry ninety-five degrees, like a blast from a furnace. Since I was hugely pregnant, I hoped to limit those invited to some of Susu's cousins and a few friends her age, but I learned it is impossible to have a child's birthday party in Syria and invite only children.

Susu first called her cousin, May, and when Susu said, "Mothers are not invited," May asked in dismay, "But who will feed us?" How my mother laughed when Susu repeated what ten-year old May had said! Of course, we caved in and all the mothers and little and big brothers and sisters and little maids were invited to the party, as usual.

When the children sat to eat, Mother was amazed to see the mothers standing behind their children and actually putting bites of cake and spoonfuls of ice cream into the mouths of their far too old children.

"Good heavens!" Mother said. "May was not joking!

To no one's surprise, after all my exertions for the birthday party, I had my baby the very next day. Tete was in bed that day with an asthma attack. I went to the hospital in the morning and the family received news of the baby's birth around two in the afternoon. Mother and Susu were sitting in Tete's bedroom when the word came that a baby boy had been born.

Tete leaped to her feet, crying out her congratulations, *"Mabruk, mabruk!"* and took Mother's hands and circled the room with her, dancing on tiptoe with her nightgown billowing around her. Her son now had a son. This was one of the happiest moments of her life her daughters told Mother who was happy, too, for me, for Tete and for herself.

Mother later wrote about this moment: "Here we were together, two mothers. Kipling famously said that east is east and west is west and never the twain shall meet. Well, we did meet, we clung together - and it was good."

That afternoon, Mohammed brought Mother, Susu and Muna to see the new baby. Muna had insisted on wearing a party dress with a hem that needed sewing and poor Mother, who hardly knew how to hold a needle had basted it up with huge inch-wide stitches.

I also had been stitched up and had to sit on a rubber tube for a few days, but I was happy that our family was now complete. We had been expecting a third girl so now we had to scramble around for a name. I rather liked "Tarek" or "Khaled", but Mother said she could not pronounce either one. Then Mohammed suggested "Omar" and everyone liked it. Actually, Mother did not pronounce "Omar" correctly either since it begins with the Arabic letter "ayn", which has no equivalent in English. However, the name "Omar" with the "ayn" anglicized to an "o" is familiar to Americans, so Omar it was.

Up to now, Mohammed and I had been called Abu Sawsan and Im Sawsan (Susan), the father and mother of Sawsan, but now, at a stroke, we became Abu Omar and Im Omar. In Damascus, parents are called *Abu* and *Im* of their first child, be it boy or girl. But if a boy comes along, (lucky you) you are definitely and permanently called *Abu* and *Im* of that boy.[7] Poor Muna, her nose out of joint, indignantly asked when it would be *her* turn.

---

7 This form of address was very common and considered very polite in the sixties. Today, many young Damascenes consider it old fashioned.

Despite the ninety degree heat and no air conditioning in the hospital, Omar was swaddled tightly just as Muna had been. He was a beautiful baby the day he was born, with a fair complexion, blue eyes and blond hair, but by the second day he had turned yellow and had heat rash all over his body and looked like a little Chinese baby with measles. We had worried about the Rh factor with every child and this time there was a problem; Omar's blood was Rh positive, while mine was Rh negative and the doctors said he might need a blood transfusion. However, after a week of ultra violet treatment, a transfusion was ruled out. Also, I had not forgotten how upset my friend had been when her baby was circumcised at nine months, so this was taken care of before Omar left the hospital.

Once baby Omar and I were home, the visits of congratulations began and the first to arrive were Mohammed's uncle and his wife who brought Omar a gold good luck charm to ward off the evil eye. Tete's brother, Ghaleb Hawasly - Khalo or Uncle to all of us - had his sister's blue twinkling eyes, but with a naughty gleam in them. His tarboosh and handlebar mustache marked him as an old-fashioned Arab gentleman and, although he was in his eighties, he had a firm step and a straight back.

The minute he walked in, he went over to the sleeping baby, waved his right hand in a circular motion over him as he murmured some incantations, bent over and puffed to the right and the left of the baby and then pinned a little gold hand studded with a turquoise on Omar's jacket. We all watched, fascinated by this performance.

I whispered to Mother what he said: "In the name of God, the Most Merciful, the Compassionate. May He protect you. May He keep you safe from the evil near you and all around you."

"Puffing is supposed to blow away the evil spirits," I told Mother. "It's an old superstition here, probably thousands of years old."

Khalo then sat down across the room with Mart Khalo (Uncle's Wife) beside him, and started talking to Mother. Susu, who loved to translate for her grandmother, did the honors this time.

"Mommy, he says he's had seven wives, but he's never married a foreigner. Now he would like to try an American wife. All his wives are dead or divorced except for Mart Khalo so there would only be two of you. He wants to know what you think about this."

While Susu was translating, Khalo beamed at Mother and Mart Khalo rolled her eyes, like a mother whose son is making a fool of himself. When Susu paused, Khalo jumped to his feet, took Mother's hand, and, with a courtly bow, kissed it. We were all rather taken aback.

He spoke again and Susu whispered to Mother, "Khalo says he wants to show you his nice house and garden." Then she added, "His house is beautiful, Mommy. I could go with you to show you the house, but Mama can't come."

Amused by her serious air, Mother asked why not.

"Because," said Susu, "Mama just had a baby and has to stay in bed for forty days."

To our relief, Khalo didn't seem to expect an answer to his "marriage proposal". He had lived up to his reputation as a ladies' man and that, no doubt, was his intention. As he left, he again kissed Mother's hand. Mart Khalo said good-bye with an exasperated look at Khalo's back as he walked out the door ahead of her.

Six days after Omar was born we made one last trip down to the souk for Mother's last minute purchases. I created a sensation when we went in one shop we had been in the week before while I was still very pregnant. When the shop-keeper saw my flat stomach, he was visibly startled. He choked out some words of congratulation, but could not hide his shock. Mother found out Susu had not been joking about the forty days in bed.

After childbirth, Damascene women actually did stay in bed. They were taken back to their parents' home where they lay in bed, dressed in white satin peignoirs and received female visitors coming to congratulate them on the new baby. When the forty days were up, the older female relatives helped the new mothers take their first bath (hopefully they were at least sponged off before this time!) and, in what was probably a throwback to some pre-Islamic custom, had them sit on a raw egg to ensure their fertility. After all this, the new mother finally went home with the baby to her husband. To go shopping, let alone to leave your bed before the time was up, was unthinkable. My in-laws were used to my strange American ways by now, but I could still shock the rest of the city.

The next day was the sad morning Mother had to leave. We piled into a taxi and drove off just at dawn while Mother looked back at Jebel Qassioun until she could see it no longer. At the airport, we kissed good-bye at the gate, but suddenly, with a nod to someone in authority, Mohammed escorted us right up to Mother's waiting plane.

"*Ma salami* - Go with safety, see you next year, *in sha' Allah* - God willing," we all said.

Omar was an easy baby; he mostly ate and then slept until the next feeding. Also Muna and Susu were not jealous, at least not that I could detect. In fact, Susu was a great help with him and loved the role of big sister. The year that began so badly had certainly taken a turn for the good.

I never knew what Muna had missed until Omar was born when I discovered the paternal relatives usually have a big party to celebrate the birth of a baby. Perhaps because Muna was a second girl, my in-laws never had one for her. Since everyone invited to this party brings the baby a gift, it is sort of a "baby shower" and is called the *imbarakay,* (the blessing), the same word used for a bridal shower. Like the bridal *imbarakay,* which is held *after,* and not before a wedding, the baby *imbarakay* is held after the baby is born.

Actually, Omar had three "showers". The first was attended mostly by young girls and young women from Mohammed's and Riad's ministries. Mohammed's pretty cousin, Ghada, started the dancing and got five or six other girls up to dance with her. It was a joyful occasion with lots of music, dancing and *zalageet*[8] – ululations, the eerie, trilling sounds made by Arab women to express happiness.

The traditional dish served at an *imbarakay* for a new baby is *caraweya* (ca-Ra-we-ah), a sweet pudding made of powdered rice and ground caraway seeds and topped with nuts. It is supposed to be good for nursing mothers, but since Kawsar knew it was one of the few Syrian dishes I really didn't like, she served ice cream, cookies and coffee, instead. I wore a blue lace dress Kawsar had sewn especially for the occasion, had my hair done and looked quite "respectable" as Mohammed says when he means "nice".

The next night an older group of female relatives came and the third night I invited my friends over. Omar slept peacefully in his carriage throughout all three parties.

Not long after Omar was born, Jill left and Adel soon followed her. Jill never returned to Syria, but I would see her again one more time in the States where she finally found happiness...

As autumn began, Anna Maria told me that she was pregnant for the fourth time. She worried it was too soon since there would only be fourteen months between her last – which was a third boy - and the new baby, but she hoped this time to have a girl. In fact, on Muna's birthday, February 18th, she was delighted to end up with not one girl, but two identical baby girls.

By September, Abdo was back from his graduate studies in England and the house was livelier and Tete was happier. His sisters began pushing all their pretty friends his way, in vain. He enjoyed being a bachelor and resisted all their efforts to marry him off.

The girls were back in school, the days began to grow shorter and the long, hot summer was finally over. It was time to fold away the summer clothes and take out the winter clothes and the heavy, wool quilts; time for Suad and I to scrub the walls, the ceilings, the chandeliers and the windows before taking down the carpets and the *sobas* from the *s'eefay* When the house was so clean it smelled of soap and you could eat off the scrubbed floor, the carpets were unrolled and the *sobas* were set up and their stove pipes installed. The cold weather could come; we were ready.

8 *Zalageet* is Damascene dialect for *zagareed,* the standard Arabic word for this odd. high-pitched, piercing sound which is so strange to Western ears.

Winter nights Tete's bedroom was turned into a living room and the family often gathered around the fire in her room. Kawsar would bring a bag of brown, fat chestnuts, slit them and put them on top of the hot *soba*. The room was soon filled with the appetizing smell of roasting chestnuts. Kawsar would keep an eye on them, turning them as they slowly cooked while we all waited impatiently to eat them. With the chestnuts, we drank scalding tea and ate wonderful *abu serra* oranges – navel oranges – that were juicier and tastier than any I had ever had.

And, as we soaked up the warmth and ate our evening snack, we talked. Often it was about our daily lives, what we had done that day or what our plans for the next day were, but sometimes someone would begin reminiscing about the old days. I don't remember how the subject came up – maybe someone mentioned Dr. Homad - but one of these cozy nights, we ended up talking about the difficult years of the French Mandate and Mohammed told of his part in protests against the French when he was just a school boy...

IV. Tales of a Family and a City, 1942-1970

"I started preparatory school in 1942 at the age of twelve. How happy and grown up I felt the day my father took me to register in the Tajheez Oula School! But these were not happy times for the country. Syria was still under the rule of France and we hated the French soldiers that flooded Damascus after World war II began. Everyone longed for independence and even we school boys joined in the struggle to end the Mandate."

* * *

In fact, the Syrian nationalists had been struggling for decades against French rule. After the collapse of the Syrian armed revolt of 1925, the National Bloc, a coalition of "urban notables" was organized in 1926 to work for independence. The goal of these nationalists was to achieve independence by diplomacy and cooperation and, when all else failed, by strikes and demonstrations.

The twenty-six years of the Mandate were punctuated by promises and concessions from the French – always made under threat of civil unrest or worse - followed by setbacks and violence. Under pressure, the French allowed the election of a Constitutional Assembly in 1928, but then objected to six of its articles and cancelled the Assembly. It took three years of negotiations and threats of violence by the National Bloc for the two sides to ratify the constitution.

From the beginning of the Mandate, the French High Commissioner had appointed the Prime Minister and there was no legislative body. However, the new constitution mandated elections for a President and the establishment of an elected Parliament. The long-awaited elections were held in December 1931/January 1932, but were suspended when the French authorities meddled in the elections. Riots and demonstrations broke out in protest and the elections were only resumed when the French promised to remain neutral.

Mohammed Ali Abed, a wealthy Damascene notable who ran as an independent, was elected the first president of Syria. There was jubilation in the streets of Damascus when, on June 11, 1932, the first Syrian flag was raised over Government House and a seventeen-gun salute proclaimed the birth of the Syrian Arab Republic. However, the country was still awash in French soldiers and the French High Commissioner had the last word in everything.

The next eight years were turbulent as the Syrians struggled for the independence and unity of their country. The French suspended constitutional government in 1934 and again in 1939. In 1938, France turned over the Syrian province of Alexandretta to Turkey and also once again proclaimed direct French control over the Jazira, the Druze Mountain and the Alawite Mountain. In fact, France had been ruling the latter two areas as autonomous areas since 1923.

Just when it seemed things could not possibly get worse, World War II broke out. After Paris fell to the Germans, the Vichy regime declared martial law and food rationing in Damascus.

On June 8, 1941 Britain and the Free French invaded Syria to prevent the Vichy government from giving the Axis Powers air bases in the country. Within ten days the Vichy government was driven out and de Gaulle visited Syria soon after. He was greeted with enthusiasm because, before he came, his representative said he was coming to end the Mandate, but this would prove to be an empty promise.

De Gaulle chose an old friend of France to be President and this man, Taj al-Din Hasani, took charge in September, 1941. It was Hasani's great achievement to get the French to restore the unity of Syria. In January, 1942, there was an official celebration to mark the reincorporation of the three "autonomous areas" into the country.

When President Hasani died of a heart attack in January 1943, the Cabinet called for general elections and a caretaker government was appointed. On August 17, 1943, Shukri Kuwatly of the National Bloc was sworn in as the third elected President of Syria. In November, the Syrians met with the French and called for an end to the Mandate, but the French said they were staying in Syria as long as the war lasted.

Food shortages and inflation had continued to be a hardship for the population since the beginning of the war. In February 1943, when the price of bread was raised, protest strikes and student demonstrations broke out. At this time, Mohammed was twelve years old, a 6th grade student at the Tajheez Oula High School.

"I remember it like this," Mohammed said: "There were student leaders in our school from the 11th and 12th grades who were connected with the National Bloc. When the politicians wanted to pressure the French, they would ask these young nationalists to organize a student demonstration. They would call a meeting, announce the current issue and we boys would walk out of our classes and take to the streets.

"In February 1943, we demonstrated against the rise in the price of bread. I remember we chanted, '*Kilo khubbiz bi tlateen/ nehnu oulad juanneen!*' ['A kilo of bread at thirty piasters/ we children are hungry!'] We marched up and down the streets of Damascus yelling until our voices were hoarse.

"In March, 1944, the nationalists declared another protest strike. I was now fourteen and in eighth grade. Our student leaders told us we were going to march to demand the establishment of a Syrian army and we cheered. This was something we all wanted from our hearts. We were sick of the arrogant foreign soldiers in our city.

"We formed into irregular lines and marched from our school down to Victoria Bridge and then turned left to Marjay, past Government House. The student leaders pulled several students up on their shoulders, above the crowd and these boys waved their arms and led us in shouting, '*Bidna jaish Arabie Sourie!*' – ['We want an Arab Syrian army!'] We went around Marjay Square, back to Victoria and up past the Gates of Salihiya. Some of the older, bolder students broke shop signs written in French, but we younger boys were content to march and chant.

"We ended up at the intersection where Parliament and the French Army Headquarters faced each other. Here, both sides of the street were lined with armed soldiers. We shouted, '*A bas la France – Vive la Syrie*' as we neared them, but actually most of the soldiers were Senegalese or Moroccan. Only their officers were French.

"The bigger boys pushed against the iron barriers separating us from the soldiers and were hit with batons. Fighting broke out and the soldiers arrested some of the older students and dragged them away with bloody heads. Then the soldiers charged into our ranks and we ran in all directions. It was exciting – and scary - to demonstrate. We felt we were doing something positive for our country."

In the spring of 1945, Syria attended the United Nations Conference in San Francisco and became a charter member of the organization. Shortly after this, yet another crisis arose. France announced it was transferring three French battalions from North Africa to Syria and President Kuwatly protested that this was incompatible with Syrian independence. De Gaulle then offered to transfer more power to Syria in exchange for permanent military bases in the country. Kuwatly refused.

At this point, the British announced they were withdrawing their troops from Syria and said they would not take sides in this dispute. To the Syrians it seemed like history was repeating itself. As in 1920, Britain was turning a blind eye while France imposed its will on the country.

Hostilities broke out on the evening of May 29, 1945 when French troops raised the French flag in front of the Parliament and demanded that the Syrian police salute this flag. When the police refused, the French soldiers fired on them. Then, shooting indiscriminately, they forced their way into the Parliament building, hoping to arrest the speaker of the Parliament. When they failed to find him, the soldiers set the building on fire and, after leaving, shelled it and other government buildings. Their cannons were also turned on the citadel and the Orient Palace Hotel. In addition, the Telecommunications Center and the power stations were broken into and all electricity and telephone lines in Damascus were cut.

Meanwhile, the Foreign Minister, Jamil Mardam Beyk (a distant relative of the Imadys), who was acting president since President Kuwatly had taken ill, was holding a press conference in Government House. As soon as it ended and the foreign correspondents departed, the building was bombed and strafed by the French air force. Fortunately, Mardam Beyk and all the government officials managed to escape uninjured.

Mohammed said, "I will never forget that night. Shells whistled, bombs thudded, the sound of machine guns could be heard everywhere and our family was frantic. That same afternoon, Bara'at had gone to tutor a student who lived on Nuri Pasha Street near the French Legation [now the French Embassy]. When the bombardment of the city began, she was trapped at this student's home. She couldn't go home while artillery shells and bombs were falling and our family had no way of knowing if she was safe. We had no telephone and, since the lines had been cut, even the neighbors with phones couldn't give us any news. Nighttime came, but it was impossible for anyone to fetch her - there was a curfew and the shelling never stopped. We passed a dreadful, sleepless night. Some of us prayed for Bara'at's safe return, some read the Qur'an and others paced the floor. The next morning before dawn, the guns went quiet and Kawsar and I set out to bring Bara'at home."

"How old were you two then?" I interrupted.

"Kawsar was twenty three and I was fifteen. The streets were completely deserted except for soldiers who let the two of us pass. Our way took us past the French Legation and we were careful to walk on the opposite side of the street. As we passed the Legation, we saw two men talking together in front of their shops. Just then, the morning call to prayer began. One of the shopkeepers looked up and frowned at the Moroccan soldiers on the roof of the Legation. 'Look at those French lackeys pointing their weapons at us,' he said. 'They should be ashamed of themselves - aiming their Tommy guns at fellow Muslims.'

"We continued on to the home of Bara'at's student and we both cried when we found her safe. Then the three of us hurried back home through the empty streets. That evening the shelling started again even worse than before. It lasted throughout the night, but at least all of us were home together."

Meanwhile, the Speaker of the Parliament slipped out of the country and reached Cairo where he reported the unprovoked attack on Damascus by the French to the

Arab League. Since Damascus was completely cut off from the world, Mardam Beyk also sent couriers on foot to the consuls of Transjordan and Egypt asking them to return to their countries and tell the world of the French attack.

Although the French controlled Damascus, in Hama, Houran and the Druze Mountain the French were decisively defeated and many French soldiers were wounded and taken prisoner.

When the British government heard of the bombing of Damascus, it decided to intervene militarily and the American government endorsed this. However, on June 1st, Senegelese troops under French command continued to rampage throughout the city. The looting and indiscriminate shooting did not stop until British forces, led by General Paget, arrived in Damascus that afternoon and a cease fire was implemented.

All in all, the French troops killed 616 Syrians and wounded another 2,083 in their four-day attack on unarmed civilians. This uncivilized end to the French occupation provoked one last student demonstration that Mohammed participated in, to an extent. The boys of his school marched to Marjay Square where they made a big bonfire of their French textbooks. To the students, their wrecked Parliament building and bombed city cast a dark shadow on the glories of French civilization and culture. Mohammed went along with them, but he told me he prudently did not throw his books on the fire. He thought he might need them the next school year and wanted to spare his family the expense of replacing them.

On August 1st, the transfer of all administrative and political powers to the Syrian government began. The final French soldiers left Syria on April 16, 1946 and the next day, April 17th, was joyfully proclaimed Syria's official Independence Day.

* * *

During Mohammed's high school years, the Homad family from Aleppo rented an apartment in the Imady building and Dr. Homad, who had a doctorate in economics from France, was elected to Parliament. This hard-working ambitious man, so different from Jowdat Effendi, drew Mohammed's admiring attention. Mohammed was at an impressionable age and the successful Dr. Homad became a role model for him. In the next few years as Dr. Homad's star rose, Mohammed would keep close track of him and their paths would repeatedly converge.

Mohammed got his first job at the age of seventeen. He told me, "Like my sisters, I could hardly wait to be old enough to earn some money for the family. When I was seventeen and still in high school, I got a summer job with the Cereal Office in Noa, a small village in Houran in southern Syria. It probably takes no more than an hour to reach by car today, but back then, Noa was a three-hour bus trip from Damascus. It was my first time away from home and I was put up in a peasant's home that lacked running water and electricity, but had a good supply of bed bugs.

"While I was in Noa, Riad and her best friend were hired to teach in a girls' boarding school in Hasake. At the end of the summer, I went with them by bus as far as Deir-Ez-Zor where they caught another bus to the school. The trip took us two days, with one night in a hotel in Aleppo and another in Deir-Ez-Zor. Back in the forties, it was very daring for a Syrian girl of twenty to take a job far away from family and home. Although Riad was unusually self-confident and independent, I worried about her in this remote place. It was good to know that she was with a close friend."

The daughters of Yisra and her sister, Bahira, were now of marriageable age. One of Bahira's girls had already married and the prospects for another daughter looked promising.

"It was like this," said Lamat. "A Palestinian government official, Mahmoud Ala'adine, and his mother came calling on my aunt's family in search of a bride. Essmat was the oldest of the Idilbi girls, so she was the one brought out. Essmat was very taken with the young man and a tentative agreement was reached between the two families. It seems Essmat fell in love with Mahmoud at first sight and began dreaming of a wedding, but her happiness ended when Mahmoud met Essmat's younger sister, Najah. He decided he had chosen the wrong sister, not because Najah was prettier, but because she was educated. Najah was studying at the Teachers' Training Institute, but Essmat was illiterate. Mahmoud had an important job as head of the municipality of Ramleh in Palestine and he preferred an educated wife. He told Khali Bahira and Abu Mustapha that he had changed his mind and wanted to marry Najah. Essmat was very upset at this turn of events. She became ill and took to her bed. Sometime after Najah and Mahmoud married, she turned her face to the wall and died.

"Mahmoud took his bride back to Ramleh," said Lamat, "to his large villa surrounded by orange groves. They should have had a happy life there in Palestine, but no. Before many weeks passed, they were back in Damascus. In fear of their lives, they abandoned their home and left everything behind, even Najah's trousseau. When they arrived in Damascus, all of us did what we could to help them out."

It almost seems as if Essmat's death cast a shadow on the newly married couple. This was the spring of 1948 and Zionist terrorists were clearing Palestine of Arabs to make way for a Jewish state. Not long after arriving in Ramleh, Najah and Mahmoud joined the 780,000 Palestinians who fled in terror after hearing news of the massacre of Deir Yassin and attacks on other Palestinian towns. All the properties the Palestinians left behind were taken over by the State of Israel and no Arab has ever been compensated for the loss of his possessions. As for Najah, this was the second time in ten years she had to flee Palestine. In 1938, her entire family escaped to Damascus so her father could evade British prosecution for his part in the Arab Revolt.

On May 15, 1948 the State of Israel came into being and what is now almost sixty years of suffering - the *Nakba* or Catastrophe – began for Palestinians.

"But," said Lamat, "Najah and Mahmoud were among the few lucky Palestinians who were able to rebuild their lives. They moved to Amman, Jordan where Mahmoud got a job in a bank and Najah began teaching in a private school. They were intelligent and hard-working and eventually, Mahmoud rose to be Director of the bank and Najah became principal of her school. Together they raised a large family of successful boys and girls."

I wondered if they ever thought of Essmat. I suppose she was just the shadowy, forgotten sister who had died suddenly and unaccountably. But Tete and Kawsar told me in all seriousness that she died of a broken heart.

* * *

When the Imady girls grew up, it seemed that history would repeat itself and that Jowdat Effendi would consider no one good enough to marry his daughters. However, one persistent suitor, Wahid Beyk Hawasli, a distant cousin of Tete's, managed to worm himself into Jowdat's affections and eventually won permission to get engaged to Lamat. Part of the reason Jowdat Effendi agreed was the friendship he felt for Wahid Beyk's father. These old-fashioned men were two of a kind: stern, difficult men, ill at ease in the twentieth century.

In the forties, Wahid Beyk and his best friend, Abdullah Ka'ed, helped to establish a political party called the Cooperative Socialist Party, a step that would have far reaching effects on the members of this party and on Mohammed who was just a school boy at the time. This party was one of the parties that backed Syria's President, Shukri Kuwatly and it was also outspoken in its criticism of a certain army general, Colonel Husni Zaim. In 1949, Zaim toppled the government and threw the democratically elected President Kuwatly into prison. He also outlawed all political parties, but singled out the members of the Cooperative Socialist Party as his particular enemies for their openly harsh attacks on his character. Wahid Beyk and Abdullah Ka'ed, along with all other members of their party, became fugitives overnight.

I asked Mohammed and Lamat what happened next and Mohammed said, "They were hunted by Zaim's fearsome *mukhabarat* (secret police), fled over the rooftops of Damascus and made their way to...

"No, no," interrupted Lamat. "It wasn't like that. Don't you remember we hid Wahid on the roof in the chicken coop? We really outwitted the *mukhabarat*! Of course they came looking for him at our house because he was my fiancé. We told them they were wasting their time – no one was hiding in our building. But in they came and tramped in their dirty boots from room to room and from floor to floor.

"When they started up to the roof, I told them 'Be quiet! Our father is sleeping in the *tayara*. He is an old man and has been sick for several days. For God's sake don't wake him up!'

"They tiptoed into the room and went over to the bed. They lifted the mosquito netting and saw Abi sleeping. He played his part well and the *mukhabarat* were satisfied we were telling the truth. They looked no further and left.

"You know how clean and particular Wahid was. Poor man, if you saw him when he crawled out of that coop with the chickens squawking angrily! He was covered with chicken droppings, feathers and straw – but alive. After that, Wahid hid for some days at his sister's house until arrangements were made to smuggle him and Abdullah to Lebanon over the mountains.

"We all thought they would be safe in Beirut, but the *mukhabarat* tracked them down. They took them back to Damascus and threw them into prison. For nine months they were in jail, suffering humiliating and dreadful treatment. The worst was the day when they put Wahid into a barrel of human excrement."

All this made an indelible impression on young Mohammed. He was completely disillusioned with political parties and vowed to himself to never join a party; to do the best he could for his country as an independent nationalist, never as a party member. He remained true to this promise throughout his career. When the Baathists came to power, he was asked to join the Baath Party at different times, but he always refused and said that party politics were not for him.

The year 1949 saw Syria ruled by three military dictators, one after the other. The first two were only in power for a few months, but the third, Adib al-Shishakli, managed to hold on for four years. When Shishakli took over the government in December 1949, one of the first things he did was to release the members of the Co-operative Socialist Party from prison, including Wahid Beyk and Abdullah Ka'ed. In February 1954, Shishakli was overthrown and a caretaker government was installed until elections could be held. The elections went ahead in 1955 and brought Shukri Kuwatly back to the presidency.

Lamat married Wahid Beyk shortly after his release from prison and not long after that, Jowdat Effendi sanctioned the marriage of Bara'at to Abdullah Ka'ed. The two sisters and their husbands moved into homes in Mohajareen and soon there were grandchildren, two little boys. Jowdat Effendi would start his mornings by walking up Jebel Qassioun, to drop in on his two daughters and see his grandsons.

At the age of nineteen, Mohammed entered the School of Law in Damascus University to please his father who wanted his son to become a judge like some of the illustrious forbears. Mohammed's real interest lay in economics and in his five years at Damascus University, he took as many courses in economics as he could.

In 1953, Mohammed graduated first in his class and then took the civil service exam for the Ministry of Finance. Again he finished first and was hired as a government employee in the Ministry where he worked for seven months before being called into the army. After his one and a half years of service, he was offered two scholarships, one by the University and one by the Ministry of Finance. Since he already was an employee of the Ministry of Finance, Dr. Homad, who was Minister of Finance at this time, insisted that his protégé be sent under the ministry's auspices and arranged for Mohammed to be given a scholarship to study in America for an MA in the field of economics.

By this time, Jowdat Effendi was a sick old man who had suffered several strokes and perhaps had a feeling he would never see his son again. However, he realized what an opportunity this was for Mohammed, so he gave him his blessing and let him go.

Jowdat Effendi never saw his son again. Furthermore, when Mohammed finally wrote home about our marriage, his father was partially paralyzed with a stroke. The letter was read to him and he was shown a picture of Susu and me. My sisters-in-law say he smiled and kissed the picture and asked to see it many times.

When Jowdat Effendi had his final stroke, he was cared for at home, as is usual in Syria. Tete had the unfailing help of her children in nursing this irascible old man. Ironically, it was Riad and Abdo who had never been their father's favorites, who bore the brunt of his care. Abdo would carry his father upstairs for his weekly bath and help scrub him and change his clothes and Riad would give him his medicine and feed him. They both say that in these last months there was somewhat of a healing of the rift that had always existed between them and their father.

Jowdat Effendi lived for nine months, unable to talk very clearly, to walk or care for himself and he died quietly in February, 1958. Abdo, as I have mentioned, continued to write letters to Mohammed in America in his father's name and never told his brother about their father's stroke or even his death.

Sometime shortly before Jowdat Effendi had his first stroke, he sold the last piece of land he owned in Kabun in the Ghouta and got a good price for it. In this way, he was able to leave each one of his seven children and his wife a modest inheritance. With their money, Inayat and Riad each bought a small apartment in a new building; while both Bara'at and Lamat helped their husbands buy an apartment. In the family building, Mohammed and Abdo each got an apartment and Tete and Kawsar shared one.

* * *

When Mohammed was a young boy, his five Imady aunts had used all their wiles to persuade him to leave his family. They promised to make him rich and said he would be their favorite nephew and their sole heir. All he had to do was leave his parents and come live with them. Mohammed was not tempted for a moment.

However, Jowdat's brother, Uncle Hamdi, still lived with his five sisters - along with his wife, Im Sado, and their four sons and a daughter - and the sisters were much more successful with Hamdi's sons. They not only won the boys to their side, they eventually were able to turn them against their own mother...

I first heard the bizarre story of Hamdi and Fatima Imady from Lamat. She began like this: "There was an Imady cousin named Fatima, a wealthy, childless widow. She had been a beauty in her youth and even at seventy she was still strikingly attractive. *Ya* Lulu - can you believe? - at her age she wanted to marry again – to marry our father, a married man. She proposed marriage to Abi and hinted at a large financial settlement that could be his if he agreed. But Abi's answer to Fatima was: 'My wife's shoe is more valuable to me than all your money!'

"But when Uncle Hamdi heard of Cousin Fatima's wish to remarry he was very interested. He decided her money could make him forget his wife, Im Sado, and even forget that Fatima was almost twenty years older than him. He started courting her and before long she agreed to be his second wife. As part of the marriage contract, she signed over some of her property to him. Their marriage was a great scandal and Im Sado was very hurt, but Uncle Hamdi and Cousin Fatima were happy and didn't care.

"But our aunts *did* care about appearances," said Lamat, "so they decided that several of them should move in with Cousin Fatima. Then, when Uncle Hamdi came calling on his wife, they could tell everyone he was just visiting his sisters.

"A year or more passed. On a fine spring day, Abdo and one of his cousins went to visit the Imady farm. As usual, Uncle Hamdi was there supervising the peasants. The boys wandered about and ended up in a field of ripe cucumbers. Abdo reached out to pick one, but quickly dropped his hand when Uncle Hamdi shouted, 'Don't you dare touch the cucumbers!'

"*Ya* Lulu, the following day, Uncle Hamdi was found dead in a building on his farm. On a window ledge near him was the peeled cucumber he had been about to eat before he died. He was only fifty-three years old.

"I suppose he died of a heart attack and of course the cucumber was just a coincidence, but some family members put a different interpretation on his very sudden, eerie death. And, *ya Allah*, who would have guessed that he would die before his much older second wife and that it would be his children and his sisters who benefited from the property she gave him?"

Lamat ended the story with Hamdi's death, but I know what happened next, having heard it from several family members. After Hamdi's death, his sisters made their nephews choose between them and a life of ease and their mother, Im Sado, and the modest life style she could provide. The boys chose their aunts. With Hamdi gone,

Im Sado could no longer bear living with her hostile sisters-in-law and her four sons who, egged on by their aunts, harassed and bedeviled her. Shortly after the funeral, Im Sado took her daughter and moved out of the Imady home. Her sons, bewitched by their aunts' money, stayed behind. As these women had indulged Hamdi's weaknesses so did they spoil his sons. Two of them ended up as utter failures in life and not one of them even finished high school.

Their mother was so hurt by her sons' unnatural behaviour that she actually cursed her own boys, an unbelievable thing for an Arab mother to do. She must have been extremely provoked to depart so drastically from the normal Syrian maternal character. Damascene mothers famously call their girls by the quaint endearment *ti'ibreeni* and their boys *ti'burni* both of which mean literally, "may you bury me" – in other words, may you outlive me. Tete used this fond expression freely and often. "*Ti'ibreeni, ya* Kawsar" and "*Ti'burni, ya* Mohammed" she would lovingly say. She would even say to me, "*Ti'ibreeni, ya* Lulu".

But Im Sado called down the wrath of God upon her boys and hoped *she* would live to bury them. And she did. Only her faithful daughter outlived her. Her sons grew up, married and had children, but then, one after the other, they died and Im Sado lived on. An important precept in Islam is to ensure your mother is well-pleased with you and to fear her disapproval. That being the case, you could say these sons departed this life under a cloud since they were certainly not in their mother's good graces when they died.

The aunts lived out their days with Sado, Hamdi's oldest son and Sado's wife and five children. He had become their favorite nephew and sole heir. By 1970, all the aunts were dead and Sado had inherited their wealth

* * *

"... It was an impersonal room as the walls were bare of pictures and there were no books, magazines or whatnots, but the Persian carpet was lovely and the heater was warming the room nicely."

This was my description of the Imady salon as I saw it for the first time. An "impersonal room", I called it and noted the absence of pictures and books. However, although it took me years to realize it, there was something more significant than books or pictures missing from that room and that was a photograph of Jowdat Effendi. A portrait of the deceased patriarch of the family is what has pride of place in almost every Damascene salon. Often the host or hostess will point out the picture and proudly tell you his name. Jowdat had been dead for two years when we arrived, but no picture of him hung in the salon, or in any room in the home. After all these years, the only member of the family who has put up his picture is me, the only one of the family who never lived with him or had to endure his temper.

Jowdat Effendi cast a long shadow. All of Jowdat's daughters, except Inayat, say that their father turned them against men and put them off marriage. Mohammed, to this day, cannot bear to hear loud voices or anyone shout in anger. He has spent his entire life trying to be many things his father was not: a hardworking professional dedicated to his job; a man who is a demonstrative father and husband; a man who speaks softly and who believes in solving disagreements politely and diplomatically.

Abdo simply says he cannot understand his father. He had every reason, says Abdo, to be happy: a loving wife, seven children, a nice home, but nothing could please him.

Tete spent almost her entire life trying to placate and soothe her volatile husband. Mohammed has always claimed that his father loved his mother dearly and probably this is true. The trouble was that he didn't know how to show it and her life with him was one crisis after another. Nevertheless, Tete gave me the impression that she viewed his ungovernable temper as an affliction he could not help and she made it clear she had loved him.

Like a man caught in a time warp, Jowdat Effendi was an anomaly; a nineteenth century Damascene notable trapped in the twentieth century. Along with sporting a large old-fashioned handlebar mustache most of his life, Jowdat never whole-heartedly adopted a modern or Western way of dressing, but stubbornly clung to the old Damascene notable's garb: a tarboosh and the *imbaz*, an ankle-length white sateen tunic, that is wrapped like a bathrobe and secured at the waist by a wide belt. However, according to family photographs, Jowdat did wear a Western frock coat for formal occasions in his younger days, but the Arab *sherwal* (baggy trousers) was his riding costume.

To the end of his days Jowdat Effendi told time in the old Arab way. Sunset was always twelve o'clock, the end of one day and the beginning of a new day. Each day he would adjust his watch a few minutes ahead or back depending on the time of sunset. He also never stopped using the *Hijri* calendar (dated from the Prophet's *Hijra* or emigration from Mecca to Medina) with its year based on lunar months although Syria adopted the Western calendar around 1920.

Jowdat Effendi was a man who, literally and figuratively, outlived his time. He might have been a much happier man and have fitted into society more contentedly if he had lived out his days in the nineteenth century. One of the most traumatic changes for him was the abrupt arrival of the automobile age. Horses had been his whole world and he was a gifted breeder of horses. This is what he did best and suddenly his talent had no value. Nothing ever replaced this passion of his once horses faded from the scene.

When Jowdat Effendi lost his horses, he also lost his mobility and freedom. On horseback he had ranged freely far and wide – all the way to Palestine - from the confining city and his stifling family of numerous females. Since he never owned a car or learned to drive, when he sold his last horse, he was never to experience this freedom again.

The world into which he had been born, the world which he understood and in which he was comfortable, had vanished along with its habits and traditions and ways of doing things and he never adjusted to the new ways. To hold down a job or to earn one's living were totally alien concepts to him. Of course, money, his rightful inheritance, would have made all the difference, but he was fated to worry about money to the end of his days. He had been reared in comfort as an aristocrat and instilled with pride in his heritage and he was quite unprepared for the way his life turned out. Sometimes it is said of a man that "he was born before his time." I believe Jowdat Effendi was a man who was born too late.

14.

The '67 War and After

In November of 1966, Susu came down with paratyphoid and, before she had completely recovered, she woke up one day with jaundice and was diagnosed this time with viral hepatitis. Dr. Oum al-Khair insisted we all, even baby Omar, get gamma globulin shots to prevent hepatitis from spreading throughout the family.

In the midst of this, the DCS, the "American School", phoned me and said their music teacher had suddenly quit with the Christmas program only a few weeks away and begged me to take over. My friend, Mrs. Bitar, was no longer the principal, but I felt I couldn't let the school down. I began teaching two mornings a week, although with a sick child, it was not easy. If I had known then what lay ahead, I would never have accepted the job.

My first day at the school, I got the bad news that, since the piano was terribly out of tune, the last music teacher had been using an "autoharp" for her classes. The autoharp was a weird musical instrument I had never seen before, but the school expected me to learn to play it well enough to accompany the children at their program in a month. I foolishly took up the challenge and practiced until I had mastered it.

Meanwhile, no sooner did Susu recover than I turned as yellow as she had been. The doctor said I probably had contracted hepatitis before I had the shot, but assured me the gamma globulin would make it a lighter case. I was so tired and depressed. It seemed we went from one illness to another and I really thought it should be someone else's turn by now.

I missed so many days at school that I didn't know how a Christmas program could be thrown together, but with the help of one of the DCS teachers and many extra rehearsals when I recovered, the Christmas program was a success.

However, by January, I was out of a job! When hepatitis forced me to miss classes, I was grateful to the teacher who rehearsed the children in my absence, never suspecting she was hoping to replace me – for this is what she had in mind. She made her proposal to the principal after Christmas and he agreed to give her the music classes. Perhaps the idea was to save money by having one of his staff take on the extra work of music teacher. Whatever the case, the principal simply told me they didn't need me any more. After helping them out at great inconvenience to myself, I thought I at least deserved a month's notice, but without Mrs. Bitar, this was a different school, and I told myself I was well out of it.

On the heels of losing my job, the possibility of a trip to the States turned up. The World Bank was running the same course Mohammed had missed out on the year before and once again he was nominated to attend. I had a cynical feeling all along that it would never come to pass so, when the Prime Minister refused Mohammed permission to go, I wasn't as disappointed as the previous year. Around the same time the trip fell through, Mohammed's seventh year of service finished, leaving only one year owed to the government.

Mother was very disappointed when our trip to the States didn't materialize and kept insisting we should come in the summer. I didn't need much convincing and this time Mohammed gave his blessing and said he would arrange the trip for me and the children. He started making the rounds of the travel agents and airline offices and soon all was ready.

We had airline tickets to New York for June 9th, but on the 5th of June, 1967, Israel attacked Syria and Egypt and all the airports closed. We could hear the heavy artillery and bombing in the distance as a fierce battle raged on the Golan Heights between the Israelis with their up-to-date weapons and planes and the Syrians who made up in courage what they lacked in technology. The Israelis had to fight a bloody war for every inch of Syrian land they overran. To intimidate the Damascenes, they broadcast on the radio, "We had breakfast in the Golan Heights and will have lunch in Damascus."

When Riad heard this, she took down her father's sword from the wardrobe and swung it bravely. "If the Israelis attack us," she said, "I'll take a few of them with me when they kill me!"

A year earlier, my in-laws had hired a little girl named Sheeha from a village in the Golan Heights. Now that the Israelis had invaded, she was terrified for the safety of her family and cried inconsolably. We kept telling her that her family would not wait for the enemy to arrive, but were probably already on their way to Damascus. This cheered her up until she remembered her grandmother.

"My old Tete will be left behind because she can't walk," said Sheeha and cried some more.

By evening, refugees began arriving in the city. All the schools were opened as shelters for them and, when they were full, the overflow moved into unfinished apartment buildings. The city of Kuneitra and all the villages around it were emptied as the Israeli army advanced. The refugees were welcomed with open arms in Damascus and for weeks the women of the city, including Kawsar, cooked double the amount of food they usually prepared and gave half to the refugees. The Damascenes knew just how to cope since this was 1948 all over again when refugees poured into Syria from Palestine.

Eventually, Sheeha's father showed up and said all members of the family were safe in Damascus, except for the Tete. It would be a month before some of her sons were able to go back and get the old lady. Like most of the Syrians of the Golan, Sheeha's family lost their farmhouse and land and were permanently displaced. They ended up in a makeshift camp near Damascus, living for a short time on UN handouts. The Golan was occupied by Israel, but it was Syria that was excoriated in the international press.

When the war started, mail service in or out of the country stopped and I knew Mother must be worried about us. Luckily, some relatives were driving to Turkey and offered to mail a letter to Mother from Istanbul. In this way, I got word out that we were safe and were still coming whenever the airports opened. It was not until June 28th that we were able to go to Lebanon by taxi and take off from Beirut Airport.

Flying to New York four and a half years earlier, I had felt I was going home. This time, I felt I was leaving home. When we landed at Kennedy Airport, I asked the children, "Who's going to be happy to see Mommy?"

Loyal little Muna countered right away with, "Who's going to be sad and miss my Baba?"

We had a wonderful four-month visit with my family. There had been no American cousins the last time we had come and now there were four: Jan and Bob's Andy and Elizabeth and Jo and Dave's Andrea and Amy. Amy and Omar were only three months apart and shared playpens and toys that summer. Muna started kindergarten at Mother's old school next door, and Susu began fifth grade at my old elementary school.

Susu told me after we were back in Damascus, that the whole time she was in Palisades she kept telling herself, "It's real – it's real. But," she continued, "that it didn't do any good. Now, it's all just a dream."

The best part of this summer was that in these four months Jo and I became close. Both of us had always gotten along with Jan, but Jo and I had never been very compatible until this wonderful summer. I'll always remember how Jo hugged me good-bye and choked out through her tears, "I've got a sister."

Outside my loving family, I was shocked at the widespread lack of sympathy Americans had for the Arab refugees of the 1967 War. Comedians mocked the Arabs on television and anti-Arab hostility in the media was common. It is true I was asked to speak in my brother-in-law's church[9] in Cambridge, Massachusetts to help raise money for Arab refugees, and found a sympathetic response, but this was the exception.

We stayed in Palisades until the end of October, and when we finally arrived in Damascus, Mohammed, the aunties and Tete were overjoyed to welcome us home. In no time, the girls were speaking Arabic again and back in their old school.

There was no American Embassy in Damascus, now. After the war, America cut diplomatic relations with Syria and its embassy remained closed for the next six years. People often asked me – still ask me - what it was like for an American in Damascus during these years. I can say without hesitation I never ran into any hostility because of my nationality. Syrians, unlike many Americans I met on my visit in the summer of 1967, are careful to distinguish between individuals and governments. Syrians will say they don't approve of the American government's foreign policy, but will go on to say they have nothing against me or any Americans and, in fact, that they really like Americans. Despite the depressing international situation of Syra and the Middle East, it was a happy time for us personally. I wrote Mother. "Mohammed and I are happy these days, I think happier than we've ever been."

March 1, 1968 was the wonderful day when Mohammed's obligatory eight years of service were up. At last, the government released the family building which it had been holding as a guarantee against Mohammed completing his service. Not only was the threat removed of losing our building, but now Mohammed was free to resign, leave the country and look for work outside. We felt as though a dark cloud had been lifted from our lives.

That summer Mohammed was invited to attend an Arab Economic Planners Conference in Beirut and I tagged along. I worried that Omar would drive Kawsar crazy, but it was actually ten-year-old Susu and eleven-year-old cousin May who ended up taking care of him. They changed him, fed him, made his bottles and he was happy with all the attention. Meanwhile, I got to wander around Beirut, haunt the bookstores, do some shopping and take in a movie.

On our return, Mohammed took a few days off and, since the children had missed out on the trip to Beirut, we took them to Zebadani, a mountain resort town near the border with Lebanon. While there, the proprietor of our hotel told me I should go visit the "American lady with three children who lives just up the road in a cherry orchard." It sounded like a good idea, so I rounded up my kids and did just that. As we reached the gate, several children close in age to mine, came whooping and running down the driveway to greet us. They carted off my children to show

9 Bob was assistant pastor at this Presbyterian church while attending Harvard Divinity School.

them around and soon all six were chattering away like old friends, switching from Arabic to English and back seamlessly. The moment I saw their mother, Laura, coming out to welcome me, I realized I had met her six years earlier but somehow we had lost track of each other.

In addition to the orchard in Zebadani where Laura and the children spent their summers, her Syrian husband, Zaid Dalati, had a farm in the Ghouta and their permanent home was in Mohajareen, not too far from us. What a lucky day it was that I met Laura once again. She was someone after my own heart, someone who loved to read as much as I did, who had a wonderful sense of humor and who shared my positive outlook on life in Damascus.

The same day we became reacquainted, Laura invited us to Zebadani the next Friday and said to bring any of our friends. We accepted gladly and took along a young couple who lived near us in Mohajareen: Sharon from Ohio and her husband who worked with Mohammed. Tall, beautiful Sharon became my good friend and was the one who introduced me to all the pop music of the sixties I had missed out on.

We soon learned that every Friday, Zaid and Laura had open house in Zebadani; come one, come all. They threw open their doors and everyone - young and old, friends and friends of friends - was welcome. "*Ahlan wa sahlan*," they would say with a smile as yet another car drew up and another family piled out bearing their contribution to the communal meal.

Our Friday trips to the Dalatis in Zebadani became an established routine in our family and it was there we met many couples who became our friends. The previous autumn we had been delighted to welcome back our Scottish friend, Janette, her Syrian husband Souad and their children. Souad had decided he would be happier in Damascus than in Glasgow, after all. We introduced them to the Dalatis and soon they became part of the regular crowd that got together Fridays in Zebadani. Fun-loving Janette was a very welcome addition to our group and kept us laughing with her irrepressible jokes told in her sing song Glaswegian accent.

There was an unpopular high government official in Syria at this time, we will call him "Abu Hisham", whose short height and thin physique had sparked many jokes. Of course, Janette had a fund of them and one went something like this:

Abu Hisham was out walking one day when a tall, beautiful blonde caught his eye and invited him home with her. He could hardly believe his good luck. She took him straight into her bedroom and told him to take off his shirt and his trousers which he quickly did. As he sat expectantly on her bed in his underwear, she suddenly shouted to her children to come into the room.

"Look, children!" she said pointing at Abu Hisham's scrawny frame. "*This* is how you will look when you grow up if you don't drink your milk!"

About the time I met Laura, Anna Maria and her family left Syria. Her husband got a job with the Arab League and they went with their five children to live in Cairo. At least, unlike all other friends who had left, they would be coming back regularly to Damascus for vacations.

The summer of 1968, Mohammed was appointed Deputy Minister of Planning and the children were thrilled to see him several times on television. Mohammed himself had mixed feelings about this promotion. Of course he was pleased, but Mohammed was ambitious and now he was afraid he had hit the glass ceiling. As he said many times, with a socialist government in Syria, there was no possibility of his becoming a cabinet minister, he had too many strikes against him: he was not a Baathist party member, he was a Damascene of the old "notable" and religious land owning class - which this government looked upon with suspicion - and finally, he had an American education and an American wife. A few ministers had foreign wives, but they were mostly from the Soviet Union and the countries of Eastern Europe.

At the end of August, Mohammed came down with another case of Bell's palsy. Five years earlier it had been the right side of his face that was affected; this time it was the left. It was a blow, but we were very encouraged when he began to recover much faster than last time; every day we could see an improvement.

The government offered to send him for medical treatment to the "friendly country" of his choice and he decided on the Soviet Union. Mohammed ended up in the Diplomat's Hospital in Moscow and was treated with cortisone, infra-red light treatment, electric shock, facial exercises and massage.

He came back loaded down with presents for everyone and looking completely cured. The Russian doctors told him to continue doing the exercises they taught him, to strengthen his facial muscles and for months he did them faithfully three times a day in front of a mirror. Eventually, even the side of his face affected five years earlier improved.

Omar, at two and a half, was a self-reliant little boy. If Muna hit him or tried to take his toys, he did not complain to me, but fought right back, sometimes fiercely enough to make Muna run. But he seldom started trouble without provocation. He was, by turns, lovable and exasperating. He broke at least one thing a day and usually blamed it on someone else. He would come and show me a broken toy and say, "Look! Break it! Muna [or Khali Suad or Susu] did it! Bad Muna!" or "Bad Khali Suad!"

Of course, Suad was still with us. Although she was not very motherly, having never been mothered herself, my children became very fond of her. They called her, still call her, "Khali Suad". In time, almost unwillingly, she began to warm up to the children, but Omar was always her favorite. Suad called Muna *malekay b'tenekay*, the "queen of the tin can", but Omar was always *habeebi*, my darling.

He was sometimes very naughty to her; he'd snatch off her scarf and dump it in her pail of water or walk on her clean floors with muddy shoes, but he was always forgiven. Suad saved Omar from many a well-deserved spanking by picking him up and dashing upstairs to the aunties with him under her arm. There, she and the aunties would hide him until his crime was forgotten.

Fall weather started; warm at noon, but chilly enough at night to light our *sobas*. It was the fig season and whenever we went to Zebadani, we would stop along the way to buy the small, sweet figs called *teen Baal*. Six thousand years ago in Syria, Baal was worshipped as the god of rain and the figs that "Baal watered", that is, those from un-irrigated trees, were called "the figs of Baal". Amazingly, this ancient name still persists.

In no time, winter was upon us and Mohammed was off on a ten-day trip to East Berlin. I worried because cold weather was bad for his face, but he promised to bundle up and got home around Christmas time with no ill effects.

We had Christmas dinner at Laura and Zaid's along with three other American/Syrian couples and the next day I had a party for fourteen children. I turned them loose at my dining room table with food coloring and icing to decorate my Christmas cookies and gingerbread men. We ended up with some very non-traditional purple, black, orange and blue "Picasso" cookies and the children had a grand time.

This year our tree was the biggest ever, perhaps fourteen feet high and we kept it up well into January. Every time I decided to take it down, Mohammed would say it still looked pretty and then I'd think of all the work involved, including taking the tinsel down strand by strand to re-use the next year, and I'd agree to another day or so.

The month of February, 1969, brought some abnormally wet weather to Damascus. Day after day the rain came down until it seemed it was going to rain the Biblical forty days and forty nights. The little Barada River overflowed its banks and Marjay Square and the street running parallel to the river were inundated with up to two feet of water. The flood didn't last long, but one night, while it was at its highest, our new friends, the Buraks, took us down in their car to see the unusual sight.

These two, Mair, a beautiful, blonde Welsh girl and her Syrian husband, Nizar, who was an ophthalmologist, seemed a charmed couple to us. They were an extraordinary pair blessed with exceptional good looks, two dear little boys, a beautiful home and plenty of money all of which might make some in their shoes self-satisfied and aloof – but not the friendly and unaffected Mair and Nizar.

Mohammed met Mair and her English friend, Maureen, in the waiting room of Dr. Oum Al Khair one day when, for some reason I forget, he, and not I, was taking

Susu for a vaccination. They heard him speaking English with Susu and friendly Mair struck up a conversation. That was the beginning of our friendship and, before long, they invited us to their home one evening and the next week we had them over. Mair had a nice voice and we often ended up singing around the piano when she and her husband visited us.

It was no surprise, but still very disheartening, when Rose and Riyad announced they were taking their children and going to live in the States. They had talked about it for some time and we knew Riyad had obtained an immigrant visa. I would sorely miss Rose who had shared so many good and bad times with me and I had a good cry after she left. For years I could not pass her old apartment building without remembering her and missing her. In fact, Damascus was filling up with "ghost buildings", apartment buildings haunted by the spirits of dear friends of mine who once lived in them.

Not long after Rose's departure, Sharon and her husband abruptly left. They went without a word to anyone except me and I only knew twenty-four hours before. It really was a blow. Sharon came to say good-bye with her collection of sixties hit music – song books and records – which she gave me "to remember her by". As if I would forget her.

By now, I'd lost count of how many friends had left and you would think I'd become used to it, but I had not. Sometimes I told myself I should keep my friends at arm's length and never get too close or too fond of anyone, but I made the same mistake over and over again in the coming years.

15.

"To God is the Homecoming"[10]

The family moved to the downstairs apartment early this year in anticipation of hot weather and because, on the infrequent occasions Tete left the building, one flight of stairs was all she could manage. Although her mind had recovered remarkably after her illness last year, physically she had grown frailer and weaker. When she got sick shortly after my birthday in April, we assumed it was the usual asthma attack she had every spring and weren't concerned until the Friday she asked for a doctor to come to the house. This worried us because usually she was very reluctant to see a doctor. The doctor came and said she had pneumonia and prescribed antibiotics, but nothing for her pain, although relief from pain was what she wanted more than anything.

The next day, two American-trained doctors came and said she might die at any moment and that she should be in a hospital. This she would not even consider so Mohammed got an oxygen tank to the house and she was given glucose intravenously. The doctors gave her a shot of some painkiller, but it didn't do much good. They said ordinarily they gave morphine for severe pain, but in Tete's case they worried it could be fatal.

The relentless pain didn't let her sleep more than a few minutes at a time and she was unable to lie down and had to be propped up with pillows. On Sunday, Lamat came to help spell Riad and Kawsar who'd had little sleep since Friday. By this time, I'm sure Tete knew she was dying. More than once she said, "No more medicine; let me die."

But she was still thinking of others. On Monday morning, Mart Khalo came and, after she left, Tete scolded Kawsar for not inviting her for lunch. Throughout

10 *The Koran Interpreted*: 35:18 (A. J. Arberry translation, Touchstone, 1955).

the day Tete's condition worsened and that night, upstairs in our bedroom, we could hear her labored breathing. In fact, this agonizing sound could be heard in every room of the building; you could not escape it. We lay in bed holding our own breath, waiting for what seemed like an eternity to hear her next breath. We were praying for each breath, willing each breath, in an awful dread of unthinkable silence.

The next day, the entire family assembled in the courtyard: her seven children; her twelve grandchildren; her sister, Yezda; many nephews and nieces; her three sons-in-law; her sister-in-law, Mart Khalo; and her only daughter-in-law - me. Khalo Ghaleb, her brother, was ill himself and unable to come. We knew this was a crisis and everyone was hoping and praying for a miracle. Tete herself was typically worrying whether the numerous relatives gathered in the courtyard had been served coffee.

That afternoon, I sat beside her in her bedroom and waited for the doctor who was expected at eight. She seemed so frail and sick I remember wondering if any medicine on earth could ever make her well. When the doctor came we told him about Tete's terrible night and begged him to ease her pain.

When the doctor said he would give her an injection I held her hand and she clung tightly to mine and said imploringly, "Please, Lulu..." Immediately after the injection, she began to gasp for breath and we knew it was morphine. The rest I don't remember clearly. I think I saw her fall backwards on the bed and the doctor trying to massage her heart. I ran from the room crying, leaving her with Mohammed and Abdo. Mohammed shut the door, but when everyone saw me run out in tears, they pushed into the room. I turned and looked back and could not believe what I saw. Instead of dear Tete who only seconds before had bravely smiled at the doctor as he joked with her about what she would cook for him when she got better, there was only a small, crumpled figure lying inert on the bed. Eyes that could no longer see, ears that could no longer hear, her voice and smile gone forever - but at last she was beyond the reach of brutal pain.

No one is ever ready for the finality of death. I cried and all around me were the heartbroken cries of Tete's bereft children crying out for her - "Immi, *ya* immi!" The day we had feared for so long had really come.

But there was little time to indulge our grief. Tete's funeral would take place the next day, as customary, and there was much to do. There are no funeral parlors in Syria; the family carries out all the arrangements. First, we removed everything from Tete's bedroom except her bed and then Kawsar took down from the wardrobe a black velvet embroidered bedspread and a sheer coverlet embroidered with silk thread which were kept for this purpose. Tete was covered with these and a Qur'an was placed at the head of the bed.

Then we began stripping the house upstairs and downstairs. Pictures and mirrors were taken from the walls and pots of geraniums and anything else red was put away. Abdo ordered a funeral dinner for eighty from a catering service and hired folding tables and chairs for the guests. The nephews ordered the death notices from the printer and, before dawn, they drove all over the city posting them on telephone poles, buildings and walls. To this day, this is still the custom. People learn of someone's death in Damascus, not from a newspaper obituary or from a phone call, but from the posted death notices.

That night, seven-year old Muna, who dearly loved her grandmother, insisted on kissing her good-bye. They had already tied her jaw so I only uncovered the back of her head and Muna kissed Tete on her pretty white hair. I kissed her good-bye, too. Inayat and Riad took turns keeping vigil beside her until morning, reciting the Qur'an and praying.

The next morning, Kawsar said, as a daughter-in-law, I could wear a gray or navy blue dress, but I chose to wear black like Kawsar and Riad and it would be for forty days, not just for the funeral. One of the cousins went out and bought black nylons for Kawsar and Riad and gray for the rest of us. All the women, except me, had on hand the long, white, chiffon scarf they wear in an *asreeyeh,* the women's condolence reception. Kawsar said I would be sitting with the family in Tete's *asreeyeh* and handed me a scarf. As I took it, I felt it was one more sign that I truly belonged to this family and this society.

Around noon the hearse arrived - not a black limousine, but an ordinary white van - bringing the woman who washes the body. Inayat supervised the washing and afterwards the two women perfumed Tete's body with various scents and wrapped her in a shroud.

Finally, Mohammed, his eyes brimming with tears, carried her frail, little body and placed it in the coffin which was then draped with a black velvet covering embroidered in gold thread with verses from the Qur'an. At the head of the coffin was placed a folded towel covered with another velvet cloth to indicate the deceased was a woman. For a man, a tarboosh would be placed on the coffin.

Everything was set and the coffin was carried down the stairs. I remembered the neighbors' wild, frenzied shrieking when their father's coffin was carried out, but Tete left her house for the last time in a dignified manner. There were plenty of tears, but no hysterics.

The coffin was put into the hearse which by now was completely blanketed with floral wreaths sent by friends and relatives. While the hearse drove slowly through the narrow streets of Mohajareen, Tete's name and verses from the Qur'an were broadcast over its loudspeaker and people gathered on their balconies to learn who had died. As is customary, only the men and boys made this last trip with Tete and a procession of their cars followed the van, first to the neighborhood mosque for the funeral prayers and then on to the cemetery. Once there, Mohammed lifted her out of the coffin and, with help from some others, carried her to her grave next to Jowdat Effendi. The final prayers were read and then her body, neither embalmed nor placed in a casket, was laid to rest in the earth.

After the burial, the men returned for the traditional funeral dinner. The tables were set for forty men in our home and forty women in Tete's apartment. We didn't have to do a thing; the caterers did it all.

Khalo, who was old and frail himself was devastated when he heard the news of his beloved sister's death. He cried, perhaps remembering with guilt, his shady transactions with Tete's land.

That night began the first *timsayeh* or the men's reception. For three nights Khalo, Mohammed, Abdo, Wahid Beyk and other close male relatives received men who came to give their condolences. Several of Tete's young nephews stood outside the open door of the apartment and ushered the men in. The usual greetings were dispensed with and only a set expression of sympathy and its response were exchanged. Two sheikhs came to recite the Qur'an for the duration of the *timsayeh*, which lasted about three hours, and a man was hired to make and serve bitter coffee. Everyone sat in silence and visitors only stayed ten or fifteen minutes. When the visitors entered and when they departed, the men of the family stood up for them. Probably sixty men came to pay their respects each night.

Before dawn of the next morning, ten of us, including Mohammed, Abdo and me, went to visit Tete's grave in that depressing cemetery I hated. A sheikh was asked to come and recite verses of the Qur'an and say the prayers for the dead as we stood around her tomb. We made three of these pre-dawn visits and I found it hard to believe that dear Tete was lying under that marble tomb in that grim place.

The day after the funeral, the first women's reception, the *asreeyeh*, was held, beginning when the afternoon prayer was called and endng at the sunset prayer. The two sheikhs who came to recite the Qur'an sat in the next room where they could not see us, but we could hear them.

So began my first *asreeyeh*. We were about twenty-five women sitting in a rough semi-circle, our chairs pushed against three walls of the large rectangular salon in Tete's apartment. All of us wore long white scarves loosely draped on our heads except for Riad and Kawsar who wore black because, as unmarried daughters, they were the principal mourners. They also sat in the place of honor at the far end of the room in the middle of the semi-circle of women and facing the entrance. Three chairs facing Riad and Kawsar were placed near the entrance for the visitors.

The door of the apartment was left ajar so no doorbell would disturb the *asreeyeh*, just as was done for the *timsayeh*. Tete's young nieces stood outside our room and ushered the callers in, lifting aside the sheer curtain put up in the doorway for the occasion. The women entered two or three at a time, or occasionally, one woman alone and their visits were very brief, not much more than a minute or two: time to enter, sit, silently recite three times the short Qur'anic verse that begins, *Qul hua Allahu ahad* ...Say, God is One...", stand up and leave.

My friend, Janette, used to tell new, green foreigners worried about making their first *asreeyeh* visit: "Walk in, sit down, count slowly to forty and then get up and walk out". I could add that most visitors keep their eyes cast down and do not stare at the bereaved.

When the visitors entered, we rose in unison and then sat when they sat. When they left, we stood up and sat down again. There even was a rule for how the visitors should file in and out and where they should sit: they entered and left in descending order of their ages, that is, the oldest was first in, first out and her chair was the farthest from the door. When callers made a mistake, someone in our group would shake her head after they left and whisper, "They probably aren't from Damascus." Each city in Syria had, and still has, its own way of doing things, including its own funeral traditions.

The curtains were drawn in the room and the lights were not lit. I thought of my mother's expression, "dim, religious light". Many visitors came and our standing and sitting went on and on. It was hypnotic and eventually tiring and I was glad when, now and then during a lull between visitors, one of Tete's nieces served us glasses of water or bitter coffee. As the afternoon slowly wore on, two things kept flashing through my head: a vision of Tete holding my hand just before she died and an old English folksong, particularly the line that went, "O, God forbid that any such thing/ Should ever pass by my side".

Meanwhile, all the women's lips were constantly moving as they told their beads, repeating a short prayer. Their goal was to say one hundred thousand of these prayers for Tete and one of the women kept track of the number with two safety pins on her prayer beads; one for the hundreds and one for the thousands. Someone would quietly tell her, "five hundred" and she would move the safety pin for "hundreds" over five beads.

Before the *asreeyeh* began, Kawsar told me if a visitor should come especially for my sake, I should get up and follow the visitor out of the room and thank her for coming and, in fact, that first day several of my friends did come and I got up for them.

I have now sat in many *asreeyehs* and have made countless condolence visits and, while I found the traditions strange at first, as time passed, I felt more and more comfortable with them. I like being able to show my sympathy by making a silent visit. Words of condolence are always inadequate, but it is comforting to see your friends and relatives coming to share your sorrow in silence. I even came to believe that all the funeral arrangements you must carry out when a family member dies serve a purpose. Just when you are most devastated and heartbroken, you must pull yourself together, get things done and face people. It helps get you through the shock of those first terrible days.

The third day after Tete died, we were all sitting in her dining room having a late supper while Abdo and Mohammed told us who had come that night to the men's reception. Abdo started describing how a cousin who had a big bottom waddled into the room and, as he was talking, his face crinkled up and he tried in vain to stifle his laughter. Suddenly he stood up and gave an uninhibited and very funny impersonation of the man and we all burst out laughing. We laughed and laughed helplessly until our sides hurt and we were gasping for breath and still we laughed some more, until, literally, we cried. This flood of laughter flushed all the tension and grief out of our systems and left us limp. Perhaps we should have felt guilty afterwards, but actually we felt better. I remember being somewhat shocked, but I felt Tete would understand.

The next day dawned and our sadness returned. Of course, we were really sad for ourselves. As Riad said, "We didn't have enough of her." However, no one who loved Tete could have wanted her to go on in such pain. Mohammed said the fact the doctor was there and couldn't save her and the fact that her last days were spent in agony were clear signs from God that her time was up; that there was nothing more we could have done. Her death was *maktoub*.

For forty days after Tete's death we were in mourning, wearing somber clothes and refraining from listening to music or attending any kind of celebration. Tete had died on a Tuesday, and, as was customary, Kawsar and Riad held open house for women every Tuesday afternoon in her memory. Friends and relatives flocked to these gatherings to remember her and pray for her. However, her death marked the end of an era. The extended family had lost its center and, from this time on, we saw less and less of the more distant relatives. The family grew smaller.

In accordance with Damascus traditions, the family held a solemn observance of the fortieth day after Tete's death by inviting the *maylaweeyeh*[11] to the house to perform their ritual dance. These "whirling dervishes", as they are called in the West, began their dance in a stately manner to the beat of a drum and chanted hymns. The pace of the music gradually picked up and they began to revolve, slowly at first. Gradually, they reached a trancelike state and whirled faster and faster, their circle skirts billowing straight out from their waists like huge, white, blossoming flowers. All at once, the drumming ceased and they stopped spinning so abruptly their skirts swirled violently around their legs as they stamped one foot and then bowed, their feet rock solid to the floor with no hint of dizziness. I was spellbound.

When Tete's health began to fail, we all tried to stop her from "tiring herself" and were surprised when this upset her. We should have realized that caring for her

---

11 *Maylaweeyeh* is Damascene dialect for the standard Arabic word, *mawlawi*. The *mawlawi* are a Sufi order whose dance is part of their striving for spiritual enlightenment.

family was what gave her pride and self-respect. The idleness we tried to impose on her made her feel useless and unhappy. In the end, we let her do whatever she felt able to do.

Although Tete was born and raised in a patriarchal society and had no education herself, she held unusually enlightened notions. She would say, "These days girls go to school, just like boys, and women have jobs and earn money, just like men. Women no longer have to depend upon men to support them, so there is no longer any reason to prefer sons to daughters!" Tete loved her sons and grandsons, but no more than she loved her daughters and granddaughters.

What is even more unusual, her kind heart knew no boundaries. I remember watching an Egyptian war film on television with the family and there was a battle scene with Israeli soldiers dying right and left all over the screen. Abdo and Riad were cheering, but Tete looked ready to cry and said reprovingly in her gentle voice, "But they have mothers, too."

Another time it was grim news from Northern Ireland of fighting between Catholic and Protestant. Abdo explained to his mother what was going on and she looked shocked. "But they are both Christians. Why are are they killing each other?" she asked.

By her own choice, Tete died penniless. She insisted on distributing everything she owned to her children years before she died. She wanted to be sure it was all done correctly according to Islamic law and that no one would be cheated as her husband had been many years ago.

Over the years, in her self-effacing way, Tete had deftly calmed down her husband's outbursts and made each child and each grandchild believe he or she was her favorite. From my first day in Damascus, she accepted me and did everything to help me feel at home in my new life. She was a remarkable woman and I am glad I came to know and love her.

Khalo had taken Tete's death very hard and had not been well since then. About four months after his sister's death, he had a heart attack in the middle of the night and died very suddenly. Now, of the five Hawasli siblings, only Yezda, the youngest, was left.

Mother had just about decided she was not coming this summer, but when Tete died, we insisted and finally she changed her mind. On July 10th she arrived in Damascus for one month. My friends Laura, Emily and Kathy had tea parties for Mother and I took her on many trips down to the souk. It was a quiet visit and we spent many days just sitting with Kawsar, Riad and Abdo remembering Tete, crying a bit and comforting each other. Mother's visit did us all good.

The Fair opened the middle of September, not long after Mother left, and the big event this year was a musical at the outdoor theater featuring the Lebanese singer,

Fairouz. I was familiar with her beautiful voice from radio and television and was thrilled to see her perform on stage. I promised myself that someday we would take Mother to hear Fairouz sing.

Thanksgiving dinner this year was at our place with fourteen adults and fourteen children, counting us. There were Laura, Kathy, Emily and Mary with their husbands and children, plus two newly-married couples. We had to rearrange the entire apartment to accommodate the crowd. I baked three turkeys with Suad's help and everyone brought something. We had a lot to be thankful for, I thought, looking around the room at our friends and all the dear children.

In November, Mohammed and I took a group of UN experts from the World Food Program on a helicopter tour to the construction site of the Euphrates Dam. When I was still with FAO, I had done the voice-over for a UN documentary on the death and destruction caused by the 1964 flood of the Euphrates River. When the dam was finished it would permanently end the danger of flooding and provide electricity for the entire country.

On our way there, we flew slowly and so low we had a perfect view of everything beneath us. We passed over villages of "beehive houses"; a huge herd of camels which scattered when frightened by the noise of our helicopter; the great citadel looming over the city of Aleppo; the Euphrates River wandering lazily through the land and the green, palm-studded oasis of Palmyra arising improbably in the barren desert. As impressive as the ruins of Palmyra are, it was the city of Damascus at night which I would remember best, glowing like a jewel at the foot of Jebel Qassioun as we circled the city several times before landing.

Early in December, I began receiving Christmas cards and letters from many of my departed friends including Penny, Holly, Jill, Sharon, Anna Maria and Rose. Rose wrote me from Colorado that now she had all the "things" she was longing for in Damascus, but had no time to enjoy them. She said it was a rat race in the States and that I should appreciate life in Damascus where you have time for your children and your friends. The trouble is, I thought, the friends never stay.

It was always emotionally wrenching when a close friend left. We foreign wives in Syria, however unlike our backgrounds, all shared the same unusual challenge of living and raising our children in a very different culture from the one we left behind. Young women with small children form strong bonds with each other wherever they live, but in Damascus, our special circumstances made us especially close.

So it was that when a friend left, I would feel bereft and, truth to tell, a bit angry. I needed this friend, I depended upon her. How could she leave? - I would fume. Then, often as not, I would cry. But whether my friends left or stayed, my life here would have been far poorer without them.

16.

The Ten-Year Blues – and Beyond

In my first two years at NYU, the folk music craze was just beginning and on weekends Washington Square Park was filled with young people singing and strumming guitars. I was captivated and wished I could learn to play the guitar and even fantasized about singing folk songs in one of the little Greenwich Village coffee shops. Then Mohammed came along and all this was forgotten - until I met Suzy. Before Sharon left Syria, she introduced me to Suzy, a bright, spirited redhead from Texas who spoke Arabic fluently. Suzy also could sing and, best of all, she played the guitar. She knew dozens of folk songs and sang verse after verse by heart. I told her of my old dream and she said I should get myself a guitar.

Christmas and the Eid al-Kabeer came close together in 1969 which meant the children were showered with new clothes, presents and money for both holidays and so, when a Christmas money order arrived from Mother, I decided to be selfish and bought a guitar. Suzy generously offered to give me some lessons "just for the fun of it" and when I took her up on it, she was kind enough to claim she enjoyed teaching me. In my usual enthusiastic way, I plunged right in and began practicing every spare minute I had. Soon the two of us were playing and singing folk songs together. Suzy would play the complicated melodies and I would strum chords; she sang the tunes and I sang the harmony. Even a half-forgotten dream can come true, it seems.

However, as I spent more and more time practicing, I began to think I was using the guitar as an escape from everyone and everything: Mohammed, the children, Kawsar, Riad and Syria, especially Syria. I was very aware that March 1st would mark the tenth anniversary of my arrival in Syria. Ten years in Syria, I thought; I had spent a whole decade here. The number "ten" seemed such a significant number. I brooded over this and felt homesick, dissatisfied and out of sorts.

It seemed as if we were going to be here forever while so many of our friends had left or were planning to leave. On top of this was the fact that I wasn't the only one depressed: Mohammed and I both had what I called the "ten-year blues".

For months Mohammed had been under unrelenting stress in his ministry as a colleague carried out a vendetta against him. The trouble began in the winter of 1969/1970, when Dr. Bader (not his real name) a communist in the Ministry of Planning, tried to get several of his fellow party members hired in the ministry. When the Minister turned them down, Dr. Bader asked Mohammed, who was Deputy Minister, for help in getting them appointed, but Mohammed supported the Minister's decision. Dr. Bader was furious and in retaliation, he accused Mohammed of giving input-output tables, which he described as "classified information", to "foreigners".

Mohammed had, indeed, worked on preparing these tables. Since converting the coefficients for these tables required stupefyingly tedious calculations, a UN expert suggested having an employee from the Ministry take the data to Cairo where they had electronic data-processing machines. This was done and calculations that would have taken months to finish in Syria were completed there in a week. Although the Minister of Planning, as well as the Prime Minister, had authorized sending the data to Cairo, Dr. Bader carried out a smear campaign to discredit Mohammed whom he claimed had made "classified information" available to non-Syrians. Although there was no truth whatsoever in this charge, many ignorant, but highly placed, people in the government believed Dr. Bader. Some people even started calling Mohammed a traitor and saying he should be tried.

We felt we were living under a black cloud. It was a very unhappy period for Mohammed and me. I agonized with him and privately hoped this would push him to look for a job outside the country, preferably in the States, but bad as things were, Mohammed could not contemplate leaving.

On the contrary, life in Syria began to look very permanent although the constraints that had been keeping Mohammed here were gone. His government service had been completed, dear Tete was no longer with us and even Mohammed's job which had always been a great source of satisfaction to him was now a big headache.

More and more, there seemed to be no future in Syria for Western- educated officials, let alone those with American wives. As time passed and nothing improved, Mohammed became very discouraged and finally began thinking he should leave Syria. I didn't push; he would have to make up his own mind.

Some of our happiest times during the dark days of 1970 were our Fridays in Zebadani where Laura, Emily, Janette, Suzy and I could talk out all our frustrations, the children could run off their bottled up energy after being confined in an apartment all week and Mohammed could enjoy being with friends who distracted him from the problems he was facing at the ministry. Laura taught us to play an exciting Arab card game and when we got tired of cards, Suzy and I would take out our guitars and get everyone singing.

This gloomy spring Omar got chicken pox and mumps in rapid succession and next Suzy told me she would soon be going to Holland with her little boy to join her husband who had been granted a scholarship there. Suzy said she would be back in six months (it was actually much longer), but that didn't cheer me up. Our music had been a great source of comfort to me and I would miss it and miss Suzy. I had sworn not to get too friendly with anyone after Sharon left, but I never learned.

By June, the situation in the Ministry was no better and Mohammed asked me to write Mother and tell her that I was coming to scout around for a job for him, as Jill had done for Adel a few years back. We planned to have Suzy mail this letter when she got to Holland. But before I even began writing Mother that the "long ten years" were finally over, Mohammed changed his mind again. I felt like I was on a roller coaster. Living in Syria was much easier when I knew there was no possibility of leaving; uncertainty was harder to cope with.

But life went on and I even found it could still be very pleasant. That summer we had a lovely four-day vacation on the beach in Latakia with many of our friends. We were six American/Syrian couples with our twenty children all staying in adjacent bungalows facing the sea. The sea was calm since we were in a protected bay; you could go out half-a-mile and the water was still not deep. It was wonderful for the children and a carefree time for the adults. Under the sun, relaxing on the beach or frolicking in the warm, blue water it was possible to forget everything and just enjoy the moment. The unstable Middle East, trouble in the ministry, homesickness – all could be temporarily forgotten on this beautiful beach with these good friends.

Susu turned thirteen on July 5th, 1970 and was now taller than me and all her aunts and was inches taller than her cousin, Yasir, who was the same age. Yasir had replaced May as her best friend since May, at fourteen, was now a young lady whereas Susu was a Peter Pan child who resisted growing up. She and Yasir happily pursued what May scornfully called their "childish fun". Even Laura's daughter, Aida, who was only nine, was already eager to grow up and get married while Susu turned her back on the adult world.

Near the end of July, news of my father's death on Susu's thirteenth birthday reached Damascus and I cried. My tears surprised me and I told myself that I cried more for the tragic waste of all his talents and abilities and for his lonely death in a Veteran's Administration Hospital than anything else. But that is not true. I have a wonderful photograph in an antique oval frame of Father at the age of four. He is in a sailor suit with knickers and his golden curls hang to his shoulders. He once told me that this was the happiest day of his small life because he was on his way to the barber to have the hated curls cut off. His eyes are leveled straight at the camera, his thumbs are hooked in his belt and his legs are sturdily straddled in the most boyish stance possible to offset the girlish curls. He looks out at the world with such innocence and intelligence that it is almost painful for me to look at it – really look at it. The truth is, I loved him and I wish things had been different for him and for us all.

At the end of the summer, Mohammed finally managed to clear his name. He was able to prove that, far from being classified information, the figures used for input-output tables are openly published in the Statistical Abstract of Syria as well as in the Statistical Abstract of the Customs Department. Also, he got printed proof that the USA and the USSR along with all other UN member states, routinely publish these tables.

After all Dr.Bader's damaging accusations had been shown to be false, the man got no more punishment than a slap on the wrist because, as a communist, he had a foreign government backing him. He was merely transferred from the Ministry of Planning to another ministry, not fired as he really deserved.

When school opened in the fall, Susu entered eighth grade, Muna third grade and Omar started kindergarten. The first week of school, Omar came home upset. He said his teacher had asked the children what their mothers did and that he didn't know what to say because as he told me, "I didn't want the teacher to know my Mama is illiterate." Apparently, being able to read English didn't count with Omar. In any case, it was a wake-up call for me. I had been thinking of studying Arabic and now I decided the time had come. Two new friends were signing up for a course connected with Damascus University and I quickly registered with them.

A new challenge always inspired and energized me and I guess the suspicion that I might be staying in Syria forever made me think it would be good to be able to read and write Arabic. So I began.

I found it a daunting undertaking although we had an excellent teacher. One shock was that much of the Arabic I spoke so fluently was not standard Arabic. I was constantly being told by the teacher, "that is not an Arabic word." How frustrating it was to try to acquire standard Arabic on top of my Damascus dialect. One sad result was that as I learned grammar and "correct" words, I lost some of my carefree fluency. I began to worry about grammar mistakes and this made me self-conscious and slowed me down. But at last I was able to read Arabic and could look up words in the dictionary. That made it all worthwhile. We had fifteen hours of class a week with three hours of homework every night. Susu helped me with my assignments and went over the weekly "essays" we had to write. Even with her help, mine came back covered in red pencil, but I persisted.

On November 16th of 1970, Hafiz Assad, the Minister of Defence and head of the Air Force, took over the government in a bloodless coup he called a "corrective movement". Mohammed got a new Minister of Planning and the country was mostly pleased with Assad's takeover. The new leader, who was a Baathist like the people he overthrew, began his rule by reaching out to those who had felt for some time that the country was run by people who only had their own interests at heart. He traveled around the country stressing the need for reconciliation and unity. Prices of basic foods were cut, the heavy hand of the security services was eased and a more liberal era was ushered in. Mohammed had a personal reason to be pleased: the new president did not trust the communists who had been Mohammed's bitter enemies and their influence was now quite diminished.

1971 began with a gala New Year's Eve party we had at our house for all our friends. Dinner was a joint affair and I contributed a roasted turkey and Suad's good *kibbeh*. We danced, even Mohammed, everything from the latest shake to the Arabic *debke* (a foot stamping line dance).

A few days after our New Year's party, Mother had a cataract operation and had to stay in the hospital for eight days because neither of my sisters was free to go home with her. Jo had her hands full with her two little girls and a colicky new baby boy and Jan was living in Chicago. Of course, I was in Damascus feeling guilty and wishing I were nearby.

In 1960, when I left New York, I naturally worried about what going to Syria might entail; about how my in–laws would receive me, if I would be homesick and if I could learn Arabic. All my worries were about myself; it never crossed my mind to be concerned about my active, independent mother with her two fulfilling jobs. It never occurred to me then that, as the years passed and Mother grew older, she might need me, and I would be seven thousand miles away. Jo and Dave, who were only fifteen minutes away by car, did everything they could for Mother, but they had three small children and Dave's elderly parents to cope with as well. There were to be many times in the coming years when I wished I could have been of more help to Mother.

In February, we phoned Mother on her birthday to ask how she was doing after her operation. We shouted at each other for a minute or two in the unsatisfactory manner of international phone calls some thirty odd years ago. Then, two months later, came more bad news. Mother had fallen and broken three bones in her foot. When Kawsar heard, she said that if *she* had been with Mother, this would never have happened. And, true enough, whenever the two of them walked together in the city, Kawsar would take Mother's arm and protectively steer her around, telling her to mind her steps if there was a pothole or a curb. Mother had always felt this concern was unnecessary, but after her fall, she may have had second thoughts.

Mother's cast came off after six weeks and we were glad to hear that she was still coming in July for her usual month. We were also relieved that this time she would not be alone, but would be flying with a friend, a young Syrian woman whose parents were our neighbors in Mohajareen.

Good news, bad news; another American friend and her family went to the States in the spring and said they did not plan to return, but Suzy and her family came back in April with a new baby boy. Since last summer, I had been working my way through the Joan Baez songbook and I was eager to show Suzy what folk songs I had learned to play.

In May, we got together with some friends on the occasion of the Prophet's birthday. This was usually celebrated in Damascus by a recitation of the birth and life of the Prophet, Qur'anic verses, prayer and song. However, we had a cake and the children insisted on candles and singing Happy Birthday. The men were slightly scandalized and I wouldn't be surprised if it was the first time in Islam that anyone had celebrated the Prophet's birthday in this way.

In June, Susu, Muna and I had our final exams and we all passed. I was so exhausted from my demanding Arabic class, that I wasn't sure I would sign up for the second year. As soon as school was out, Laura, Zaid and their three children went to the States and we and all the old "Zebadani gang" missed them sorely. Laura said they would be back in time for school in September, but I worried that we might never see them again. In fact, they did not come back until January of the next year by which time I had lost all hope of their returning.

On July 15th Mother made her fourth visit to Damascus and Wahid Beyk drove us to pick her up from the airport. As his car drew up in front of the family building, Kawsar and Riad were leaning out of the windows, waving at Mother with smiling faces and the children were running down the stairs shouting, "Mommy, Mommy!" We never failed to give Mother the "Great Greet".

As we hugged and kissed and warned the children not to knock Mother over, we marveled to see how well she had recovered from her fall. The only concession she made was that her inevitable high heeled shoes were a bit lower. Now Kawsar even took Mother's arm as she walked around the apartment and Mother graciously indulged her although she privately told me it made her feel like a feeble, old lady.

Mother's visit seemed over far too soon. She met my new friends Ailsa, Robbie, Sally and Suzy. Of the "old friends" she had met before, there was only Emily and her family. Suzy and I played our guitars for Mother every chance we got and she and the children sometimes joined in.

A new resort had opened in Latakia and we took Mother there for a few days at the end of July and stayed in a cabin right on the beach. I brought my guitar and we had several sing-alongs on the sand under the stars. The children picked all their favorite songs and taught Mother the ones she didn't know. We spent as much time singing that month as we did talking.

Not long after Mother left, Mohammed told me the wonderful news that Mother and I would see each other again in just a few weeks. He said he was attending a UN conference in Ecuador scheduled for the middle of September and that we would fly together to New York where I would stay with Mother and he would get another flight to Ecuador. He promised to join me in Palisades for one week when the conference ended. Kawsar and Riad said they would take care of the children and, for once, there was no last minute disappointment. As our plane took off I realized it was our first airplane trip together. We had been married fifteen years, but we had only flown together on our helicopter flight to the Euphrates Dam.

I spent three weeks in Palisades and, as it turned out, I arrived exactly when I was needed. A few days after I came, my brother-in-law, Dave, rushed Mother to New York City Medical Center with excruciating pain from kidney stones. She spent four days in the hospital and I visited her every day. Since she came home with a urinary tract infection, it was good I was there to take care of her.

By the time Mohammed joined me in Palisades, Mother was much better and we spent a happy week with my family. Jan, Bob and their children came from Chicago to be with us and Mohammed and I had a good time getting to know and love my sisters' children. There were Jo's Andrea, who was five, her little sister Amy and baby David as well as Jan's Andy, who was also five, and baby Elizabeth. Jo borrowed a guitar for me and I taught the children, especially Andrea and Amy, several folk songs. Their favorites were *The Fox* (went out on a chilly night) and *The Three Little Pigs* (who died of the felo-de-se). Every time the children, even baby David, tried to grunt like the mother pig in the song we would laugh ourselves silly.

One unforgettable night we three sisters and our husbands went out for dinner to the Bear Mountain Inn where they had a band. All six of us danced and Jan and Bob were so impressed by Mohammed's trendy dancing, that they said they were going to take lessons.

The next day, as we all sat around talking at Mother's, Mohammed casually dropped a bombshell into the conversation. He said he had applied for two jobs with the United Nations, one with UNDP, the United Nations Development Program, in Libya and the other with FAO in Egypt! This was a complete surprise to us all, even to me.

Mohammed said while neither of these jobs would bring us any closer to Palisades, they would pay international salaries and provide a very comfortable life. In addition, there would be benefits such as health insurance for us all and educational allowances for the children. Knowing Syria and Mohammed, I didn't let myself get too optimistic about these possibilities, but Mother, my sisters and my brothers-in-law became very excited and began to envision a future where we would easily be able to visit each other every year. Mohammed said it would be several months before he would hear anything from the UN and I privately determined not to give it a second thought in the meantime.

Back in Syria, it was good to be with the children, Kawsar, Riad and Abdo again and they were glad to see us and get their presents. After all the gloomy weather during the trip, we also truly appreciated the Damascus sun and clear, blue skies. It had been rainy or cloudy almost the entire time I was at Mother's and Mohammed's weather in Ecuador had been no better.

Christmas this year was overshadowed by Riad's exciting preparations to go on pilgrimage and, the last week of December, armed with provisions for the three-day journey, she set off by bus to Mecca. She traveled with several girlfriends from her ministry and would be gone about three weeks. Before she left, she promised us that she and Kawsar would come out of mourning when she got back. It would be three years in April since Tete's death and although we had tried to persuade them it had been long enough, they were still wearing black.

We celebrated New Year's Eve 1971 with what was becoming a family tradition: a big family party with Abdo, Mohammed's sisters, their husbands and most of the teen-age cousins. I served an early dinner and then May put on her records and we danced. She and Yasir taught all of us, (well, *almost* all), the latest dance craze in Damascus, "the jerk".

Not long after our New Year's party, Mohammed came home with the news that he had received two definite, official UN job offers. One was from UNDP for the position of head of the Economic Planning Group in Libya and the other was from FAO for the job of economic adviser in Cairo. After we talked over the pros and cons of both jobs, Mohammed sent word to UNDP that he would accept the job in Libya provided his government gave him permission to go. Now that my dream of eleven years was within our grasp, I should have been ecstatic. Instead, to my surprise, I was having second thoughts.

In fact, I was ambivalent about both offers. Cairo would be a better place to live and our good friends Anna Maria and Haidar were already there, but the better paying job was in Libya; Mohammed's salary there would be a fortune to us. However, the more I heard about Libya, the less I liked the sound of it and I felt the only good thing about it was the money. Also, it looked less and less likely that the government would let Mohammed go, and if they did, I worried that he might not be happy and maybe even the children and I would not be happy. It would mean uprooting ourselves and leaving Kawsar, Riad, Abdo and all the rest of the family we loved so well not to mention our dear friends and the children's schools. Eleven years in Syria had taught me to take life as it came. I told myself, it is out of my hands and would be decided one way or the other before long. If Mohammed didn't get permission to leave soon, the posts would be given to someone else.

To my amazement, in February, Mohammed got permission from his minister to leave Syria and he notified the UN he planned to arrive in Libya sometime in April. No sooner had he done this, when the chance of a job in Washington D.C. suddenly materialized! I was thrilled, but dared not pin my hopes on such a wonderful possibility. In March, the World Bank sent us airline tickets to Paris where some of their officials would interview Mohammed for a job with their bank in Washington. Although Mohammed had accepted the job in Libya, he said he wouldn't hesitate to turn it down for the opportunity to work in the States. We left Damascus on March 10th and, as we boarded the plane, I tried not to think ahead. I told myself whatever happens, we would get to see Paris together.

We had four days in Paris and, like so many before me, I fell in love with this beautiful city even though we arrived in the middle of a taxi strike. We took the Metro to the stop nearest our hotel and then, after we lugged our suitcases up endless stairs, we emerged into pouring rain. By the time we had walked the one block to our hotel, we were drenched and I was crying. Even after this inauspicious beginning, the city enchanted me and Mohammed and I had a wonderful time seeing all the sights. We counted it as yet another of our "delayed honeymoons".

But the job in Washington was not to be. When Mohammed had his job interview, the World Bank officials said he was "over-qualified for the available position", but said they would keep him in mind if something more suitable turned up. I was glad I had remained skeptical about this possibility, but still I was very disappointed. So was Mohammed.

From Paris we flew to Vienna where Mohammed attended a UN meeting grandly called "The High Level Experts' Committee on the Reorganization of UNIDO" (the United Nations Industrial Development Organization). While there, we were invited to a show at the famous Spanish Riding School. We enjoyed the show, but both of us kept thinking how much more Jowdat Effendi would have appreciated seeing the amazing Lippizaner horses put through their paces.

17.

A Dream Comes True

Our flight from Vienna landed in Damascus at midnight on March 22nd, and we planned to start packing for Libya the next day. Again, it was not to be. At three a.m. that morning, the phone rang and a very groggy, sleepy Mohammed answered the phone. It was the office of the President, and the President's secretary said, "*Mabruk*, Your Excellency! You have been appointed Minister of Planning."

Mohammed managed some kind of reply, hung up the phone and turned to me with a dazed look on his face. He said, "I'm the new Minister of Planning," and I hugged him and shouted, "*Mabruk*! *Mabruk*! You did it! You did it!"

Mohammed's dream had come true; his schoolboy ambition to follow in Dr. Homad's footsteps and become a cabinet minister had been achieved. Although he had been looking for a job outside the country for months, in his heart I knew he really wanted to stay in Syria. One of the reasons he reluctantly decided to leave was that he felt he had reached the top rung of the ladder when he became Deputy Minister. For an ambitious man who was only forty-one, it was very frustrating to think you can go no further. Now, the impossible had happened and he was a minister.

That was the end of any sleep that night. We ran upstairs to tell Kawsar, Riad and Abdo the good news and with all the excitement, the children woke up and were told. Telegrams and phone calls of congratulations started pouring in and I could hardly believe it. Somehow the news spread quickly because before breakfast several "frogs" showed up to say, "*mabruk*" and make their requests to the new minister.

Aside from feeling it was all unreal, what were *my* feelings I asked myself in the midst of all the excitement. Strange to say, I felt at peace with this turn of events. An American wife and an American education were two counts against Mohammed in this socialist government. Unfairly or not, I had felt it was "my fault" that Mohammed had reached a dead end in his career. Now, I no longer had any reason to feel guilty. President Hafiz Assad had recognized Mohammed's outstanding ability and loyalty to the country and did not seem to care that he was not a Baathist, that he had studied in the West or that his wife was an American.

Oddly enough, I had never really believed we would live in Libya. Whenever I tried to visualize life there, my mind would go blank. In fact, both Mohammed and I had never been enthusiastic about going there. We viewed it as a stepping stone to a better position in a more appealing place. But no job outside Syria, I was sure, would ever make Mohammed as happy as he was now.

Just to give us a proper dose of reality, the bad came with the good. Mohammed arrived home from his first day as minister and learned Riad had been knocked down by a hit-and-run motorcyclist in front of her ministry. Mohammed and Wahid Beyk, spent the entire afternoon with Riad at the hospital where the X-rays showed she had a broken arm. After her arm was put in a cast, her cut lip was stitched up. Eventually, she would have to see a dentist because she had lost three teeth, but for now her whole mouth was so swollen she couldn't eat at all and could only drink with a straw. When Riad got home, Susu appointed herself as her aunt's nurse and stayed at her side, waiting on her and trying to comfort her.

Now, we not only had people pouring in with congratulations, we also had visitors coming to commiserate. Riad was in no danger, but she was very uncomfortable and in a lot of pain and it put a damper on our happiness.

Next morning, the arrival at our building of Abu Gassem driving the black ministerial Mercedes signaled a new chapter in our lives. Since we still did not have a car of our own, this was an immediate and enormous improvement in our life style.

Many routine things that are done easily in the States, are complicated and time consuming in Syria. Electricity, water and phone bills all had to be paid in cash at certain offices where you often had to wait in line for a long time. Renewing your identity card, paying your real estate taxes, registering your children in school, all these were processes full of red tape and all involved more than one trip to more than one office. Life became much simpler when Abu Gassem took over all these duties for us, as well as for Kawsar, Riad and Abdo. Having a driver and a car, especially an official Mercedes, was a huge advantage. The path was always smoothed for a minister's driver.

When Mohammed became minister, nine spindly little trees appeared overnight on our block. Mohammed ordered them to be planted because I missed the trees that lined the streets of Palisades. I was touched and although Muna promised to water them every day, it was actually Kawsar who watered them for years until she became too ill to carry the pails of water. Now these trees have grown sturdy and tall. I am sure no one guesses they are there because an American woman was homesick for trees.

Several days after Mohammed became Minister of Planning, Shasho, our local sidewalk vendor, spoke to him: "I hear there is a minister on our street now, so I guess I better close up here and go somewhere else."

Mohammed assured him that it was all right for him to stay where he was; that he had been there a long time and would be missed if he left. Shasho bowed and smiled and stayed on his corner. I had never forgotten that Shasho was the first person I saw as we drove up to the Imady home the day I arrived in Syria. As the years passed, every morning Shasho continued to carefully arrange his fruit and vegetables on the corner he had claimed for his own. He was still there in 1976 when we left Mohajareen and moved to Tejara in the east of the city. Not long afterwards, we heard that he had been killed by a hit and run driver. Shasho left behind his pretty wife, several children and memories in our old neighborhood of a friendly, honest, little man.

In May of 1971, Mohammed went to China with a big Syrian delegation headed by the Minister of Foreign Affairs. In Beijing, in fact in every city they visited, the Syrians were given a tumultuous welcome, with school children and ordinary citizens lining the streets in the thousands, cheering and waving the Chinese and Syrian flags. Nixon had made his historic visit to China three months earlier and he was driven from the airport into Beijing through quiet, empty streets in stark contrast to the welcome given the Syrian delegation. In 1949, when Mao came to power, Syria had been the very first country in the world to recognize Communist China and the Chinese greatly appreciated this and never forgot it.

Mohammed had meetings with Prime Minister Chou En Lai and their conversation took on a much warmer note when Mohammed mentioned that his wife and mother-in-law were neighbors and friends of Edgar Snow[12] and that they had introduced him to the journalist and his wife in the mid-fifties. Chou En Lai said words to the effect that any friends of the Snows were friends of his and of China's.

Laura and Zaid Dalati had finally returned from their long stay in the States and we and all their many friends were very relieved to have them back. Now that we had Abu Gassem and the Mercedes, our Friday trips to the Dalati's in Zebadani became almost a routine. There was always a group of us there, new friends and old, with our children. We could almost feel our worries slip away as we turned into the driveway. Everyone contributed to the meals and Laura often cooked a tasty lentil dish called *mujadera*.

---

12 The journalist, Edgar Snow, author of *Red Star over China*, and a personal friend of Mao Tse-Tung and Chou En Lai, lived in Palisades in the fifties and sixties and he and his wife were our friends.

Arab hospitality is deservedly renowned, but the generous way Laura and Zaid shared their home in Zebadani was truly exceptional. They threw open their doors to all their friends every Friday without fail, month after month, year after year and it was a haven for us all. All were welcome in their mountain home: Syrian neighbors, relatives of the Dalatis, but most of all, the handful of Syrian/American families in Damascus, for whom it became a Shangri-la. Some of the younger children, I believe, thought it was their very own Friday kingdom.

At the height of the cherry season, Laura invited Emily and her five and me and my three to spend several days in Zebadani to help pick the cherries. There were twelve children with Laura's three. No men – no room for them. We climbed the low trees and picked and ate the fat red and yellow cherries until our hands, lips and clothes were stained and we all had upset stomachs. We filled quite a lot of the little baskets to send to market, but we probably ate as many cherries as we picked.

During these long ago spring days, we three friends shared our thoughts and worries in what I remember as perfect harmony and the children, when they tired of climbing trees and picking cherries, had a fine time together laughing, crying, playing and squabbling. The weather was beautiful, the cool mountain air refreshing and in the distance you could see the snow-capped peaks of Jebel Sheikh, the Biblical Mt. Hermon. It was a magical time.

In June, Susu, Muna, Omar and I had our final exams; I had signed up for the second year of Arabic after all. Omar passed to second grade, Muna to fifth grade and I was 9th in my Arabic class whereas my friend, Emily, came in second. More than half the class failed, so I didn't do too badly. As for Susu, her marks would not be announced for a month because this was the year she took the national brevet (9th grade) exams.

At the end of June, Suzy, her husband, Bourhan, and their two boys moved into our building. Abdo had built a "penthouse" on the roof and although it was too small for a family of four, they were going to be his first tenants until they could find a bigger apartment. There was a housing shortage in Damascus at this time and Suzy and Bourhan's landlord had won a case against them and evicted them so this was a happy solution for them and for us. Now Suzy and I had only to go up or down two flights of stairs to play and sing together.

In July we had Abu Gassem drive us, along with cousin Yasir, to Latakia where we stayed for three days. Susu and Yasir were both fourteen now and still the best of friends. We stayed in the same place as last year when Mother was with us and this year Emily, her husband Mohammed and their five children joined us.

Almost as soon as we arrived, Omar began begging to go see the big ships. Since the port was a restricted area, we weren't sure they would let us in, but when our driver said, "The Minister of Planning wants to see the harbor," everyone immediately stood at attention, saluted and said, "*Ahlan wa sahlan*, Your Excellency!" The children were thrilled.

Omar loved the big ships and ran excitedly from place to place looking for the best spot to see the cranes loading and unloading. As I watched, I remembered 1960 when the *Hellenic Sailor* was anchored in Latakia harbor for six hours and our deck cargo was off-loaded – all those cars thickly smeared with grease. Now I saw the action from the same shore that had looked so mysteriously enticing back then, and I saw it as the wife of the Syrian Minister of Planning. How surprising life could be!

Back in Damascus, we started swimming twice a week now that we had Abu Gassem to drive us and usually took Suzy and her children along. Often Janette and her three would also be at the pool. The children, for the first time ever, instead of their usual burns, got sun tans and looked healthy and brown. Susu and Muna both learned to swim and Muna could even dive. Omar was happy to paddle around in his rubber octopus. The pool we went to was new and very tastefully designed with beds of blooming rose bushes and bougainvillea everywhere.

Sometime in August the results of the brevet and baccalaureate (12th grade) examinations were published, a very critical time for students in Syria and their families. The marks were printed in the newspapers and crowds thronged the streets to buy that issue. We were all anxious since, depending upon Susu's results, she would enter either a general education high school or a college preparatory school in the fall. Fortunately, she did fine and was entitled to start 10th grade in the same preparatory high school where Lamat was in the administration and where May was an 11th grade student.

It was also in August that Jihan Sadat, wife of the Egyptian President, visited Syria with her four children and for the first time in Syria's history, the ministers' wives, including me, were asked to go to the airport to officially welcome them. There was only one other foreign wife among us, the French wife of the Minister of Health and I was nervous about meeting these ministers' wives. However, they greeted me warmly and it turned out that one of the women, the wife of the Minister of Public Works, was the mother of one of Muna's school friends.

Jihan Sadat was beautiful, elegant and distinguished and I thought she compared favorably with Jackie Kennedy. We were lined up to greet her by the protocol people, according to the rank of our husbands. Since Mohammed was a new minister and not a Party member, that meant I was near the end of the line. Jihan walked down the line graciously shaking all our hands while a protocol official whispered to her – not our names, but whose wife we were. I, of course, was "the wife of the Minister of Planning". That night there was an official ladies-only dinner for Mrs. Sadat and, two days later, the Egyptian Embassy gave another ladies-only dinner in her honor. At the latter invitation, one of the Syrian minister's wives said, in introducing me to Jihan, "This is Im Omar from America," and Im Basil, the President's wife, who overheard, corrected her and said, "She is now *our* daughter."

Today, while writing about Jihan Sadat's visit, I reminded Mohammed of this night and he said, "You came home flying." That is true. I had been accepted when I arrived in 1960 by Mohammed's family, but now even the country, in the person of the First Lady, had claimed me as one of its own.

It took us the entire summer to convince Mother to visit us this year and she didn't arrive until September 3rd, much later than usual. Mother was impressed with our efficient driver, Abu Gassem, who retrieved her luggage and whisked her through the airport formalities. Although it was not one of his official duties, he fancied himself a bodyguard and gave Mother a glimpse of the pistol he carried in the car to defend Mohammed.

She heard Abu Gassem calling Mohammed, "*Ya sidi*" and her interest was piqued when the children told her it meant "My Master". I quickly explained that although "My Master" was the literal meaning, it was really the equivalent of "Sir" in English.

Susu showed Mother the khaki uniform which she would wear for her three years of high school: a long-sleeved belted tunic over trousers, both made of heavy twill material. Under the tunic came a tailored khaki shirt and a tie and with the outfit came heavy boots and a little cap. It was all very military and very severe. Mother felt sorry for her, but Susu said she didn't mind because all high school students wore this same uniform.

Susu also told Mother about the military training that she would have. All high school students were required to take a one-hour class, three days a week in which drill sergeants taught them to march, shoot, dismantle and reassemble rifles and machine guns, treat wounds and crawl under barbed wire. Without this training, girls and boys could not graduate.

Of course we took Mother to Zebadani where she had a good time with Laura and Emily and the rest of the Zebadani gang. We also took her to Zaid's farm in the Ghouta to admire his cows and we even managed to find a camel on our way back so Mother could pose for a picture with it.

Our next outing was to Maloula. Mother said ten years ago she had promised the nuns there to return and return she did in grand style, as mother-in-law of the Minister of Planning, riding in our official black Mercedes with Abu Gassem at the wheel.

The International Fair was in full swing and this year Mother and I decided the Chinese pavilion was the most impressive and artistic. At the entrance was a blown-up picture of the Syrian delegation with the Chinese leaders taken during their visit in May. In the picture, Mohammed stands next to Chou En Lai, Edgar Snow's old friend.

We were provided with a smiling young Chinese woman to show us around the pavilion. She was supposed to know English, but although she managed to explain the exhibits in barely comprehensible English, she didn't understand a word we said. However, Mother was determined to tell her that Edgar Snow was our friend. She said it once and then said it again in simpler English, but was met only with a baffled look.

Mother said it one more time, very clearly and very slowly, and the face of the young woman broke into a wide smile and she exclaimed, "Ed-gah 'No, Ed-gah 'No! Good flend China peepur!"

Then she hugged and kissed my mother. We saw the rest of the exhibits with her arm hooked in Mother's.

The weather was still hot when October began and Mother's visit ended. The night before she left, Zaid took her on a whirlwind trip through the dark and narrow winding streets of the Old City in his van. She always found it exhilarating to step back in time once more and pass the old buildings that have stood for hundreds of years with their courtyards, fountains and bitter orange trees. At times the van could barely squeeze through the narrow streets, but finally we turned on to a wider street, the Street Called Straight and drove down towards the Eastern Gate.

Suddenly we smelled something wonderful. We slowed down and, sure enough, there in a little shop was an old man baking bread in a round earthenware oven. We stopped and bought some and he handed it to us wrapped in newspaper. We ate it hot and finished it quickly. It was delicious.

We all cried in the airport the next morning when Mother left and we watched her plane flying over the mountain until it was out of sight. Outside the city, on our way back from the airport, we saw three camels laden with wood for sale. They were roped together single file and led by a man on a donkey. This used to be a common sight when I first arrived, but now they are banned from the city. I wished Mother had seen them.

School started, my Arabic classes resumed, Suad's husband was in the hospital once again with his bleeding ulcer and our hot weather continued. It seemed summer would never end, but then overnight the temperature dropped, a cold wind blew from the snowy peaks of Jebel Sheikh and we put down our carpets, got out our heavy quilts and lit our *sobas*.

December was a Chinese box of surprises. First, Riad announced she was going to take Kawsar on pilgrimage and they would be leaving the end of the month! This trip, said Riad, was for Kawsar's sake because Kawsar would never have the courage to go alone. The hajj is obligatory on all Muslims who are able to perform this rite and Riad wanted to make it possible for her sister to go. Kawsar, who had never traveled before, was both excited and a bit nervous at the prospect.

Next, came the news that May, who was just sixteen and in her third year of high school, would be officially engaged in January to a second cousin, a grandson of Tete's sister, Bahira. Fawaz was twenty-seven years old, blond and handsome, and a construction engineer with his own company. I was planning to have my usual big New Year's party for the relatives this year and I told May to bring her fiancé along.

Most exciting of all, on December 23rd, Mohammed was appointed Minister of Economy and Foreign Trade! This was one of the four most important ministries in the country and Mohammed would have 30,000 employees under him. Under his jurisdiction would be all the banks, including the Central Bank and his signature soon appeared on all the Syrian paper currency. He was in charge of all import and export; the harbors and maritime transportation; the tobacco monopoly; the cotton ginning and marketing monopoly; the insurance companies; some nationalized companies; the Aleppo Fair; the International Fair of Damascus; and finally, economic relations with foreign countries and international organizations. It seemed such an enormous responsibility that I was almost scared, but Mohammed was not; he was in his element. As for the children and me, the most thrilling part of Mohammed's new position was that he now was in charge of the Fair.

* * *

April 2007: Three times a week, as I drive back from the pool after my early morning swim, I pass the grounds of the razed International Fair, now a forlorn vacant lot on the south bank of the Barada River. Every time I drive by this site, I recall when, for three weeks every year in September, the International Fair was Mohammed's fief, his kingdom and sometimes his headache. There was a time when the Fair was the most exciting occasion of the year, the most anticipated annual event, for our family and for the rest of the city.

The entire fair with all its buildings and employees was under the supervision of the Minister of Economy and, for the twenty-four years Mohammed was the Minister, he represented the President at the official opening of the Fair, an event of pomp and pageantry. Mohammed's arrival was announced by the sirens of his motorcade and, upon alighting from his Mercedes, he was ceremoniously greeted by an officer of the honor guard. Everyone stood at attention as the military band played the national anthem and then Mohammed, along with the officer and the chief protocol official, inspected the honor guard. Finally, Mohammed was led down the red carpet, into the theater of the fair.

Mohammed's speech on the state of the economy, which he always wrote himself, was the main feature of the opening day of the Fair. Not a seat would be empty as all the notables of the city eagerly waited to hear what had been achieved in the country the past year and what the prospects for the future were. This speech was, in a way, the equivalent of the American president's State of the Union speech.

I would always attend opening day, sitting on the end of the front row, next to the Director of the Fair and his statuesque French wife, Nadia. The rest of the front row would be filled with VIPs, ministers of economy from the different participating countries, ambassadors and such like. I was very proud of Mohammed who always radiated total confidence as he gave his speech and reeled off statistics on all aspects of the economy without recourse to notes. The members of the family who were not present would be glued to their TV screens, watching the goings-on...

The theater still stands, but a large empty lot is all that is left of the rest of the fairgrounds where once stood the pavilions of some thirty odd countries. Gone also are the two restaurants, the open air handicraft section, the Bedouin tent and the amusement park...

The fair was open in the morning, closed in the hot midday and afternoon and open again in the evening. The entrance fee was so low that poor workers and peasants could afford to come with their families and they came in droves, cleanly scrubbed and dressed in their finery. Side by side with the city folk, they walked from one pavilion to another, each representing a different country and each bursting with consumer and industrial goods of all kinds which were solemnly inspected by young and old. The walkways from one pavilion to another were flanked by colorful flower beds and here and there several large decorative fountains sprayed cooling water into the sun.

After Mohammed became Minister of Economy, Mother always came to Damascus when the Fair was in full swing. Night after night we dressed up to attend the opening reception of one pavilion or another. Afterwards, Mother, the children and I invariably headed for Mother's favorite area, the outdoor handicraft section, which teemed with the activities of many local artisans: frail elderly men weaving fine silk brocade on ancient looms – "Who will take over their craft when they die out?" frets Mother - and young muscular glass blowers, now puffing with chipmunk cheeks, now swinging their long metal blowpipes from which bloomed vases, pitchers and glasses, all red hot and still pliable from the blazing furnace. When they cool off, they end up in deep shades of blue, green and amber and then some are decorated in gold arabesque patterns. For a handful of change, Omar and Muna buy drinking glasses and have their names inscribed on them in gilt paint. Peasant women with tattooed patterns of dots on their faces sit and weave large straw trays and baskets. Carpenters, carefully incising wood for an inlay of mother of pearl, work next to young men filling bottles with colored sand that cleverly portray scenes of palm trees and camels.

Finally, when we get tired, I sometimes lead our little troop to the "coffee shop" which is fittingly in a "house of hair," the Arabic name for a Bedouin tent. We sink down gratefully on cushions and are first served hot tea "to cool off," as they say, and then the tiny little cups of bitter coffee laced with cardamom. When we raise our eyes, there are the lights of Mohajareen and a new moon rising over the mountain.

Other times, when Mother has bought all the souvenirs we can carry, we head for the benches facing the river to cool off. As night falls, jets of water are shot into the air from the river and illuminated by colored lights. Adding to the holiday air, enormous flags of all the participating nations flap crisply above us on their tall poles and music floats from loudspeakers, mostly the mournful songs of Fairouz

I never remember the fair without recalling the lovely, haunting voice of Fairouz. The performances presented at the theater were the best part of the fair and the biggest attraction was the annual appearance of the Lebanese troupe of Mansour and Asim Rahbani. Each year the Rahbani brothers would stage a new musical extravaganza which showcased Mansour's wife, Fairouz. The talented Rahbanis wrote and directed the plays and all the music; I am not sure who choreographed the wonderful dances. The Rahbanis composed in the Arabic tradition but with a subtle touch of Western influence. Their songs, always sung by Fairouz, are popular in the Arab world to this day and their music is also the most appealing Arabic music to Western ears.

Every year, Mohammed was given a large batch of tickets to all the events at the theater and it was hard to not hurt feelings when it came to passing out tickets for Fairouz's performances. All the family members wanted to attend and there were never enough tickets to go around.

How we looked forward to these events! I recall our anticipation as Mother, Susu and I got "all torched up", as Janette would say, for one of Fairouz's musicals. Abu Gassem drives us to the theater and we are escorted into the office of Nazem Beyk, the Director of the Fair, where he and his wife, Nadia, graciously receive us. Fairouz is notified that we have arrived and she and her husband join us for a cup of tea before the performance begins. Fairouz comes out larger than life in full theatrical make-up and costume and the rest of us look pale and washed out by comparison. She is surprisingly shy and conversation would be rather halting if it were not for the expansive and sociable Nazem Beyk who cracks jokes and puts everyone at their ease. Mother asks Susu in a whisper what the name of tonight's performance is and Susu whispers back, "Mays Ar-Reem".

After our short visit, we walk to our seats in the first row; Mohammed and I leading the way with Susu and her grandmother trailing behind. My long straight hair is lifted by the breeze and my long silk gown swirls around my ankles. People step forward smiling to greet Mohammed - and the rest of us as an afterthought. Happiness, anticipation and pride in Mohammed – all these emotions wash over me and I straighten my shoulders as I feel all eyes upon us.

I sit down with a rustle of my skirt between Mohammed and Mother and have one of those rare and fleeting moments when you actually observe yourself as if from a distance and realize that you are living through one of the supremely happy events of your life. "Enjoy it!" says that observer who is - and is not - you. And as the orchestra directly in front of us begins the overture, my heart beats in time with the *derbekka,* the Arabic drum, and my spirits soar.

"Mays ar-Reem" ... after all the years that have passed, I know every song by heart...

* * *

The winter Riad and Kawsar went to Mecca – the winter of 72/73 - was cold and very dry up until the Eid al-Kabeer, which fell in January. No sooner did the Eid begin, than the dry spell ended with a bang. First, heavy rain fell, then the rain turned to snow and finally the snow became a snowstorm. Snow is rare and exciting in Syria so we had Abu Gassem drive a carful of us - our children, two cousins, Mohammed and me - to see the snow. We planned to go to Zebadani where there is always more snow because of its higher elevation but when we got to the Beirut-Zebadani turnoff, we couldn't go any further. The wind was howling and the snow was coming down so thick and fast that you couldn't tell the earth from the sky or see the road. It was a real blizzard and there was already at least a foot of snow on the ground. Naturally, the children wanted to get out of the car and play in the snow, but after two minutes outside they ran back to the car, covered in snow and freezing cold.

On the drive back we found a good spot where the wind was not as fierce and the children did run around and throw snowballs for about fifteen minutes. When we got back to Damascus, we were disappointed that the snow didn't stick, although it snowed on and off for two days in a row. After countless sunny days, the earth was too warm for the snow to last.

Besides this very unusual snowstorm, it was a strange Eid in other ways. It seemed very queer not to have Riad and Kawsar upstairs and the building was empty without them. Also, Inayat and Hassan were in Beirut with Hassan's family during the holiday so Muna didn't have her cousin, Ammar, to play with. May was completely pre-occupied with Fawaz now they were engaged and even Mohammed wasn't around much because he was busy with a delegation for most of the Eid.

While Kawsar and Riad were gone, Abdo, who was even lonelier than we were, had his meals with us and spent most of his time in our apartment.. Before Riad and Kawsar returned, Lamat, Suad, Susu and I cleaned all the apartments in the building and scrubbed the stairs. Everything was made ready for the return of our *hajjays* (pilgrims).

They didn't get back until ten days after the Eid and, since the journey from Mecca to Damascus by bus is a grueling trip, they arrived exhausted. Even the rites of the pilgrimage require quite a bit of stamina. Suad and I had a welcoming feast ready for them when they arrived and they were ravenous. It seems their meals on the hajj had been mostly hit-or-miss. I told them they needed to rest and insisted they have their meals with us for at least the first three days.

The day they returned, we got an electrician to hang the customary strings of light bulbs on the outside of the building in celebration of their safe return from pilgrimage. The lights hung from the roof all the way down to the first floor. That night, as we lit the lights, they blazed out the news that our *hajjays* had returned. All over the city buildings were similarly lit up as pilgrims returned, adding a holiday sparkle to almost every street.

All Damascene women had a certain day set aside for their *isti'bal*, a monthly reception or "at home" day for their women relatives and friends. Everyone knew Kawsar and Riad held their *isti'bal* on the first Thursday of the month and that visitors were welcome that day after five in the afternoon. The first *isti'bal* Kawsar and Riad had after they returned from hajj was a grand affair and about fifty women came. Women *hajjays* wear white as they receive guests and Riad and Kawsar looked like brides in their long, white and silver dresses especially made for the occasion. I also had a new black and violet dress which Kawsar had sewn for me earlier. In addition to the usual juice and coffee, for this special *isti'bal* Kawsar and Riad served individual dishes of a festive pudding covered with almonds and pistachios as well as small glasses of *Zam Zam* water[13] from Mecca and Saudi dates. They brought back presents for everyone and many people gave them presents in return.

For Kawsar, this trip was extraordinary and almost overwhelming. Riad said that if someone had offered Kawsar a return ticket the first day they arrived in Mecca, she would have come straight back! She had never left home before and the crowds, the heat, the strangeness of it all caught her by surprise. She was accustomed to having people depend upon her, but suddenly she and Riad were totally dependent upon their friend and traveling companion, Aida, who had made several pilgrimages and knew her way around. Riad said Kawsar was also constantly worrying about all of us back in Damascus and wondering how we were managing without her. Truth to tell, life without Kawsar wasn't easy.

The sisters were full of stories about their adventures in Mecca. They had a bad scare when they got separated for about six hours from Aida and couldn't find their hotel or even remember the name of it. However, there is an agency that helps lost pilgrims and one of its employees was able to locate their hotel and escort Kawsar and Riad back there to the great relief of their friend, Aida. She was terribly concerned about them and had started calling hospitals.

---

13 *Zam Zam* water is from the well that miraculously gushed forth for Abraham's wife, Hajjar, when she was left in the desert with her young son, Ishmael. Pilgrims often bring some of this blessed water home with them.

Another day, while they were walking near their hotel, a cat fell or was thrown from a high building. It fell "like a bomb", as Riad said, and missed her head by inches. Riad, who is no cat lover, almost fainted away. The three women stood transfixed, staring at the "dead" cat for a few minutes when suddenly it shook its head, staggered to its feet and walked, not limped, off. Aida, who is fond of cats, said it was probably going on hajj and was determined not to die until it finished its pilgrimage!

Kawsar said the enormous crowds at the Kaa'ba overwhelmed her and whenever they prayed, there was always someone directly in front of them, behind them and on both sides, penning them in. However, she was thrilled to have gone and, like every returning pilgrim I have ever known, wanted to go again as soon as possible. She told me they both prayed for Mother to come to Damascus next summer and assured me prayers made on hajj will be granted.

Although Riad had promised she and Kawsar would stop wearing black after making her pilgrimage last year, it was not until the April after this hajj, the fourth anniversary of Tete's death, that the sisters, to our great delight, finally put away their black clothes and began wearing gray. However, ending their mourning was a long process as they slowly went from black to gray to navy blue before returning to ordinary clothes of any color.

Twenty religious sheikhs were invited for dinner on the fourth anniversary of Tete's death and, afterwards, they recited the Qur'an from beginning to end in her memory and did a little joyful dance, quite different from the whirling dance of the *maylaweeyeh* order. This group stood in a circle with their arms on each others shoulders and swayed right and left chanting, *Allah hay! Allah hay!* (God lives! God lives!).

* * *

A Syrian cabinet minister has sweeping powers which can be used for good or bad. Mohammed always said one of the important satisfactions of his job was that it gave him the ability to do much good for many people and the power to right many wrongs. One of the first people Mohammed helped was Suad. He was able to remove her from her legal limbo as a stateless, undocumented non-person and have her officially registered as a Syrian citizen. What a joyful day that was! When she was issued her own identity card she was finally able to register her marriage with the civil court. She had had a religious marriage, but only now could it be officially recognized. After that, she fulfilled another long-time wish of hers: she went over the border on a day trip with some friends to Beirut, Lebanon. Best of all perhaps, her fear of ending up as a cadaver in the School of Medicine was finally gone. We all rejoiced for her.

When Omar and Muna had their tonsils out in May, Suad bought a huge, expensive, red bicycle for Omar as a get-well present. It was big enough for me or

Susu and far too big for Omar, but we couldn't give it back. Omar would have been disappointed and Suad would have been hurt. We solved the dilemma by giving her a new radio which cost slightly more than the bicycle. We were proud of Muna for not being jealous. She realized the bicycle was partly Suad's indirect thank-you for getting her status legalized.

It is now forty-five years since Suad first came to work for us. She is still living in the same apartment she and her husband moved into when they married, but now she is alone. Even her loving care could not prevent her husband's ulcer from killing him in the end.

When you walk into her two room apartment, you are ushered into her "parlor". A small square room, it is lined with French style chairs and a sofa. Clean curtains frame the one window, geraniums are in the window box and potted plants are set on the immaculate tiled floor. A large photograph of her husband has pride of place in this spotless room.

Suad has finally retired and I hope her life is easier now. I visit her from time to time and always take her money which I consider her well-deserved pension. I have never forgotten all she did for us and I am not alone; the in-laws of my friend, Penny, have also never forgotten her.

She always said she had given birth to a girl and that she had never seen the baby since it was a few days old. However, there was always a young man she talked of and bragged about. She said he was studying abroad, but that he visited her when he was in Damascus. She said he was the son of people she had worked for but we always wondered. Could he be her son? I hope so. It would be nice to think that her very own son keeps in touch with her and cares about her.

* * *

In October of 1973, I went with Mohammed to Nairobi, Kenya for the annual joint meeting of the World Bank/International Monetary Fund (IMF). Almost all countries send the governor of their central bank to represent them at this meeting, but the Central Bank of Syria is under the jurisdiction of the Minister of Economy, so Mohammed was Syria's Governor, the country's designated representative to this meeting.

I had no idea when we went to Kenya that this was to be my introduction to a new world of international conferences and official governmental trips that would take me to countries I never dreamed I would see and in which I would meet people whose names were world famous.

At the opening ceremony of the conference, hundreds of native dancers from all over Kenya gathered in the huge city square to sing, dance and welcome Jomo Kenyatta and his wife as they drove up in their open limousine. It was very colorful and gay with the dancers wearing brilliantly printed native costumes. Kenyatta, a silver fly whisk in his hand, opened the conference with a brief welcoming speech and then Robert MacNamara, who was head of the World Bank, made a long speech in which he passionately made all kinds of promises to eradicate poverty and help the people of third world countries. People whispered that after his part in the Vietnam War, he was having an attack of conscience. I hoped he would accomplish some good, but I wasn't very hopeful.

The government of Kenya went to great trouble to ensure all the delegates and their wives had a good time. We stayed at the Intercontinental Hotel and had a car and driver assigned to us. A special sightseeing program was prepared for the women and the four Syrian wives and I planned our tours together. Since our ladies didn't speak English, I was the self-appointed translator.

All the delegates and their wives were issued tags with their name and the name of their country and I was no exception. On the tour bus that first afternoon, I smiled to myself when several people read my tag, "Mrs. Mohammed Imady of the Syrian Arab Republic" and complemented me on my good English.

This meeting in Kenya was the first of twenty-six World Bank/IMF meetings we attended during the twenty-four years Mohammed was Minister of Economy and the six years he was head of the Arab Fund. The usual venue of the meetings was Washington D.C., but every third year the meeting would be held in one of the member countries and Mohammed and I traveled the world as we attended World Bank/IMF meetings in Canada, Germany, Hong Kong, the Czech Republic, Thailand and Spain. 1976 was the exciting year Mohammed was elected Chairman of the Board of Governors to preside over the joint meeting of the World Bank/IMF meeting held in Manila in the Philippines. Over the years, in conjunction with these World Bank/IMF meetings, we were invited to receptions given by Ferdinand and Imelda Marcos, the King and Queen of Spain, the King and Queen of Thailand, Vaclav Havel and his wife and the Mayor of Hong Kong and his wife.

I will never forget when the wife of the Mayor of Hong Kong asked to have her picture taken with me because I was wearing a glorious, silk Chinese wedding dress; bright red with birds and dragons embroidered on it in glittering silver. Mohammed bought it for me on his first trip to China and neither he nor I had any idea it was a wedding dress, but when I wore it in Hong Kong to official World Bank invitations, I created a sensation. Everywhere I went the Chinese turned their heads and said, "Oh, beautiful bride!" I was seriously asked by several people if we had just been married. My picture was taken and appeared on the front page of several Hong Kong newspapers. But all this was far in the future...

Our first World Bank/IMF meeting ended and we flew from Nairobi to Beirut where Kawsar, Muna and Omar were waiting in the airport with Abu Gassem to drive us home. When we left Nairobi, the jacaranda trees were blooming and even the streets were littered with their violet petals; in Damascus it was the red and purple bougainvillea and the white jasmine that were in bloom.

It was so good to be home. I welcomed the pellucid sky and the September sunlight which had lost its summer ferocity. There is something about the dry, clear air and the crystalline quality of light in the autumn days of Damascus that never fails to lift my spirit.

It was the 29th of September when we arrived home so we had about a week of calm before the war began.

18.

My Home, My Country

On October 6, 1973, Syria and Egypt initiated a daring, surprise attack on the Israeli occupation army. Assad hoped to recapture the Syrian Golan Heights which had been seized by Israel in the '67 War and Sadat hoped to regain the Egyptian Sinai, which was lost in the same war. Also, after this recent humiliating defeat, both presidents wanted to restore their countries' self-respect.

The war began well as the Syrians broke through the Israeli defenses in the Golan and the Egyptians successfully stormed over the Suez Canal, but then the Egyptians dug in and for a week Syria was left to fight alone. This enabled Israel to direct all its might against Syria and its forces, armed with the latest weaponry, began to drive the Syrians back from land they had recaptured. We were getting up-to-the minute reports on radio and TV and knew the Syrian losses were high, but the Israeli army suffered great losses, as well. However, the tide turned decisively when Israel began a bombing campaign of Syria. On October 9th, the oil refinery in Homs, the port of Latakia, and other strategic targets in the country were attacked.

The next day, October 10th, was the worst day of the war for us; the terrible day Damascus was bombed. Rumors flew that the building of our friends, the Buraks had been hit. No one was surprised since their building was too close for comfort to the Ministry of Defense. When several people called and told me this, I was sorry the Buraks had lost their beautiful apartment, but not yet concerned about them because, the day before the war began, Mair herself had phoned me and said that she and her two boys were staying with Diana, an English friend who had a safe, basement apartment, far from any possible targets.

A few days later, just two days before the bombing, Mair called me again and asked if we were all okay. She and her friend, Maureen, were both nurses, and Mair told me they had tried to help the war effort by volunteering for hospital work, but they had been turned down. She also said not to worry about them; that she, Maureen, their children and several other British women were all staying in Diana's apartment. She also said her husband (an eye surgeon as well as an ophthalmologist) was sleeping at the military hospital where he was operating practically round the clock on wounded soldiers. The day before the raid, Mair's younger son, Ayman, celebrated his fifth birthday with a little party down in this basement apartment.

On the fourth morning of the war, Nizar showed up at Diana's place and said he had a few hours of leave and wanted to sleep at home. He collected Mair and the boys and asked Maureen and her children to come, too. She said she'd come later, for lunch. Mair went home to clean and cook and at 11:30 she called Maureen and reminded her not to forget lunch and asked her to bring the jam and Nescafe she had left at Diana's. That was the last anyone would ever hear from Mair. At 12:10 their building had a direct hit. Actually, instead of falling down straight, the bomb, a vacuum bomb, went horizontally into their apartment where it exploded.

By chance, at that very moment, I was on the roof of our building with Suzy's son and husband, Bourhan. We saw two Israeli Phantom jets screaming towards us and climbing steeply to clear the mountain, then saw several large, black clouds of smoke puff up in the city and, seconds later, heard the awful explosions. I shouted, "They're bombing Damascus!" Bourhan grabbed his son by the hand and rushed down the stairs. I hesitated a moment as the heart sinking thought raced through my mind that one of those explosions looked terribly close to Mohammed's Ministry and then I frantically started to follow Bourhan, but slipped and fell heavily. At the time I felt nothing, but that night I found I had a huge, painful bruise all down my left side. I picked myself up and ran down to Kawsar's apartment where the first thing I did was to phone Mohammed at his office. Thank God he was safe and, when the bombs fell, he had been signing a trade agreement with the Chinese Ambassador.

Then Bourhan called Suzy who was at work in the office of the United Nations Development Program (UNDP). She said a bomb had fallen nearby and that dazed and wounded people dripping in blood were staggering into her office. At least five locations were hit, all in the vicinity of the Ministry of Defense, but the ministry itself was spared. Instead, civilian targets were bombed including the Medical Syndicate, the home of the Pakistani Ambassador, the Teachers' Training Institute, Mair and Nizar's building and the Omayad Circle. Three planes carried out the attack, but I don't know how many bombs they dropped.

When Mohammed came home his face was set and pale and he said the Burak's building had been hit and the entire family had died. I refused to believe this and insisted over and over that Mair and the children were at Diana's and Nizar was at the hospital. Mohammed told me that wasn't true, but I was in shock and denial. Such terrible things didn't happen. Not to people we knew. Not to this charmed couple. Not to our dear friends. Impossible.

That night I couldn't sleep. I kept remembering a February night four and a half years ago when the Barada flooded and Mair and Nizar drove us down to see this unusual sight. I remembered Mair saying with her charming Welsh lilt, that now they were our friends, and we would see what loyal friends they would be.

The next morning, like a demented person, I took Susu and we got in our car and I asked the driver to take us to the Burak's building. I had some irrational idea that I would find Mair there and she would tell me everything was fine. The car could not get very close because of the rubble in the street so we got out of the car and walked to the building. The top two floors were flattened like an accordion and chunks of cement blocks, and all kinds of debris, including household effects filled the street. Nizar's two brothers were there standing on the rubble in front of that desolate ruin waiting for something, for someone to be found. One of them was crying.

We had to watch our steps as we picked our way through the remains of the building and suddenly I saw at my feet what looked like a large book covered with dust. I picked it up and found it was a photograph album with a partially charred cover. I turned some of the pages and saw, through tears, pictures of Mair, Nizar, their wedding and their children. It was a shocking and heartbreaking find. This album with its smiling, doomed faces finally brought home to me the reality of what had happened and Susu and I both began to cry. With tears streaking my face, I stumbled over to one of the brothers and wordlessly handed the album to him. Weeks later I regretted this when I heard that Mair's parents, the Blythins, had not been sent a single thing to remind them of their only child and only grandchildren.

That night one of Nizar's brothers and Mohammed along with Mair's friend, Diana, went to the morgue and identified what was left of the bodies of Nizar and his younger son. They had been sleeping together at the time of the attack and they died together, the child in his father's arms. Although Nizar's body was badly mutilated, in death his arm was still protectively holding his son tight and both were wrapped in a sheet from their bed. They were found first because they had been blown outside the building by the blast. Diana was able to make a positive identification mostly because she recognized the English sheet.

Mohammed never forgot Mair saying that she and Nizar were our loyal friends and he proved himself a true friend to them even after death. He got the Governor of Damascus to bring in the demolition workers and the big machinery and checked on their work every day until everyone in the building was found. It took ten days to find seven-year-old Akram and eleven days to find Mair, who could only be identified by her wedding ring. Her family had asked to have her body flown home to Wales at first, but by the time she was found, they had had second thoughts and said to bury her with her husband and children. Mohammed and I attended the solemn memorial service held for her in a Protestant church in the old city. The church overflowed with the Burak's many friends and some of Mair's British friends told us they had obtained permission for her to be buried with her family in a Muslim cemetery in Aleppo, the home city of Nizar.

Thirty hours after the Burak's building was hit, a man and his wife were taken out alive and mostly unhurt from that collapsed ruin of a building, thanks to the round-the-clock work of the demolition crew Mohammed had brought. The couple had three children, none of whom had been at home at the time of the raid and they were delirious with happiness to be reunited with their parents. The morning Susu and I stood in front of the building, this couple was still trapped inside. No one who had seen that building could believe anyone would be taken alive from it. It seemed like a miracle.

A few days later we heard of another tragedy caused by this same attack. Susu had only one good friend in all her years in primary school, a cute freckled girl called Juhaina. This girl and her sister, Samia, who was two years older, came to many of Susu's birthday parties and I remember commenting on Samia's flawless, alabaster complexion. At the moment the bombs fell, Samia, a young mother of eighteen, was pushing her one-year old in a stroller in front of the Medical Syndicate. Her baby boy was killed, vaporized, and her beautiful face was permanently scarred with deeply embedded shrapnel.

The children's cousin, Mazain, also just escaped death. He was riding his bicycle around the Omayad Circle behind a truck full of tomatoes when the attack came. The blast threw him and his bicycle into the Barada River and saved his life. Neither he nor the bicycle had a scratch. However, the driver of the truck just in front of him was killed and his tomatoes were cooked and sprayed all over, mixed with blood. When Mazain climbed out of the river and found himself unhurt, he ran to help some badly wounded people out of their damaged cars, including a very pregnant woman. Military cars quickly arrived from the adjacent Ministry of Defense and transported the dead and wounded to the nearest hospitals. Mazain said the smell of cooked tomatoes will always remind him of this terrible day of death.

We were safe in Mohajareen, but so many were not. Our children were greatly affected by these tragedies, particularly since the children who died were their friends. Muna, Omar, Ayman and Akram had been in the same school and Omar and Akram were in the same class. Omar kept saying if only their school had not closed, Ayman and Akram would still be alive. I knew better, but was not going to try to explain the concept of *maktoub* to a seven-year-old.

I had my hands full with Omar who started having temper tantrums, partly from fear and partly from being cooped up in the "downstairs apartment" for days. When the war started Kawsar, Riad and Abdo had all moved downstairs to the safer first floor apartment and the children and I were with them most of the time. Also, every day Inayat brought her three children, Ammar, Usama and Ola, to Kawsar and they, along with Omar and Muna would spend long hours during air raids in the windowless room dug into the slope of the mountain. The children were now terrified of airplanes and we had air raid warnings daily, sometimes five or six a day. Also, there was the unspeakable noise made by Phantom jets breaking the sound barrier as they flew over the city. To make the children feel safer, Riad told them their Jiddo (Grandfather), Jowdat Effendi, had prayed two *rikkas* (prostrations) of thanks to God for every tile laid in that room. Nothing bad could happen in it, she said. In fact, Jowdat had prayed in this way for the entire building, not just that one room, but Riad wanted them to feel it was special.

During one of the interminable air raids, ten-year-old Ammar and seven-year-old Omar started playing with knives they had sneaked from the kitchen, bragging how they would attack the enemy soldiers if they came. To demonstrate, Omar threw his knife and by chance hit five-year-old Ola, in her chest. The children were horrified to see it pierced the skin and drew some blood. A shocked Omar shouted "Sorry!" while Ola cried, and Ammar and Muna comforted her, cleaned up her dress and put a bandage on the cut. They made her swear to never tell anyone and brave little Ola kept her promise. It is good my children didn't tell me this story until years had passed and they were grown. I was worried enough about Muna and Omar as it was.

Another of my worries was for Susu who, with a handful of other high school girls, had volunteered to help in the Moassat Hospital where wounded soldiers were arriving daily. Although these teen-age girls were mostly sterilizing equipment for operations and did not actually care for the soldiers, they saw them as they were admitted to the hospital with their dreadful injuries. One day a bomb fell close to the hospital and, shortly after, two busloads of wounded soldiers were brought to the hospital. It was announced that the hospital might be targeted next and all those who could do so were ordered to go the bomb shelter. That night Mohammed said a hospital during war was no place for a sixteen-year-old and forbid Susu to return.

Our nerves were on edge and it didn't help that we constantly heard artillery guns booming in the distance as the fighting continued in the Golan. We all got cabin fever. Mohammed went to work every day, but of course the rest of us didn't leave the house for a long time. The children were frightened and bored and Kawsar, Riad, Susu and I tried to keep them distracted and entertained.

There were other bombing raids on outlying areas near the city, but after the one attack on the heart of Damascus, the enemy was never again able to bomb the city thanks to our SAM missile defenses. In fact, several enemy planes were shot down and their pilots ejected over the city in full sight of all the inhabitants. The first time this happened, it triggered a dramatic moment of truth for me. As the Israeli pilot slowly parachuted down, practically every man, woman and child in Damascus was on the roof tops watching his descent and clapping and cheering. He landed in the Ghouta and was captured by some peasants who turned him over to the authorities.

That day, standing with my children on the roof as the pilot descended from the sky, an extraordinary revelation washed over me. I felt at one with all the Damascenes on their roof tops at that moment and I realized Syria was now irrevocably my country. Its tragedies were mine and its triumphs were mine. America was, and always would be, my native land, but now I had two countries to call my own and Ruth's words truly said it all:

"...where you go, I will go; and where you lodge, I will lodge; your people shall be my people, and your God, my God. Where you die, I will die, and there will I be buried..."

Epilogue

At least one important goal of President Assad in this war was achieved: the country regained its self-respect as our soldiers fought bravely and stubbornly and civilian morale remained high. However, the Golan Heights remained in Israeli hands. Before the month was up, the October War ended in a ceasefire but, to this day, Israel is still illegally occupying the Golan. Even worse, in violation of international law, Israel has annexed this integral part of Syria and the world turns a blind eye.

* * *

In 1973, I stood on that roof in Damascus and was stunned by the realization that Syria, for better or worse, was my country. That same year, the Syrian government conferred citizenship on me making me officially a citizen of both Syria and America.

Thirty-four years have passed since that day on the roof and so many things have happened they could easily fill another book. Fifty-one years have passed since Mohammed and I were married and I have been in Damascus for the grand total of forty-seven years. During these years our children have grown up, married and had children of their own. We are now patriarch and matriarch of a "tribe" of twenty-one: our three children, eleven grandchildren and two great grandchildren plus the spouses of our children and our two married grandchildren.

My Syrian family also has also grown as my sisters-in-law, Bara'at, Lamat and Inayat have all been blessed with grandchildren. Like us, Lamat also has several great grandchildren. All three sisters-in-law also lost their husbands in the last six years. The saddest loss of all came when our beloved Kawsar died in 1981 of heart failure only eleven years after her mother's death. She left a tremendous gap in the family circle and Riad, who had expected she and Kawsar would grow old together, mourned her death for years. However, Muna's children have "adopted" Riad as their Syrian grandmother; they call her "Tete Riad" and are the joy of her old age.

The same building in Mohajareen which Jowdat Effendi bought with such pride in 1931 is still home to Abdo and Riad and in the nineties it once again rang with the laughter of children as Abdo's son and daughter were born and raised there. Abdo married late and moved into the "downstairs apartment" where he, his wife and their grown children are still living with Riad above them, in our old apartment.

Friends continue to arrive in Syria, become like sisters to me, and then leave forever. Of all my friends from the earliest days, only Dolores and Anna Maria remain in Damascus. However, I have kept in touch with many of those who left, first by mail and now mostly by email and a few good friends – Jill, Laura, Penny, Ruta and Jocelyne - I have even visited. The world is smaller these days and keeping in touch is easier.

In addition to Mair, three of my well-loved friends from the old days, Janette, Holly and Jill have died, but are not forgotten. Adel is now happily married to a Syrian woman who has also become a good friend of mine.

Mother made a total of ten trips to Syria, the last one in 1979 when she was seventy-eight. She lived to see eight grandchildren and five of her great-grandchildren and died at the age of ninety-four, still worrying about the unstable Middle East, her dear "Sham" and all her beloved Syrian family members.

In 1993, when I was fifty-nine and brother Jim was sixty-seven, my son Omar got us together for the first time. I had known about my father's son, my half-brother, since I was sixteen and it was my dearest wish to find him. Omar tracked him down in Omaha, Nebraska and when we met it was amazing to discover how much we had in common. We truly felt like brother and sister. Mohammed, my children and my grandchildren welcomed "Uncle Jim" into their lives with open arms on his two visits to Damascus. We all feel our lives have been enriched and blessed since Jim became part of our family. Like us, Jim and his wife Barbara head a large clan of children, grandchildren and great grandchildren.

My dear sisters and brothers-in-law, who now have a total of ten grandchildren between them, have visited Syria twice and I have visited them almost every year in the twelve years since Mother died. We bridge the distance between us with emails and our love.

Susu and Omar were both in the States for ten years whereas Muna was in France for six years while they and their spouses were studying. But although our children lived abroad for years, they all came back to Syria and are settled in Damascus. I would like to think this is partly because of the positive image I gave them of their country.

Mohammed was Minister of Planning for nine months and then served twenty-four years as Minister of Economy, from 1971 to 2001 with six years as head of the

Arab Fund for Economic and Social Development in Kuwait sandwiched in-between. He retired for four years beginning in 2001 during which time he wrote four books.

He is now back working full-time at the age of seventy-seven, as Chairman of the Board of the Commission on Financial Markets and Securities which is charged with setting up a stock market in Syria. He is also head of the Board of Trustees of the Arab International University and Chairman of the Board of Directors of Dar al-Naeem Orphanage. Not one of these long, impressive titles represents a comfortable sinecure; on the contrary, all these posts are demanding and require ability, hard work and patience. Mohammed's habits of a life-time continue as he gives his utmost effort to each position. He still works a six-day week although the country went over to a five-day week in 2004. He is not the man to rest on his laurels and, *in sha' Allah,* his health will not fail him.

During our six years in Kuwait, I finally obtained my college degree and began teaching English at the British Council there. On our return to Damascus in 1985, I was one of the two teachers hired to start the American Language Center (ALC) which opened in 1986 with sixty students. The ALC proved very successful and now has over one thousand students. I continued teaching there until the late nineties when I retired to write a book about my mother which I called *Postscripts from Palisades.*

Among our eleven grandchildren are six granddaughters, four of whom range in age from sixteen to twenty. Mohammed recently said his fondest wish for them is that they marry husbands who will love them as much as he loves me.

Mohammed still lights up any room for me when he enters and the best part of each twenty-four hours is the moment I fall asleep in his arms. He has given me a wonderful life and I cherish our memories together.

How surprising, how improbable that the girl from Palisades and the boy from Damascus would meet and marry and how unlikely that they would still be together after more than fifty years! I can only say it was written: it was *maktoub,* or, as the Qur'an says, "There befalls not any happening in the earth or in your souls except it is in a book before We [God] manifest it."[14]

14 *The Koran Interpreted,* 57:22 (A. J. Arberry translation, Oxford University Press, 1964).

Family Photos

Mohammed and me in Palisades, December, 1955 - Our first photograph together.

Susu and me on the Hellenic Sailor, February, 1960.

Jowdat al-Imady with his brother, six sisters and mother, around 1904. Jowdat in riding clothes (sherwal).

Jowdat in formal dress, around 1909.

Jowdat with five of his children: (l-r 1st row) Riad, Mohammed, Inayat: (top row) Lamat, Bara'at, 1932.

A lane in the old city of Damascus.

At the Pyramids, Giza, Egypt, 1961.

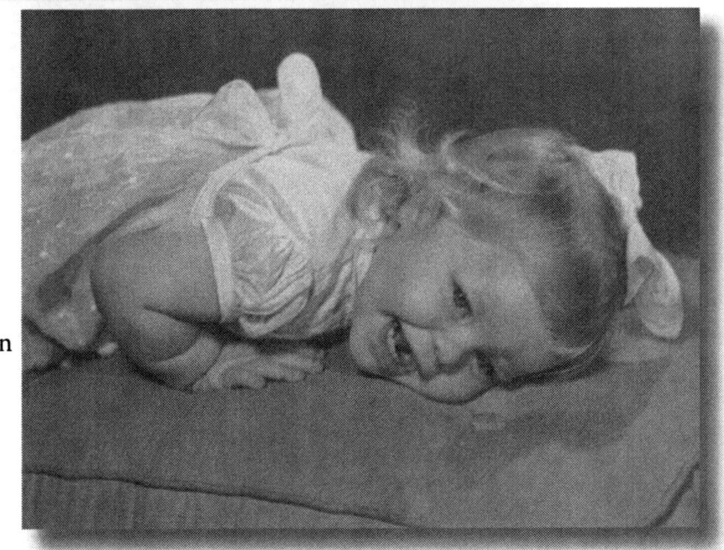

Muna at eighteen months, 1963.

On the roof (l-r) Inayat, Kawsar, Tete, Abdo and Riad, 1961.

Mother on the roof with Jebel Qassioun in background, summer 1961.

Haidar's Garden with his sons, Gihad and Anas, 1964. Today, a city block of apartment buildings stands in the place where this vanished garden once was.

Our winter picnic in the Ghouta (1st row l-r) Yasir, Muna, Tete, Mazain, Mahair, Ma'an: (2nd row l-r) Riad, Lutfia Khanum, Mohammed, me, Lamat: (3rd row l-r) Susu, May, Sheeha, Wahid Beyk - Kawsar behind May - February, 1966.

The two of us with Susu, Omar and Muna, 1967.

Abdo drinking coffee with Tete, 1967.

Omar at two years, 1968.

Kawsar (right) and friend Aida on Hajj, 1971.

Suad on our balcony, 1971.

Mohammed with Chou En Lai, Beijing, China, 1972.

The two of us at the World Bank/IMF Meeting in Nairobi, Kenya, 1973.

Elaine and Mohammed in their garden around 1991.

Bibliography

Fawaz, Leila Tarazi, *An Occasion For War: Civil Conflict in Lebanon and Damascus in 1860*, I. B Tauris Publishers, London, 1994.

Lovell, Mary S., *A Rage to Live*, W. W. Norton, New York, London, 1998

Mardam Bey, Salma, *Syria's Quest for Independence*, Ithaca Press, Reading, UK, 1994.

Moubayed, Sami M., *The Politics of Damascus, 1920-1946: Urban Notables and the French Mandate*, Tlass House, Damascus, 1999.

Schilcher, Linda Schatkowski, *Families in Politics: Damascus Politics and Estates in the 18th and 19th Centuries*, Franz Steiner Verlag, Stuttgart, 1985.

Seale, Patrick, *Asad: The Struggle for the Middle East*, University of California Press, Berkeley & Los Angeles, 1989.

Books in Arabic

Imady, Omar, *Min al-Fusul al-Imadiyah ila al-Fatawa al-Hamidiyah: Thaman Qurun Min Tarik Usrah Dimashquiyah*, Dar al-Tlass, Damascus 2003

al-Murabet, Muteeah, *al-Nour wa al-Nar fee Maktab Anbar*, Dar al-Fikr Dimashq, Damascus, 1991

al-Tantawi, Sheikh Ali, *al-Jame' al-Umawee fee Madinat Dimashq*, al-Manara, Jeddah, 1990

Mustapha, Shaker, *Madinatun Lil'ilm: Aal-Qudama wal Salihiya*, Dar al-Tlass, Damascus, 1997

Other Books by MSI Press

Achieving Native-Like Second-Language Proficiency: Speaking

Achieving Native-Like Second-Language Proficiency: Writing

Blest Atheist

Communicate Focus: Teaching Foreign Language on the Basis of the Native Speaker's Communicative Focus

Diagnostic Assessment at the Distinguished-Superior Threshold

How to Improve Your Foreign Language Proficiency Immediately

Individualized Study Plans for Very Advanced Students of Foreign Language

Mommy Poisoned Our House Guest

Puertas a la Eternidad

Teaching and Learning to Near-Native Levels of Language Proficiency

Teaching the Whole Class

The Rise and Fall of Muslim Civil Society

Thoughts without a Title

Understanding the People Around You: An Introduction to Socionics

What Works: Helping Students Reach Native-like Second-Language Competence

When You're Shoved from the Right, Look to the Left: Metaphors of Islamic Humanism

Working with Advanced Foreign Language Students

Journal for Distinguished Language Studies (annual issue)

LaVergne, TN USA
24 February 2010

174124LV00009B/64/P